ENTREPRENEURSHIP
CREATING AND MANAGING NEW VENTURES

THE BEST OF LONG RANGE PLANNING

The aim of this series is to bring together in each volume the best articles on a particular topic previously published in *Long Range Planning* so that readers wishing to study a specific aspect of planning can find an authoritative and comprehensive view of the subject, conveniently in one volume.

Whereas each issue of *Long Range Planning* normally contains a 'horizontal slice' of Long Range Planning at a particular time, in different fields and in various kinds of organizations across the world, each volume in the new series will take a 'vertical slice' through more than a hundred issues, pulling out the outstanding articles on a given subject.

Other titles in the *Best of Long Range Planning Series:*
Strategic Planning — The Chief Executive and the Board (Number 1)
Edited by Bernard Taylor

Making Strategic Planning Work in Practice (Number 3)
Edited by Basil Denning (forthcoming)

Planning for Information as a Corporate Resource (Number 4)
Edited by Alfred Collins (forthcoming)

Later volumes will deal with other topical themes, such as:

● Strategic Management in Major Multinational Companies.

● Developing Strategies for Competitive Advantage.

● Strategic Planning for Human Resources, and

● Implementing Corporate Strategy: Turning Strategy into Action.

Each volume will contain 10–12 articles, and about 120 pages. In due course they will provide a comprehensive and authoritative reference library, covering all important aspects of Strategic Planning.

The titles in this series are available individually, or can be obtained on annual subscription at an advantageous rate. Further details can be obtained from Brian Cox, Journal Sales Director, Pergamon Press plc, Headington Hill Hall, Oxford OX3 0BW, UK.

A Related Journal
LONG RANGE PLANNING★

● The international journal of strategic management and corporate planning.

The Journal of the Strategic Planning Society and of the European Planning Federation.

Editor: Professor Bernard Taylor, Henley — The Management College, Greenlands, Henley-on-Thames, Oxon RG9 3AU, UK.

★Free sample copy gladly sent on request to the Publisher.

ENTREPRENEURSHIP
CREATING AND MANAGING NEW VENTURES

Edited by
BRUCE LLOYD
Independent Consultant, London

PERGAMON PRESS
OXFORD · NEW YORK . BEIJING · FRANKFURT
SÃO PAULO · SYDNEY · TOKYO · TORONTO

U.K.	Pergamon Press plc, Headington Hill Hall, Oxford OX3 0BW, England
U.S.A.	Pergamon Press, Inc., Maxwell House, Fairview Park, Elmsford, New York 10523, U.S.A.
PEOPLE'S REPUBLIC OF CHINA	Pergamon Press, Room 4037, Qianmen Hotel, Beijing, People's Republic of China
FEDERAL REPUBLIC OF GERMANY	Pergamon Press GmbH, Hammerweg 6, D-6242 Kronberg, Federal Republic of Germany
BRAZIL	Pergamon Editora Ltda, Rua Eça de Queiros, 346, CEP 04011, Paraiso, São Paulo, Brazil
AUSTRALIA	Pergamon Press Australia Pty Ltd., P.O. Box 544, Potts Point, N.S.W. 2011, Australia
JAPAN	Pergamon Press, 5th Floor, Matsuoka Central Building, 1-7-1 Nishishinjuku, Shinjuku-ku, Tokyo 160, Japan
CANADA	Pergamon Press Canada Ltd., Suite No. 271, 253 College Street, Toronto, Ontario, Canada M5T 1R5

First edition 1989

Library of Congress Cataloging in Publication Data
Entrepreneurship: creating and managing new ventures/
edited by Bruce Lloyd.—1st ed.
p.   cm.—(The Best of long range planning: no. 2)
Articles reprinted from the Long range planning journal.
1. New business enterprises—Management.
2. Entrepreneurship.
I. Lloyd, Bruce.   II. Series.
HD62.5.E58   1989   658.1'1—dc20   89–4036

British Library Cataloguing in Publication Data
Entrepreneurship: creating and managing new ventures.
(Best of long range planning; no. 2)
1. Entrepreneurship
I. Lloyd, Bruce   II. Series
338'.04
ISBN 0–08–037108–6 Hardcover
ISBN 0–08–037407–7 Flexicover

Printed in Great Britain by BPCC Wheaton Ltd, Exeter

Contents

Page

INTRODUCTION: Entrepreneurship: Creating and Managing New Ventures
Bruce Lloyd 1

PART 1   NEW THINKING IN VENTURE MANAGEMENT

SECTION 1   THE STRATEGIC MANAGEMENT OF INNOVATION

The Innovative Firm
H. Igor Ansoff 27

Change in Management and the Management of Change
Robb W. Wilmot 29

Planning vs. Strategy — Which Will Win?
Michael A. Carpenter 35

SECTION 2   DEVELOPING NEW PRODUCTS AND SERVICES

Strategies for New Product Development
Frederick D. Buggie 41

How to get New Products to Market Quicker
G. B. M. Mathôt 51

Competing with Japan — The Rules of the Game
Merlin Stone 62

SECTION 3   STRATEGIC PLANNING FOR RESEARCH AND DEVELOPMENT

Directing Technological Development — The Role of the Board
Simon Willder 79

SECTION 4   STRATEGIES FOR DIVERSIFICATION

Diversification — the Key Factors for Success
Jean-Pierre Detrie and Bernard Ramanantsoa 87

SECTION 5   NEW VENTURES AND SMALL BUSINESS

Strategic Management: New Ventures and Small Business
Arnold C. Cooper 97

The External Corporate Venture Capital Fund — A Valuable Vehicle for Growth
Knut Bleicher and Herbert Paul 104

Alliance: The New Strategic Focus
Barrie G. James 111

SECTION 6   NEW VENTURE MANAGEMENT

Venture Management — Success or Failure?   119
B. C. Burrows

The Delusion of Intrapreneurship   135
C. Wesley Morse

**Corporate Development — Preferred Strategies in U.K.
Companies**   139
D. A. Littler and R. C. Sweeting

**Piggybacking for Business and Nonprofits: A Strategy for
Hard Times**   146
Richard P. Nielsen

**PART 2   NEW VENTURE MANAGEMENT IN PRACTICE:
COMPANY CASES**

New Venture Development at Du Pont   155
A. B. Cohen

Regaining Your Competitive Edge   159
Michael E. Naylor

New Venture Management in an Electric Utility   165
Gilbert D. Harrell and George O. Murray

**How Elf Aquitaine Provides Technological Assistance to
Small Businesses**   173
Jean-Pierre Turbil

Can we Plan for New Technology?   176
Gerard Fairtlough

Entrepreneurship: Creating and Managing New Ventures

Bruce Lloyd, Independent Consultant, London, U.K.[†]

The management of change and new business development is central to corporate survival and success but is far from easy to achieve. The selection of papers in this volume offers a number of guidelines for the transition from the initial opportunity to the move into the new market and the effective management of the new venture. The authors highlight the important place of entrepreneurial initiative and motivation in the implementation of product development and diversification policies.

This extensive introductory article provides a detailed overview and analysis of the wide selection of papers which have been published in the *Long Range Planning* journal in this crucial area. Taken together, they provide invaluable insights into the problems and opportunities relating to the critical strategic issues that arise in managing change in general, and creating and managing New Ventures in particular.

The Strategic Management of Innovation

Managing Change

Managing change and new business development are central to corporate survival and success. It is a subject that is considered implicitly by many of the articles published in *Long Range Planning*; yet it is rare for it to be examined explicitly and it is, perhaps, even more surprising to find not only has no article using the title of this special study been published previously in the Journal, but there is not even a category for New Ventures or New Business Development in the special 100th Issue Index.

About twenty years ago, in one of the first issues of the Journal, Ansoff wrote of the problems of 'The Innovative Firm'[1]*. He argued that among the problems encounted by business firms are:

---

1. Perception and anticipation of the changes which are taking place in the environment.

2. Within the firm, the problem of stimulating creative behaviour, as opposed to the more common attitude of promalgation and extension of previous models of behaviour.

3. The problem of processing an invention from its inception through the various parts of the firm.

4. The problem of introducing new products alongside old and established products, and devoting an appropriate amount of management attention to each.

5. The problem of timing entry into the market.

6. The problem of the timely divestment of established products, which are not unprofitable as yet, but which are facing a declining future.

7. Finally, the problem of resource budgeting: how much to budget for innovation, for capital assets, for investment in success of current operations, and for dividends to the shareholders.

Ansoff concluded: 'It is difficult enough to design a firm which is efficient in exploiting an established product–market position, or to design a firm which is inventive in creating new positions. It is doubly difficult to design a firm which can successfully perform both tasks.'

The basic issues highlighted by Ansoff are the same today as they were when he originally wrote his paper. Drucker[2] supported this view when he argued: 'We must therefore learn how to make existing large companies capable of innovation'. These are themes that continually recur throughout this collection of papers. However, although the problems are essentially the same as always, there

1

have been changes in the techniques used in an attempt to identify and resolve them.

On a similar theme Martin[3] found that:

> One major area of business planning was found to be missing from practically all the companies studied. While systematic analysis and planning of current operations was being undertaken, no structural thought was given to planning for change . . . companies which do plan for 'change' tend to view 'change' in terms of diversification and acquisition. It is rare for a company consciously to plan any alteration in the present business and its environment, so that its profit making potential is enhanced.

He maintained that the planning system needs to:

☆ Provide a logical basis for thinking.

☆ Ensure that comprehensive consideration is given to each alternative.

☆ Keep the necessary re-cycling of the parts of the plan to a minimum.

☆ Be practical, workable, and allow business planning to grow naturally as a function within the company.

A recent comprehensive attempt to look at these issues was undertaken by Carnall,[4] who identified and discussed an integrated approach to the management of strategic changes. He developed two main themes:

(1) What are the managerial skills required for effective organizational change?

(2) As change is disruptive and disturbing, how do people experience change and how may they be helped to cope with the pressures of major changes?

and argued:

> Any significant organizational change demands that existing ways of thinking about and talking about what we do can be overturned. Dominant views must be usurped. Experience tells us that the first attempt to articulate an alternative view, a novel concept, will fall on barren ground, very often. More likely it will meet opposition and even outright rejection. To overcome such opposition or rejection neither logic, evidence nor participation of all concerned, appears to be enough.

Three skill areas were identified: (i) managing transitions; (ii) dealing with organizational cultures; and (iii) the politics of organizational change. Only by synthesizing these three areas did the author believe it possible to 'create the environment in which creativity, risk-taking, learning and the re-building of self-esteem and performance' could be achieved.

In coping with change individuals go through a process that starts with *denial*, moves onto *defence*, then *discarding*, before achieving *adaption*. In order to move through that process, satisfactory understanding is essential, as is re-building of self esteem, which can only be achieved by combining intelligible information, new skills, support and empathy.

Strategic Business Units or New Ventures

All the above issues are succinctly put into an overall corporate strategy context by Taylor[5] in his thorough survey of the overall corporate strategy issues. He highlighted the inevitable decline in sales or profits on the basis of a do-nothing approach and that the difference between that decline and any growth objective must be filled by a combination of increased internal efficiency, new products, new markets and new business (internally or externally generated). The sections of his paper (II to VII) covering the corporate life-cycle, devising a corporate strategy, strategies for growth, business as a portfolio of investments, a wider view of strategy and the development of management systems, are not only as relevant today as they were over ten years ago (when the paper was originally published), but they continually recur as themes discussed later in this study. Taylor suggested that in a diversified business there should be strategy centres as well as profit centres:

(1) For purposes of strategy and resource planning, diversified business should be divided into Strategic Business Units (i.e. a unit of the company with its own mission and its own competitors and capable of developing an independent long-term strategy).

(2) Strategic planning should be concerned with the allocation of managerial as well as financial resources.

(3) The emphasis in the managerial system should also be tailored to the stage of development in the business:

(a) New ventures will require entrepreneurial management, a flexible organization structure, informal systems for information, communication, performance measurement and control, and the financial resources to enable them to develop and introduce new products into a rapidly growing market.

(b) Businesses which have passed the introductory stage, require professional management to install more formal systems to improve communications within the growing organization and to keep control of costs, production, sales etc. They are likely to be self-financing but they need to make use of sophisticated management techniques such as operational research and organization development.

This division is very useful, but, in the longer term there is inevitably movement and overlap between these two categories, and the dynamic nature of the organization — and the associated management problems — should never be underestimated.

Although there is scope for precise definitions, in general the literature has used the terms 'Divisions', 'Strategic Business Units' (SBU's), Wissema's[5a] 'Product Market Combinations', or 'New Ventures' loosely, and the Boston Consulting Groups' (BSG) portfolio matrix can apply almost equally well to each word.

However, creating New Ventures is more about encouraging change and innovation; they are essentially corporate vehicles designed to exploit more effectively new ideas, products or markets. Unless otherwise deliberately stimulated, human nature appears to show that all organizations become increasingly conservative, concerned with their own internal needs and objectives. This process inevitably inhibits innovation and change. The concept of New Ventures is one way to help overcome this tendency to inertia. It is, however, important to recognise that this approach can — especially at the early stages — result in additional difficulties in the continual battle between the existing core businesses and the new business areas.

The key question here is: How do you create and organise New Business Ventures that, one day, will grow into the next generation of Strategic Business Units? If successful, New Ventures can be an invaluable vehicle for the corporate transformation that is essential for corporate survival and success over the longer term.

However, as Schwaninger[6] argued:

> The strategic planning process should be designed in a different way from the operational planning process. Experience suggests a procedure which seems to gain increased acceptance in companies with several business units. Instead of planning for all SBU's (Strategic Business Units) in one annual planning cycle, periodic strategy meetings are held several times a year, for example at monthly or bi-monthly intervals. During each meeting, previous strategies of one or two business units are reviewed, revised and formulated anew. The frequency with which business units are planned is handled flexibly. It varies from unit to unit depending on their specific dynamics — those with intensive competition or high rates of innovation (short life cycles need to be dealt with more often than the ones in which less change is taking place). In addition conferences to develop overall corporate strategy are necessary.

Some of these organizational issues were discussed by Hegarty and Hoffman,[7] building on the three general types of strategic decisions identified by Miles and Snow,[8] which must be made to adapt the firm to its environment. These decisions were : (1) choices of products and markets; (2) selection of technologies for supplying, producing and distributing goods/services; and (3) administrative choices of structures and management systems.

The purpose of the Hegarty/Hoffman study of 407 European top managers was to attempt to answer two broad questions:

(1) *Who* has primary influence over different types of strategic decisions made in organizations?

(2) *What* powerbases enable departments to exert decision influence?

Although the concept of New Ventures was not mentioned, this paper recognised that 'power and influence in strategic decision-making is a complex process', and that the organizational issues cannot be ignored. The paper also showed how difficult it is to introduce a New Venture concept into a traditional organization structure even if it had top management commitment.

Another useful general introduction to strategic issues and their organization and development within the corporation was given by Skipton,[9] but he too did not specifically discuss New Ventures.

Corporate Transformation

A general weakness of much business literature is that it fails to recognise the key elements in the corporate renewal cycle, which are:

(1) Exploit the first specialization.

(2) Identify the point where the first specialization is beginning to become deficient.

(3) Identify a second specialization for which there is a demand and for which the specialist knowledge and experience developed in stage (1) could be appropriate.

(4) Transfer from the old specialization to the new, without ending up as a diversified group that has no specific skills.

(5) Exploit the second specialization.

One obstacle to the effective implementation of this renewal cycle is that the corporate culture, managerial style and approach to strategic planning could well be different for stages (1) and (5) when compared with (2), (3) and (4). This is why it is essential to recognise both the importance of managing change and the need for flexibility in any approach to strategic planning. The needs of effective 'cloning' in the growth phase can be radically different from the pressures of managing a turnaround or corporate transformation. Consequently it is not only a matter of the effective management of each element of the process and the movement from one stage to the other, but it also involves the management of different stages and cultures within a single organization.

Ideally the innovative corporation would successfully integrate both approaches and styles but, unfortunately, that appears to be the exception rather than the rule. Several authors have, however, rightly emphasised the need for flexibility: 'Those involved in the planning activity need to be clear where the organization stands in the cycle at any one time and thus be aware of what is most wanted from planning at that point';[10] or as Leontiades asserted:

> The message is clear: planning must exist in more than one dimension. Planning must be flexible to cope with fluctuations in a dynamic environment. In some periods planning for nothing more than maintaining the momentum of existing businesses may suffice. But when management perceives the need for fundamental changes in strategy the intensity, as well as the character, of planning will shift to encompass variable as well as fixed aspects of planning.[11]

Similarly, Pearson,[12] when he reviews the strengths and weaknesses of the product life-cycle and gap analysis in the context of new product development, concluded that organizations must:

> Concentrate continually on reposturing the division or business to meet significant long-term changes in the environment and maintaining as much flexibility in the business as possible to meet continuing, but different and sometimes quite unexpected, changes in the future. This is achieved by a results-oriented project management approach which develops the business or division by a series of specific projects; the exact balance depending on the unique needs that the business or division faces within a paticular environment.

Most corporations are delayed in stages (1) and (4) of the progression and they operate as a result in a range of different businesses. The particular problems and conflicts in diversified companies were discussed by Goold and Campbell,[13] who identified three main 'styles' of management: strategic planning (core business), strategic control (diverse businesses) and financial control (manageable businesses). All three approaches require some kind of basic business unit and even those who organize their core businesses along product lines are likely to define the peripheral businesses as New Ventures, if for no other reason than it is easier to effect their disposal. The financial control approach accepts the concept of a fully independent (although usually wholly owned) corporate structure, with the business areas operating as subsidiaries to the holding company, who is essentially operating as a conglomerate. Here the key resource is usually quality of management. Often groups organized in this way are active in the acquisition/disposal business, and that is essentially the definition of their core business.

The diverse business philosophy can be viewed as an inbetween state, either moving away from the traditional core [stage (1)], or towards a new core [stage (5)]. It is here that New Ventures often get the greatest opportunity as 'this philosophy entails creating groups of more homogeneous businesses, and delegating much of the strategy responsibility to those groups'. Goold and Campbell[13] also found that 'the companies classified as following the diverse business philosophy have seen a lower average level of profitability but have enjoyed particularly rapid improvements in returns in recent years'. This could be accounted for by the fact that it is likely that these groups are moving into a later stage of a corporate turnaround where, once a sound profit base has been established (usually by a crash cost cutting programme) the emphasis is switched to a concerted search for new business areas as the basis for future growth. As can be seen again, the management of New Business areas (including New Ventures) is the key to successful corporate metamorphosis and long term survival.

Pearson[14] discussed the problems of setting and sustaining effective corporate objectives within the context of changing cultures and managerial styles by, among other things, comparing Maslow's hierarchy of human needs with a hierarchy of corporate needs. He concluded the corporate hierarchy with 'The need to achieve and maintain a leadership position in a chosen field'. His analysis failed to emphasise sufficiently that in a dynamic changing world the need to manage the process of *changing* fields is critical over the longer term. Many (if not all) mature industry problems arise because this issue is not recognised and/or it is badly managed by top management.

At the corporate level of multi-unit firms (irrespective of how the unit is defined) the central strategic questions are the same: namely, what mix of businesses should be pursued? and how should priorities be determined?

'Today's most common word in the manager's vocabulary is that of change,'[15] pronounced one article, while another asserted that 'good planners don't plan, they enable good managers to plan.'[16] Both articles — and others[17] — emphasised the importance of managing change and, by implication, the importance of setting the right framework for New Ventures (and there are few places where getting the framework right is more important than in New Ventures) but none of them discussed the issues explicitly. Planning flexibility was also emphasised by Cartwright:[18] 'The key to success in planning lies in the fine art of balancing what you really want and need with the ways and means actually available for achieving it'.

However, as Robinson[16] noted, 'in the very first article published in the Society's journal we read: "The purpose of long range planning is not so much having a plan but developing attitudes, processes and perspectives which make planning possible." *Plus ça change, plus c'est la même chose*'. Yet the task of deciding what precisely is changing and why, and what is staying the same is, unfortunately, as difficult today as it was twenty years ago. On the other hand it is reasonable to assume there are some universal truths and they are usually simple ones too.

Some of the problems experienced in turnaround are illustrated by Zimmerman,[19] who identified a number of common themes in the process:

☆ Turnaround is a multifaceted process.

☆ A 'referent' organization is necessary [to regulate present relationships and activities, as well as to establish base values and operating ground rules. In addition, it needs to foster the appreciation of emerging trends and issues and to develop a shared image of a desirable future, and provide infrastructure support in the form of new resources, information and the direction of special projects.]

☆ A new and additive view of the environment is an essential step.

☆ The process of examining the environment needs to be systematically approached.

☆ Values need to be clarified and articulated. Old values should be preserved as new values are added. Traditional values can have a considerable influence on the speed and direction of change.

☆ The systematic withdrawal of resources can often be a vehicle for improving organizational performance.

These factors illustrate the problems of creating and sustaining New Ventures under such conditions, despite their crucial role over the longer term.

Another approach[20] to turnaround identified four elements to any overall strategy: management strategies; cutback strategies; growth strategies; and restructuring strategies. In his analysis of the Management Process of turnaround O'Neill found that it involved:

☆ Being preceded by a change in top management's redefinition of the firm's business.

☆ Changes in most areas of the organization.

☆ Growth strategies were less used by firms which are highly diversified.

☆ In unsuccessful turnarounds, there is less attention to re-structuring strategies.

☆ Often unsuccessful turnarounds are newcomers to planning.

☆ Turnaround success is affected by competitive position product life-cycle and general market conditions.

☆ The cause of the decline is an important determinant of the turnaround strategy.

He concluded that 'a turnaround represents a new "strategic era!" '. As an increasing number of companies are partly or totally involved in a turnaround strategy, it is essential that there is understanding of how this impacts on New Ventures and New Business development if the company's longer term prospects are not to be sacrificed to short-term interests.

Dowdy and Nikolchev[21] considered how industries mature and the role technology can play in reversing the trend, as well as exploring alternative techniques managers can use to determine whether the application of new technology can revitalize a particular product line or service and how to determine which technology should be developed or applied. As has already been mentioned, these are essential elements in the vital process of corporate metamorphosis. However, most turnaround approaches can easily put any existing New Venture strategy at risk as their payback is usually too long-term for them to be initiated at the early stages of any recovery. This paper illustrated the difficulty of overcoming either — or both — of these constraints.

Nevertheless, the analysis of symptoms of Maturity and evidence of premature Senility discussed by the authors are invaluable in providing a framework for understanding and managing the situation.

Maturity Symptoms:	Market saturation
	Inelastic demand
	Overcapacity
	Product displacement
	Technological obsolescence
	Customer sophistication
Senility Evidence:	Management inflexibility
	Overoptimistic projections
	Complacency
	Morale problems
	Mismanaging the experience Curve
	Inappropriate performance
Measures:	Overstaffing
	Poor communication
	Financial mismanagement

In their paper[21] these factors were combined into competitive product profiling, involving analysis of functional performance; acquisition cost; ease of use; operating costs; product reliability; service ability; and system compatibility.

In the final section the Management Challenges were evaluated, but no mention was made of possible re-organization, or more precise definition, of the basic business units. In many situations this is an essential prerequisite of the whole analysis. The authors considered that:

> depending on the importance of the technology and the time criticality for its availability, the range of options includes:
>
> ☆ Acquisitions
>
> ☆ Internal research and development
>
> ☆ Licensing
>
> ☆ Internal ventures
>
> ☆ Joint ventures
>
> ☆ Strategic and innovative alliances
>
> ☆ Venture capital investments and nurturing
>
> ☆ Educational acquisitions
>
> The most appropriate or desirable approach depends on the particular circumstances involved.

It should, however, be recognised that most — if not all — these options are long-term. More detailed consideration of the 'particular circumstances' is covered by other papers in this collection.

This paper[21] goes on to argue:

> American companies are constantly looking for new methods to capture advancing technologies from small entrepreneurial start-up companies. Many are establishing innovative alliances with such companies. For example, Tektronix, Acme-Cleveland and Caterpillar Tractor have established strategic alliances with small high-technology firms hoping both to obtain new technology for use in traditional product lines as well as create an entrepreneurial environment within the company.

Such an approach can be invaluable; but 'hope' will not be enough to be successful in itself; it will need to be combined with an understanding of the special conditions necessary for success, including an appropriate corporate structure, which is discussed in more detail elsewhere.

Board Involvement

One simple, yet often forgotten axiom, is that the Board and the Cheif Executive Officer (CEO) should be involved in any significant innovation that is being undertaken by, or within, the organization. This statement is made not only because the Board and its operation is the critical element in determining the future success of the corporation, but also because change and innovation are invariably associated with significant risks — and without the active support of the Board and/or CEO any significant innovation is almost inevitably doomed to fail.

But to include the Board in this comment is not to ignore the view expounded by Bavly[22] that, in practice most Boards are extremely ineffective. Or as Drucker put it: 'The Board has become an impotent ceremonial and legal fiction. It certainly does not conduct the affairs of the enterprise'.[23]

Yet the 1983 Korn/Ferry annual Board of Directors survey identified Strategic Planning as one of the most important issues facing the Board, ranking second only to Financial Results.

Pinnell[24] suggested that in developing objectives and strategies the Board should answer the following questions:

(1) What growth in pre-tax profits is to be achieved and by when?

(2) How far can this growth be achieved by the existing business? What strategies (e.g. in marketing, capacity expansion and cost reduction) would be required?

(3) If the existing business cannot achieve the profit objective, what type of structural change should be planned?

    (a) Collaborative strategies, e.g. Joint ventures or licensing?

    (b) Acquisition of more promising businesses? or

    (c) Divestment or closure of unprofitable activities?

Rosenstein[25] also supported the view that Boards were not sufficiently involved in strategy. Again neither of these articles explicitly recognised the importance of managing change and innovation, let alone that New Business Development and New Ventures were a key Board responsibility.

This omission is also reflected in other articles, such as that by Steiner and Kunin,[26] which identified 14 qualities for a CEO, and went into a long discussion on the need for increased awareness of public policy issues, but did not mention the key role of the CEO in new business development and in managing change and innovation.

Another approach by Wissema[27] looked at the management changes expected in the 1980s and found that management archetypes did not necessarily coincide with corporate culture and that there was a need to synchronize management development planning with strategic planning. 'This link is logical but is nevertheless absent almost everywhere'.

In practice New Business Development and the management of change is a key CEO responsibility. But 'in many companies the principal obstacle to the integration of strategic planning into the management process is the CEO.'[28] However, a survey of UK and Canadian companies between 1974 and

1979 found that 'the most significant change with regard to the responsibility for planning appears to be a move to increase the involvement of the chief executive officer'.[29]

In most cases top management have been promoted to their positions because of technical skills demonstrated in the core business and this can often present additional problems as the New Business/Core Business debate easily gets caught up in other organizational and personality issues. Such a development produces a whole range of personal selection and training issues that are rarely dealt with satisfactorily, partly because it is a difficult and sensitive area to research.

To understand the process of cultural change, let alone effectively manage that change, is not easy, particularly for a mature company in crisis. It is much easier to manage rapid growth during a corporation's initial entrepreneurial phase, Any attempt to move from the entrepreneurial to the professional stage, or to mix the two cultures, requires a deep understanding of the issues. The importance of a mixture of corporate cultures was discussed by Scholz,[30] but he avoided any discussion of possible conflicts between the Core (traditional) and New Business (innovative) areas — and how these might be resolved.

One example of the positive influence of the Chief Executive is cited by Wilmot,[31]★ who advocated an approach to innovation and accelerated organizational change, with particular emphasis on realizing rapid competitive benefits from the implementation of strategic information systems. He believed that 'change has become associated with reactive rather than pro-active behaviour, and this is completely inappropriate. It is viewed as miserable rather than exciting, depressing rather than exhilarating'.

Wilmot also maintained that 'the investment gap is in management of innovation, not R & D' (a subject referred to in more detail later). Further, he believed that 'the process of networking is one of the most cost-effective and dynamic ways that exist of keeping change on the agenda and is a tremendous stimulus to innovation'. The 13 points identified in his 'Changes in Management and the Management of Change' checklist are shown in the first page of his paper and are strongly recommended.

Wilmot concluded:

> It may just be that many of yesterday's star companies are coming to the end of their eras, that what they were good at may no longer be relevant. Their tremendous belief in *their* particular recipe may be *their* downfall and *your* opportunity.

Very few corporate innovators survive decades of bureaucracy, although notable exceptions do emerge to meet the challenge of urgently needed turnarounds.

Historically, planning has been more an exercise in co-ordinating organizational and operational activities, than a vehicle or catalyst for managing change. It has been used primarily by corporate 'clones' who were managing rapid growth, rather than by those companies either in their initial entrepreneurial phase, where the original entrepreneurial vision tended to dominate, or by mature companies attempting to manage a turnaround.

Today this pattern is changing, partly because the limitations of the 'cloning' approach are becoming increasingly recognised, and partly because the management of change is becoming more widely accepted as being at the very *core* of management. This does not mean that the traditional Strategic Performance Indicators[32] do not apply. It is always important to ensure that the planning system meets operational needs; is indicative of desired performance; is acceptable to subordinates; and is as reliable, timely and simple as possible. It is, however, increasingly important for the strategic planning and control system to focus on the identification and effective exploitation of New Business opportunities. Even when the Strategy Consultants are evaluated[33] the key element of New Business development is rarely mentioned. The 7–S McKinsey Framework (Strategy, Structure, Systems, Style, Staff, Shared Values, Skills) recognises the importance of having all the elements pointing and working in the same direction, but the analysis that goes with this approach rarely identifies the importance of change, innovation and New Business Development as the ultimate priority.

Carpenter[34]★ used his experience at General Electric to bring these issues together when he suggested that 'strategy and planning are two words that should not be juxtaposed'.

Strategy is concerned with the workings of a business and winning against one's competitors.

Planning, on the other hand, tends to focus on the development of specific, detailed programs for a product line, for facilities, for marketing etc. that follow from the strategy.

The strategic development process must focus on making the strategy explicit, making the assumptions clear, and testing the strategy's validity. The fundamental questions of strategy mentioned in his paper are:

☆ How can competitive cost or price advantage be obtained?

☆ What are the structural shifts — technology, market or competitive — that are occurring in the environment and how can they be exploited?

☆ What are competitors' strategies and their implications?

☆ What do we have to do to win?

Strategic management must get back to basics by de-emphasizing the *process* and *bureaucracy* of strategic planning while re-emphasizing sound strategic thinking and effective implementation.

Carpenter also argued that 'to increase the value-added of our profession, corporate planners must direct their activities towards strategic thinking and away from planning systems; towards vision and away from volume; towards insight and away from forms and formats; and towards creativity and away from control and bureaucracy'.

Other authors[35] have also recognised the existence of different styles of strategic planning, each with their own business philosophy, set of planning approaches, concepts and techniques. In this case 5 styles were identified, each with a different focus:

☆ Allocation and control of resources

☆ Developing new business

☆ Managing organizational change

☆ Mobilizing power and influence

☆ Explanation of the future

Unfortunately for the effective management of change invariably elements of each approach are required, and this more integrated and comprehensive approach was developed by Taylor in his survey of 'Corporate Planning for the 1990s, The New Frontiers'[36]. He concluded that to achieve superior competitive performance, Corporate Development needs to be seen as an Integrated Process designed to manage strategic change at all levels of the organization. This involved:

☆ Leaders who make a public commitment to a company philosophy and specific goals.

☆ Competitive bench-marking to set the performance standards.

☆ Internal marketing programmes to explain the business objectives and strategies to employees.

☆ A business philosophy and strategy to provide a framework for individual action.

☆ Project teams and task forces which are accountable directly to top management for the detail.

☆ Segmented organization structures which divide businesses into smaller autonomous units, which allow the development and operation of entrepreneurial managers who are held accountable for profit and growth targets.

☆ Staff training and team development to build the capability for improved performance.

☆ Employee involvement programmes, performance appraisal and incentive schemes to motivate and reward individual and group achievement.

In evaluating the papers in this area the three papers included in this volume stand out as particularly relevant to the core issues involved in the strategic management of Change and Innovation.

☆   ☆   ☆

In the next four sections covering New Product Development, R & D, Diversification and the Relationship with Small Companies, there is a wide selection of papers covering various aspects of the subject, although few authors have specifically focused on the New Venture theme. This dilemma is repeated when the case studies are considered. However there are two key papers in Part 1, Section 6 that deal specifically with Venture Management, and, taken together, the papers provide invaluable insights into the problems and opportunities relating to the critical strategic management issues that arise in managing change in general, and creating and managing New Ventures in particular.

Developing New Products and Services

In general the papers published by the *Long Range Planning* journal in the area of New Product Development deal with the theoretical or analytical issues relating to the products themselves. Very few examine directly the issues relating to the business or organizational structures (such as New Ventures) which are necessary for the successful exploitation of new products.

The papers included in this section do not specifically concern the role for New Ventures within the overall strategy of new product development, but they provide invaluable insights and essential background, to the theme.

Buggie[37]★ provides a comprehensive set of guidelines that enable more effective new product development. Much of his analysis overlaps closely with that applying to New Ventures — i.e. cost curves, organizational requirements and risk factors, as well as being an invaluable starting point for defining a product-based venture in the first place.

To meet the need to get new products to the market more quickly, Mathôt[38]★ argued for the need to establish multi-disciplinary *Innovation Groups* whose main ingredients are:

☆ The right mix and size of the Group (and that the chairman of the Group should be the Managing Director)

☆ 'Hard' agreements on frequency and duration of meetings

☆ Efficient discussion techniques

☆ Planning the innovation activities

The Innovation Group should evaluate the prospects for new products within an initial feasibility study which is then — if appropriate — developed into a detailed Business Development Plan. In this exercise the following subjects should be considered:

☆ The product; its characteristics and components.

☆ Product development; problem areas and costs.

☆ Marketing; geographical strategy and distribution channels.

☆ Production; used/bought issues and costs.

☆ Finance; selling prices, costs, investment requirement and funding sources.

These elements are very similar to those mentioned in the discussion on the role of business plans in the New Venture Management Section. It is on the basis of this plan that *Top Management* can *decide* to set the development of the new product (venture) in motion. It is also an invaluable document against which subsequent progress can be monitored; and it should be regularly updated.

The issues surrounding New Product development inevitably overlap with those relating to R & D, which are discussed in more detail below. Pilditch[39] reflected a widely held belief when he maintained

there seems to be a gap, doesn't there, between inventiveness and a capacity to develop market-winning new products; one may *not* be the fruit of the other . . . with few exceptions, the firms that place too great a faith in R & D will be disappointed, increasingly . . . while we win Nobel prizes we lose markets.

He recognised the importance of regarding innovation as 'the whole process by which products or processes move successfully into the economy', and he went on to argue the undeniable importance of satisfying the needs and wants of customers.

However, in his otherwise convincing approach to developing new products, Pilditch made no mention of the organizational issues that invariably hamper effective exploitation of new products. These factors can be critical in many cases and this can produce the need to consider — and answer —

such questions as: Is the product in question really new? Or is it a modification of an existing product that can be dealt with satisfactorily within existing channels and structures? Or does the product need to be taken out of the existing structures to give it any chance of success? (i.e. does it need a New Venture approach?) How is that to be done? Do those operating the New Venture approach really know what they are doing? — if they do not, the product has even less chance of being successful.

The points made by Pilditch about UK industry also relate to other parts of the world, such as Germany:

In future, technological change will lead not only to growing competition in terms of innovation but also to shorter product and technology life-cycles in the industries producing technology-intensive consumer goods. This has considerable consequences for the companies' product strategies. First, the aim must be to keep the products technically attractive for the market, and secondly, to ensure that they can be produced and sold profitably. Short product life-cycles mean that the period during which investments must be amortized becomes shorter and therefore that the level of return can only be improved if the manufacture of high-technology products also leads to an increase in the value added they yield during their life-cycles. This pattern of development indicates that product-strategy risks grow as the level of competition or innovation increases . . . market growth and market share is the outcome of the realization of success potential within strategic product technology management.[40]

Stone[41]★ provides an extensive analysis of the New Product Development approach of Japan, which includes a useful nine-phase process for understanding the behaviour of 'Mechatronic Markets'. This process starts with the recognition of the initial opportunity and ends by moving onto the next market; in many ways these are similar stages to those identified in the section on Corporate Metamorphosis above. Understanding — and learning from — the Japanese experience in New Product Development must be one of the top priorities for any CEO and this paper is an excellent starting point.

In another paper,[42] Stone supported the need for a flexible approach to planning, as outlined above. He believed that 'in competitive markets, the winners will usually be companies which take a *horses for courses* approach by using different kinds of planning for different markets, technologies and businesses'.

However, in Stone's detailed New Product Marketing plan format that was developed within the overall New Product Planning and Launch Process, there was no discussion of the (perhaps critical) issue of the Corporate Structure itself within which these new product marketing decisions were to be taken.

Further papers[43,44] look at various aspects of New Product developments and Planning but without considering the organizational issues.

Barksdale and Harris[45] provided a comprehensive paper that combined

> the product life cycle and portfolio Matrix models to provide an exhaustive system for classifying and analyzing a diverse assortment of business units. Classification of products according to this model reveals the relative competitive position of products, indicates the rate of market growth; and enables the visualization of strategy alternatives in a general sense if not in precise terms.

The detailed analysis of 'infants; stars; problem children; cash cows; dogs; war horses and Dodos' is an invaluable framework for developing an effective role for New Ventures (and SBU's). The organization issues appeared to be taken as given, although the paper did emphasise in general that product/market strategy was a fundamental element in the process of adapting an organization to the changing market.

It is impossible to undertake an exercise such as the 'Risk Return Approach to Product Portfolio Strategy'[46] unless well defined business units (or ventures) exist. The more these units are defined the more flexibility will arise in exploring options for acquisition or divestment. James[47] provided a valuable introduction to the corporate life cycle which highlights the 'frightening spectacle' of the 'Inertia Phenomenon' that is at the centre of any understanding and/or management of corporate change, which is itself critical to any strategy concerned with New Business or New Product development.

Strategic Planning for R & D

The UK has an excellent tradition for Research but has been continually weak on exploitation. One explanation for this weakness is reflected in the continued discussion[48,49,50,51] of technology and R & D, without any consideration being given to the organizational issues involved in exploitation. It is easy to mention in passing the need for SBU's or New Ventures (although this is rarely done); it is another, much more difficult task, to ensure that they operate successfully.

Allen's[52] approach to R & D assessment was essentially project based and contained a number of similarities to that of New Venture evaluation, except that the latter is likely to be more formally structured. The approach to Project Cash Flow is particularly similar.

Sethi, Movsesian and Hickey,[53] showed how technology can be planned and managed using formal techniques similar to those used in business and capital investment planning. They argued that 'together with business strategy, the technology strategy defines how resources can be used most effectively to achieve a sustainable competitive advantage'. But, again, there was no discussion of a role for a New Venture strategy within that strategy.

The importance of integrating business strategies with the strategic management of technology was emphasised by Frohman and Bitondo.[54] They recognised that a technological strategy must cover such items as objectives; technology selection; investment level; external assessment; acquisitional analysis; as well as organizational and policy issues (i.e. it is very similar to the elements included in a basic business plan). In order to undertake this process successfully the manager must know: the key performance parameters of the product as seen by the customer; the competitive developments in the product market; and the manufacturing process.

The importance of integrating product research with production research was also highlighted by Prentice.[55] His detailed comparison with the Japanese approach emphasised the importance of top management commitment to quality; efficiency; R & D; and long-term strategies, as well as the need for consistent (relatively a-political) co-operation with the Government. Prentice concluded that at least part of the Japanese secret was due to the fact that 'R & D is directed to specific end targets that are products or production systems with world markets in view'.

The importance of Government policy was also identified by Smith.[56] He discussed the role of macroeconomic cycles (including the Kondratieff cycle) and argued that

> Government should use its unique position to encourage longer term results which will come from basic interventions helped along the route to experimentation, development and finally commercial exploitation as a basic new innovation. The problem is the selection of the right adjustment policies and the right points in the innovation process to inject money and motivation.

In the UK at least there is little evidence to suggest the Government is an effective vehicle for 'picking winners', or that any significant attention is given to the organizational issues involved in the effective exploitation of R & D. However, there have been recently some signs that attitudes are slowly shifting in the right direction.

Willder[57]★ used the Product Champion, rather than the Venture Manager, concept, although there is considerable overlap between the two approaches. He argued that 'two major forces act on a technology-based business: first, the pull of a relatively-known market place whose requirements a business endeavours to satisfy; secondly, the push which the development of more advanced technology creates to meet requirements not necessarily extant in the existing market'.

Willder further emphasised the importance of Research Management Reviews of research activities, which should have the following objectives:

☆ To define programmes in the first instance, specify their scope and chart progress.

☆ To ensure that all programmes have an identified sponsor, preferably from among the business divisions, charged with the responsibility for subsequent exploitation and sales.

In order to exploit the new product or idea requires the organization and management of the development process, which can be viewed as the formalization of the specification, design, development, testing and launch, which should be managed by a 'Product Champion'; and choosing the right Product Champion is an important issue for the Board/CEO.

The Board also needs to establish an environment within which the Product Champion can operate. Willder recommended 'The Greenhouse' concept operating under a New Business Director. Again this approach is not dissimilar to that of Venture Management. He maintained: 'Finally, the New Business Director must be a strong creator of the Greenhouse environment, be able to analyse and present the cases carefully and well, and be prepared to re-parent the successful ventures into other parts of the company'. The latter point cannot be over emphasised and is often complicated by intense internal political manoeuvring. It is also important to emphasise that the New Business Director is not the only source of innovation and new business development within the company. The broader the base and source of innovation within the corporation the better.

Van Gunsteren[58] used the strategic classification of Licence Giver, Licence Taker, Jobber or Consultant as a basis for re-structuring the organization. Although there was no specific discussion of the New Venture concept, he did, however, maintain that

the basic identities can flourish alongside each other within one corporation, as long as the associated organizational units are kept separate and their autonomy is sufficient to allow them to develop their own appropriate approach to business problems (along with a general corporate spirit).

One of the benefits that was found to arise from this more rigorous separation into different business units was that 'buck-passing and internal quarrelling came to an end and profitability was restored.' If only it was that easy!

In two papers Petroni[59,60] examined the problem affecting the R & D function caused by its lack of integration with the enterprise, which makes it difficult to pass from invention to innovation — that is, to turn the invention into processes and products to be exchanged on the market. He recognised

that the degree and significance of the innovative output which is the institutional goal of an industrial research organization will be *directly proportional to the integration of the structure called upon to produce it*.

The soul of corporate strategy is innovation, i.e. the capacity of the enterprise to keep up or renew itself continually in a competitive situation where the rules of the game change rapidly and constantly.[59]

He went on to argue that 'the relationship between innovative and improvement research was of the utmost importance if there was to be efficient structuring.' In order to attempt to overcome the almost inherent 'difficult' relationship between Strategy and Research a number of alternative approaches were considered, including: the presence of a person responsible for Research and Development on the Board of Directors; the separation of improvement research assigned to the various 'profit centres' while explorative research is entrusted to the central research group; and integration through the formation and operation of 'business teams'. There is nothing incompatable with any combination of all three approaches and, although it is not discussed specifically, the 'business team' approach has some of the essential elements that would arise if a New Venture concept was applied. The possible areas of conflict are usefully explored, with the ultimate suggestion being a matrix organizational structure; however,

an essential condition for the success of the matrix model lies in the choice of a project leader (Product Champion) with a strong managerial capacity, and a capacity for actively motivating and obtaining collaboration. In this way one can overcome, at least partially, the structural conflict situations latent in the matrix approach suggested.[59]

In his second paper Petroni[60] again emphasised 'the ability of an organization to produce innovations which help the development of the business, depends on how well the R & D function is integrated with the rest of the business; it must be possible for innovations to find their way from the R & D department into the wider organization where they can be 'commercialized' as new or improved products'. To create an environment in which this 'commercialization' can take place, managers must provide:

☆ A clear division of responsibility between R & D and other company functions, as well as between the core of the company and individual divisions.

☆ Methods of personnel management which take into account the particular values and attitudes of researchers and technicians.

☆ An efficient planning and control system for R & D activity.

Again the difficulties of integrating the Business Plan and R & D activities were considered, with Petroni concluding that 'many organizations, feeling the need to improve their productivity and profitability, have recently been led to re-examine the quality and quantity of resources that they invest in R & D. In particular, they are looking for a tighter link-up between research activities and their business development plans.' Petroni also added that there was

> a precise basis for differentiating between technology-push and demand-pull organizations. In the former, the planning mechanism is of a top-down nature, and is put into action under the leadership of R & D and top management. In demand-pull organizations, the planning process is driven by portfolio analysis, and identification of product needs; in these cases the Marketing department must lead the way, and the process is 'bottom-up' in nature.

Although there was no consideration in this approach of the New Venture concept, there are many common strands, and it is essential that any New Venture structure is at least as much market led as it is R & D driven.

It is in the nature of radical R & D results, and radical innovations of any kind, that they rarely fit neatly into existing corporate structures. It is also not uncommon for new products to challenge the markets of the existing product range.

In examining the overall problems associated with the effective exploitation of R & D, Ward[61] identified the need for more Planned Opportunism; Interactive Dialogue; Channelled Innovation and Successive Focusing. His paper also showed that long-term corporate survival and success depended on more than just trying to answer the age-old question: 'What Business are we really in?'. It required an effective product-development procedure that matched capabilities with needs. And such a process

> should enable any commercial enterprise to:
>
> ☆ Plan its future continuously and systematically.
>
> ☆ Make the most of its existing assets.
>
> ☆ Keep in close touch with its market environment.
>
> ☆ Make product decisions with minimum delay.
>
> ☆ Exploit whatever unexpected opportunities may come to light.

This approach is also relevant to non-profit organizations.

Strategies for Diversification

Diversification is a Catch 22 problem for most companies. Without it no company will survive over the long term; sooner or later it is inevitable that it will have to undergo a significant corporate metamorphosis. Yet all the evidence suggests that few companies manage to undertake this process successfully.

Some of the basic issues of diversification (i.e. Horizontal, Vertical and Lateral) were discussed in early papers in the Journal. One[62] quoted ITT as 'an example of complete diversification by making clever use of the company's management and finance know-how as its major resource'. Events a decade later illustrated how vulnerable these 're-sources' could be.

A thorough systematic approach to Diversification was provided by Malmlow[63] who considered the idea and information phase, as well as the organization of diversification projects.

Another analytical system for assessing opportunities for diversification and acquisition was provided by Younger.[64] But his approach, like many others including Thomas,[65] while useful as far as they went, tended to over-emphasise modelling and statistical techniques and underestimate the human factor. In retrospect, the failure rate of acquisitions, relative to meeting their original expectations, is extremely high; and results appear to show that financial opportunism is the main criterion for success, and lack of attention to the people issues the main cause of failure.

Having a policy that involves a New Venture (or SBU) approach can assist companies in developing a strategy and implementing a programme of corporate restructuring of whatever form, in acquisition[66,67] and divestment[68] strategies, or in other areas such management buy outs[69,70,71] and joint ventures of various kinds[72,73].

Clarke and Gall[68] found that there were three reasons for increasing the efforts spent on divestment: (1) to give a more balanced overall strategy whereby funds are efficiently moved from inappropriate to attractive investments; (2) to ensure that the impact of disposals is correctly assessed; and (3) to release the maximum amount of resources from divestments. But none of this restructuring could take place unless the businesses, or parts of businesses, were in an appropriate corporate structure.

The management of turnarounds is a difficult and painful process. Situations differ by industry, the culture of the organization involved, technology and a variety of other factors. However, essentially the crisis has arisen because, in the past, the corporation had an insufficiently innovative culture and that has encouraged complacency and inertia. The solution to this problem requires the injection, either by a change of management or policies — or more usually both — of a more innovative approach. While New Ventures have a long term role in this process, often in the short term they are actually put at risk, since the first priority in most turnaround situations is to cut costs and consolidate. Under those circumstances New Ventures that are not, at least, cash flow positive run a considerable risk of being abandoned in the interests of short term profitability and recovery. The corporate health of the parent usually has a far reaching influence on the long term prospects of the New Ventures Strategy, and the damaging effect of cyclical influences cannot be over emphasised.[74] New Ventures usually get started in good times, but are often the first to get cut back when the wind changes, unless they have established deep and powerful roots in both managerial and cash flow terms.

Robinson[75] studied over three hundred industrial businesses in declining markets using the PIMS Data Base, which is critically dependent on getting reliable information from defined business units such as SBU's or New Ventures. He concluded that with respect to profitability and cash flow, three out of the four factors relating to good performance (i.e. strong market position, low capital intensity, high relative product quality, and low costs) would help support traditional businesses and mitigate against New Ventures if used as a basis for future decisions on resource allocation. This is a common situation in the continual battle between New Ventures and the core business areas over the allocation of resources.

Detrie and Ramanantsoa[76]★ provided a strategic analysis of Diversification policies, which can have different objectives depending on the specific strategic position of the individual company and these are particularly relevant (and difficult) if the company is in its maturing or declining phase. Several types of diversification were observed: Investment Diversification; Branching Out Diversification; Support Diversification and Survival Diversification. Their paper provided two valuable tables, one of the five steps in the Diversification Decision Process, the other of the key factors in success and failure. The authors highlighted five rules for success:

☆ Make the Management Aware of the Importance of the Diversification Decision.

☆ Ensure that the firm has the Skills suited to Market Needs.

☆ Test before going Broadscale.

☆ Identify the point(s) of no return in marketing, finance and organization.

☆ Take account of the human problems.

A major exercise in diversification requires new skills, while 'having the necessary competence is certainly necessary but it is not enough by itself'. There are a number of motives for diversification and it is the final step of a four stage process of product development that begins with market penetration, followed by geographical expansion, then moves onto the development of complementary products before the company embarks on entry into new fields of activity.

Although this paper did not consider a role for New Ventures as such, these structures could comfortably be incorporated into the approach taken.

The key to post-war Japanese success has been their ability to exploit new technology and products. However, there is little evidence to suggest that this success has arisen through the use of a formalised New Venture structure as it is generally defined; quite the contrary. The Japanese tradition of an informal corporate structure has dominated their approach in the past 30 years. Nevertheless, it can be argued that a critical factor in their ability to exploit new technology and products arises because their overall corporate philosophy is dominated by a willingness to welcome change. As a result, many Japanese corporations act implicitly as a whole as if they were New Venture operations; without requiring the same formalities, and without risking the potentially harmful conflicts between the New Business areas and the more traditional sectors. Some of these advantages could be due to deep cultural factors, while others could be explained by the fact that more Japanese companies have been in their entrepreneurial/growth phase, which is generally more conducive to a collective, innovative approach. The real test comes in the challenges presented in the more recent post-oil crisis period, where the need is to restructure their maturing, traditional industries.[77]

New Ventures and Small Business

The development of links between large and small companies is an attempt to get the best of both worlds; to combine the wisdom, experience and resources of the large corporation, with the enthusiasm and innovative capacity of the smaller company. Today there are an increasing number of ways in which this can be achieved, from licensing and joint ventures, to links through venture funds and strategic alliances.

Another way to develop the links between the large company and small company sectors is through the setting-up and the use of an external corporate venture capital fund.

Some of the largest U.S. Corporations are now among the participants in various venture capital programmes. Of the 61 corporate programmes currently active in the US, 15 have non US parents.

In recent years there has been a move away from passive partnership investments towards focused corporate programmes.

In looking at venture capital as a business development tool there are several different approaches:

☆ Traditional venture capital partnerships

☆ Speciality venture capital funds

☆ Internal venture groups

☆ External focused venture programmes

However, it is often the case that internal venture divisions do not live up to their original goals and a classic case study of the pitfalls of diversification through venture capital was that of the Exxon Corporation's use of Exxon Enterprises to gain a foothold in specific new industries.

Bleicher and Paul[78] gave five Guidelines for setting up an External Focused Corporate Venture Fund:

(1) Assuring Top Management Commitment

(2) Establishing Clear Understanding of Objectives and Time Frame

(3) Select an appropriate Venture Capital Firm as partner

(4) Formulate an Investment Charter

(5) Set up Internal Organizational Structures and Procedures

These guidelines were discussed in detail in their paper and they have been designed to minimize both financial risk and the near-term organizational cost associated with setting-up an external focused venture fund. Once a successful external venture programme has been started, direct investments can often be profitably made alongside the venture capitalists.

However, it should be emphasised once again that a venture capital fund does not replace existing corporate new business development activities; it can only be a challenging, powerful and beneficial way of augmenting the other more traditional business development efforts.

> New and small firms provide a distinctive environment for the formulation and implementation of strategy ... new ventures within established firms have many of the characteristics of new and small businesses.[79]

The decision to found a new firm seems to be influenced by a combination of three broad factors: the entrepreneur, the organization, and the environment. Essentially, these factors mirror those relevant to establishing New Ventures, where the equivalent of the entrepreneur is the New Venture manager. One major advantage of the new firm is that

> it can innovate, without worrying about the effect on existing sales. This coupled with the talents and drive of the founding group is undoubtedly one reason why new and small firms have been such remarkably fertile sources of technical innovation, accounting for major innovations out of all proportion to their R & D expenditures.[79]

The management of the later growth stage is one area where entrepreneurs often become painfully aware of their shortcomings and it is precisely this area where the more professionally orientated venture managers should have an advantage. Unfortunately, combining the best of both approaches is not easy.

Cooper[79] found that a number of writers have suggested that large firms seem to be better at developing existing businesses than growing new ones.

> The large firm can bring great resources to bear upon new opportunities and can absorb failures. However, performance measurement systems often penalize these divisions and executives who assume risks. New ventures often require different kinds of people and facilities and an orientation towards working closely with customers, short production runs and continually changing technology ... New Venture department organizations may range from *ad hoc* task forces, with no formal training, to departments with established budgets, to separate legal entities ... They usually can call upon the resources of the larger organization, although this sometimes presents problems because of lack of authority over other departments. The performance measurement systems may be modified to place less emphasis on short-run profits. If the product is promising or becomes firmly established, it may be transferred to an existing department or become the basis for a new department.

Research indicates that new venture departments usually evolve, becoming operating divisions, staff departments, or new venture departments which differ in size, objectives and corporate impact from their earlier versions. Sometimes the departments are disbanded. The two major influences upon the evolution of a New Venture department appear to be the changing nature of the firm's strategy and its political support within the organization.

☆   ☆   ☆

An extreme form of venture management might be termed 'sponsored spin-offs' in which, with the parent firm's blessing, a separate new enterprise is created, possibly with the parent company holding some of the equity.

In general, these approaches have demonstrated some success (and some failures!) but many companies are increasingly experimenting with different ways of creating an environment for intra-corporate entrepreneurship (intrapreneurship). Some of the limitations of this approach are discussed later (see reference[89]★).

Developing Strategic Alliances complements the other venture capital oriented initiatives and 'are now becoming the rule rather than the exception'. This approach is reviewed in detail by James.[80]★ Alliances are used to develop new technology and/ or penetrate new markets; they can be an alternative to licensing or a complement to it, and internationally they are often established in response to political pressures for local manufacture (see reference[102]).

> In many industries, competition has reached a point where, apart from surrender, only two options are open to companies if they wish to survive — either join the competition or form an alliance with other contenders to fight the competition on more favourable terms.[80]

Unfortunately there are drawbacks to the use, and limits to the value, of alliances. 'There are great difficulties in tracking experience; accountability is weak; communications are often slack; and joint decision-making takes too long and is frequently tackled in an *ad hoc* manner'.[80]

'Alliances hold up only as long as the conditions which favoured their formation remain in force and the interests of the partners are homegeneous'. Not a very reassuring pre-condition in a changing world, unless the process of managing the change is well understood. James[80] also concluded that

> while alliance strategies under the right conditions can be valuable competitive manoeuvres they are a means to an end and not an end in themselves. The use of alliance strategies in business to the exclusion of other strategic moves robs a company of the flexibility to manoeuvre in the market place. Alliance strategies, while playing a useful role, must be considered a part but not the core of the central strategic theme for most companies.

This must be emphasised. Also from earlier remarks it can be seen that the alliances should only be part of an overall innovation strategy for *all* rather than 'most' companies. It would be an extremely risky strategy to just rely on Alliances for all new business development.

One of the first requirements of a successful relationship between a large and small company is for each party to understand the other's position — and their strengths and weaknesses.

The stages of growth of a small, rapidly growing company are likely to resemble closely the pattern for corporate life cycles in general, discussed earlier. However, small companies tend to experience a number of special problems:

(1) There is invariably emphasis on immediate profits, as the cash flow demands of rapid growth are often difficult to resource.

(2) Management is invariably stretched and red tape, bureaucracy, endless meetings and administrative demands are both frustrating and counterproductive.

The above issues — among others — were usefully discussed by Scott and Bruce.[81]

O'Neill[82] considered the tasks of the entrepreneur and emphasised the need to: study present operations as a basis for assessing future opportunities; define and exploit a competitive advantage; and finally develop an appropriate management system. He then went on to argue that there were four essential steps in developing a strategy which will create the management infrastructure: First, identify the key function in the firm; second, hire or promote people to manage each of these key functions; third, train these managers in the specifics of the department; fourth, provide opportunities for these managers to develop strategic skills.

The special opportunities and problems of managing business strategies in small High Technology companies are dealt with in a paper by Grieve Smith and Fleck.[83] They maintained that 'the underlying and frequently stated objective of the founders of these firms is not just to develop their new products or technologies in a profitable manner but to achieve and maintain the independence and freedom of action associated with the management of a small company'. Such attitudes do not make it easy to enter into co-operative arrangements with large companies.

Another paper[84] on this subject found:

(1) While the majority of firms did not have a formal business plan when started, relying instead on personal experience and intuition, they have adopted some form of planning once the company was in operation.

(2) As the companies have grown, the planning processes utilized have become more formal, structured and participatory to assure continued organizational effectiveness.

(3) The majority of the CEO's prefer an active and strong involvement in their company's strategic planning, rather than delegating that responsibility to other members of management.

(4) Most CEO's feel that improved time efficiency, company growth and a better understanding of the market will be achieved through planning.

(5) The strategic planning activity tends to be primarily concerned with the short run, updated regularly and operationally orientated.

(6) The absence of perceived benefits accruing to the company from planning endeavours negatively influenced the CEO's attitude towards planning in general, as well as the nature and extent of planning utilized in the future.

(7) Small company strategic planning is still in its formative period and its development will continue as more practical experience is acquired.

Wilson and Gorb,[85] in a paper that considered the advantages and disadvantages of collaboration between large and small companies, challenged the traditional view that most small companies are flexible and adaptable; instead they argued that many are highly dependent on relatively few large customers and are poor innovators. Fortunately there are a large number of small companies, which results in a wide spectrum of approaches and results. Inevitably there is also always considerable scope for improvements in performance in this area.

New Venture Management

Large organisations need both order and diversity in strategy for their continued survival. The role of entrepreneurial activity is to provide the required diversity. Whereas order in strategy can be achieved through planning and structuring, diversity in strategy depends on experimentation and selection. The task of strategy management is to maintain an appropriate balance between these fundamentally different processes.[86]

Business plans are the essential framework between the parent and the New Venture; they are similar to the documents that would be required to secure a potential venture capital investment and, although there is no exact formula for a business plan, any such plan should include these key points:

(1) A brief history of the business or project.

(2) A synopsis of the career histories of the entrepreneur/venture manager and the other managers.

(3) A description of the business's products or services, their markets (including growth prospects) and the present or likely competition.

(4) A summary of the technology involved, including manfacturing processes, and a review of the likely threats from technological obsolescence or competing new technologies.

(5) A financial history (if any) and forward projections of turnover, profits, cash flow and borrowings for at least a two-year period.

(6) If possible, the proposed deal structure for the funding sought, together with preliminary views on the preferred exits.

The issues that arise in the interaction between the parent and the New Venture relate to:

1. Organization

2. Profit Expectations and Cash Limits

3. Speed of Development

4. Freedom of Action

5. Management Evaluation

6. Outside Assistance

7. Inter-company Resources at 'Arm's Length'

8. Top Management Support (i.e. 'Godfathers').

In particular big company/small company cooperation requires business plans and agreements to cover:

☆ Overall Objectives and Strategy, including Funding and Review Procedure

☆ Intercompany Trading/Links

☆ Contracts for Key Personnel

☆ Exit Routes

☆ What Happens if/when Things go Wrong?

One critical and difficult issue concerns motivating and rewarding venture managers and this requires guidelines to cover the following:

(1) Measure performance using the business plan framework.

(2) Policies should apply throughout the venture not just at the top.

(3) Financial rewards are only one element; group recognition is often equally important.

(4) What are the limits on outside recruitment?

(5) There are often fundamental differences in corporate culture.

(6) The long term career development of venture managers can present problems.

(7) It is essential to combine flexibility and consistency in personnel and other policies.

The importance of the selection and training of Business Development Executives/Venture Managers is considered in some detail in a paper by Pearson[12] discussed earlier.

These guidelines can be distilled into a series of recommendations:

☆ It is important to establish goals against which performance can be measured.

☆ A review/appraisal system is required.

☆ The 'reward' package should combine public/social recognition, as well as the 'appropriate' financial package.

☆ Changes should be discussed with the Venture Managers.

☆ It needs to be recognised that each situation is different and, as long as guidelines are adhered to, the emphasis should be on being as flexible as possible to meet needs of each individual situation.

Ultimately any New Venture policy will only be successful if it is undertaken and operated with the full support of the traditional/core business, but the interface between the two needs careful and systematic management.

Burns and Stalker[87] were among the first to identify the correlation between organizational structure and operational efficiency. They found that a group of companies, working in the highly turbulent world of electronics in the 1950s which survived and grew, showed as a whole an informal, interactive and free pattern, while those of the opposite type — bureaucratic and highly formalized — were less successful. The two types at the ends of the scale were called 'organic' and 'mechanistic'. In broad terms these two approaches overlap with New Venture and core business management approaches, unless the core business had adopted a totally innovative approach. The challenge is not only to get the different approaches to operate successfully in their respective areas, but to get the — in many ways even more difficult — interface between them successfully managed.

Burrows[88]★ provided a comprehensive survey of the studies and publications in the Venture Management area; covering in more detail many of the issues discussed earlier in this introduction and in the other papers. He identified early users of the term 'Venture Projects' (Don C. Wheaton, 1961) and the link between the theory of innovation and the product champion (Donald A. Schon, 1963), as well as surveying 61 other significant references in the field (of which only three had appeared in *Long Range Planning*). Burrows' paper is the starting point

for anyone wishing to undertake detailed work in this area and is the focus for this publication. He quoted other research that looked at the difference in perception between top management and venture managers, particularly when considering the causes of venture failures. Ten Guidelines, similar to those mentioned earlier in this section, are developed:

1. Formulate a venture charter.

2. Indoctrinate top management concerning the contribution to long term corporate growth.

3. Adapt a standard format to be followed in developing venture plans.

4. Maintain a limited number of ventures at different stages of development.

5. Assign each venture its own budget.

6. Formalize the relationship between top management and venture management.

7. Install as head of each venture team a person who has demonstrated both competence as a manager and championship of the product assigned to the venture.

8. Ventures earmarked for transfer to operating divisions should not be moved until earnings are far enough above the breakeven point to satisfy the divisional managers concerned.

9. Allow division managers at least five options in disposing of their new development projects.

10. Include the venture team manager in the revue process at the end.

The extensive work of Norman D. Fast in 1979 (*The Rise and Fall of Corporate New Venture Divisions*) is highlighted. Fast defined a New Venture Division as an organizational unit whose primary functions are:

(1) The investigation of potential new business opportunities.

(2) The development of business plans for new ventures.

(3) The management of the early commercialization of these ventures.

And organizationally Fast saw it as essential that:

(1) A centre of responsibility for new business development is created to ensure it receives sufficient attention.

(2) The organizational climate and structure is appropriate for the new business development.

(3) The new business development activities are insulated from dominant values and norms of the parent company.

The venture group should have a clearly defined charter setting out its objectives and how these are to be achieved, as argued earlier. Despite this, it has been found that there is a high failure rate among New Ventures, although it is some consolation that the success rate still appears to be higher than in centralized R & D. The aims of the venture group are long term but before a group can prove itself, a company will undergo several crises which will make it alter its long term strategy. As has been mentioned earlier, when this happens the venture group is frequently in danger of being restricted or abandoned.

Even if venture groups are successful they can easily be caught up in internal political problems that arise from:

☆ Resentment by the rest of the organization and the resulting attempt to cut off resources to the venture group.

☆ Conflict with the rest of the organization because of perceived favouritism shown to the venture group by management.

☆ Infringement of traditional territory in the rest of the organization.

☆ Promotion on the back of success, which can be seen as a short cut by those involved in the traditional hierarchy.

All these issues are central to the fundamental problem of managing change within any organization, except, perhaps, for those who have a totally innovative culture.

Burrows also discussed the role of New Ventures within the context of encouraging Innovation in the New Towns, with particular reference to Milton Keynes.

There are, however, those who believe there is a fundamental conflict between the management style of the large corporation and that of the entrepreneur or Intrapreneur (internal entrepreneur).[89]

It seems clear to me that in the absence of a company-wide culture specifically designed to encourage entrepreneurial activity, large firms are well advised to consider other means to stimulate innovation. *Large companies with bureaucratic systems cannot hope to provide either the expectation of reward, or the personal autonomy which will attract and hold the best entrepreneurial people.*

These reservations need to be considered seriously and understood by anyone concerned with the strategic management of change issues, and/or New

Venture development of any kind. There is a stong case for maintaining that there is a fundamental incompatibility, but if corporations wish to survive, some compromises must be achieved. No corporation can afford to be solely concerned with the administration of the status quo and some accommodation is essential, despite the difficulty of reconciling extreme positions. No large bureaucratic organization should be encouraged to think that intrepreneurship, or new ventures, will solve all their problems. They obviously will not; but as part of a comprehensive programme for managing change and innovation, they should help. Doing nothing will guarantee failure.

Another way of looking at the cultural differences between the core and new business/venture areas is to consider the core business approach as concerned with detailed analysis that attempts to take the 'right' decision essentially through discussion and information (i.e. Bureaucratically). In contrast the New Business/Venture approach is essentially entrepreneurial, where individual effort is much more likely to be the determining factor in whether or not decisions can be 'made right'.

In his book *On The Psychology of Military Incompetence* Norman Dixon argues that the very characteristics needed for successful leadership in war — the ability to tolerate uncertainty, spontaneity of thought and action, and an open mind — are the very antithesis of personality traits that are needed to meet the requirements of military life and attract recruits in the first place — obedience, orderliness, fear of failure, a need for approval. The system makes little allowance for innovation, initiative, and independent thought. That analysis and situation has many similarities with corporate life and the personnel issues dealt with in this volume.

Littler and Sweeting[90]★ undertook a survey in 1983 in which 88 UK companies (within the 1981 *Times Top 1000*) responded to questions about how they developed new business. Although acquisitions and licensing were also considered, special attention was given to Internal Venture Development. A fundamental problem found with internal corporate ventures was that they were frequently 'technology' rather than 'market' driven and that they 'often originate from a research and development project that apparently cannot be commercialized in any other way'. Other problems frequently found were lack of clear objectives for the venture activity, and pressures for short-term returns. In the case of the latter it is worth noting, once again, that new business/venture projects are often particularly vulnerable to being cut back because it may take 10–12 years before they produce comparable returns on investment to those of the mature businesses.

Ward[91] identified the importance of CEO commitment, combined with the need for imagination and perseverance, when he analysed the case study of Pilkington's float-glass, which took 12 years to achieve a cash flow break-even position. Ward emphasised the continual need to develop a corporate structure that was concerned with *making things happen*.

Littler and Sweeting[90]★ concluded: 'It may be premature to dismiss internal corporate venturing as an ineffective means of developing new businesses because of its lack of success to date; the problems may lie more with the implementation rather than the concept'.

Another useful approach was discussed by Nielsen[92] who developed the concept of 'Piggybacking', which involved

> investing in and/or developing a new area for the institution business that is relatively unrelated to the institution's primary mission, but that is sufficiently compatible with current market opportunities so that it can generate revenues to help support in the short-term the primary mission activities that are less compatible with current market opportunities.

New Venture Management in Practice — Company Cases

The formal use of a New Venture concept originated in the U.S., although the process has been implicitly operated by organizations since organizations were first introduced some thousands of years ago. One of the first explicit exponents of the New Venture approach was du Pont.[93]★ In the past decade the approach has been developed to cover a wide range of activities, partly as a mirror to (and a way of interacting with) the venture capital industry. Monsanto was an early company to achieve success in making these links. Other companies that have been systematically active in the area — with varying degrees of success — include Emerson Electric, 3M, Control Data Corporation, Mitsubishi, Olivetti, Standard Oil of Ohio, Diamond Shamrock, Anolog Devices and Ferranti.

The motives for this approach to a New Venture strategy were:

☆ Capital gain

☆ Identification of potential acquisition candidates

☆ A window on New Technology and Markets

☆ A mechanism for changing corporate culture

☆ A vehicle for developing strategic alliances.

On the basis of the experience of these companies (and others) the requirements for success were:

☆ Clear objectives

☆ Strong Top Management Support

☆ Patience and Understanding

☆ A supportive internal and external network

☆ Early success (Extremely helpful in establishing and reinforcing the credibility of any innovation).

Du Pont was one of the first companies systematically to establish a New Venture Management Approach. In 1970 when Cohen's paper[93]★ was written, the company had eleven industrial departments/strategic business units and R & D activities were grouped into three broad categories:

(1). Improvement of Established Business.

(2). Exploratory Research.

(3). New Venture Development.

Many new products reached commercialization without going via the new venture route. In order to assess their credibility new ventures were analysed against:

☆ Market opportunity

☆ Profitability

☆ Development Timing

☆ Development Costs

☆ Investment Schedule

☆ Proprietary Position

and these were integrated into a venture plan. Cohen discussed the successful development of RISTON as a New Venture case study.

(It is interesting to note here that it was recently reported[94] that Kevlar, du Pont's superstrong, lightweight fibre invented in 1965, cost $700 million in capital expenditure and another $200 million in operating losses before it began to make 'a fair and reasonable profit' three years ago.)

Cohen concluded that

> a New Venture Development provides an ideal environment for making and carrying out decisions involved in introducing new technological developments. It combines the advantages in mobility and communications enjoyed in a small, venture-orientated company with the strong technical and financial advantages of a large company.[93]★

This is what is supposed to happen in theory; unfortunately it does not always work out that way in practice.

In a valuable contribution, Naylor[95]★ discussed his experience within the General Motors Corporation. He analysed their response to the increasing pressures for change within his industry and their corporate response, which included the development of Strategic Business Units. Each unit was characterized by having a unique, clearly defined mission and it should operate in a unique market segment. 'The business unit team recognises that they all share in the responsibility for developing and implementing the business strategy and in the rewards for a successful effort — a real combination of the three R's (risk, responsibility, reward)'.

Each SBU develops its explicit mission and objectives, the related competitive strategies and a five year business plan. The strategic planning process covers:

☆ Business Definition.

☆ Key Success Factors.

☆ Situation Analysis.

☆ Strategy Development.

☆ The Business Plan itself.

Naylor quoted Alfred Sloan's views on business management, which are equally relevant to the issues relating to New Venture development.

Harrell and Murray[96]★ described the challenges facing mature industries with a close look at an electric utility company (Detroit Edison) that used a new venture approach as a way of stimulating business growth.

The company had recognised the limited opportunities for growth in its traditional business — electricity generation — and had developed a 10 step New Venture evaluation process as a way of moving into new areas. For promising candidates that survived a rigorous screening process a project proposal was drawn up, essentially covering the Business plan elements discussed in the previous section.

If the new venture proposal passed the screening, a task force was formed to develop the idea and draw up the business plan.

There were two main requirements of the task force and the absence of either would jeopardize the new venture evaluation process. First, there should be a clear leader with clear responsibility for the output of the task force and the authority to assemble a functioning organization. Second, the task force members must be given some release time from current assignments to function properly and be recognized for their work.[96]

This paper gives two short examples that illustrate how the process functioned in practice; and the authors conclude

No process can ensure success, but a process that efficiently addresses the critical elements in venture management can speed the amount of time required to find and launch potentially successful ventures. In the final analysis, the New Venture Process is a people intensive business activity.[96]

Turbil[97]★ showed how Elf Aquitaine offered its accumulated knowledge and expertise in research, development and innovation to other small and medium size businesses in the Aquitaine area. Its success led to a similar service being offered in the Rhone-Alps region, and other large industrial groups have followed the lead in other districts. The scheme had benefits all round: Elf Aquitaine's research benefited from a widening of outlook, the area saw increased industrial activity, and smaller businesses found technological support.

According to Katz,[98] IBM activities are grouped into a number of operating units which, where feasible, have profit/loss responsibility. Operating unit management is responsible for the development and implementation of its plans, but business policies are controlled at the corporate level and this provides the broad framework within which all operating units function. At that time the company had three business areas (Data Processing, General Systems and Office Products) and 6 operating units organised in a matrix where there were strong dependencies among the units, and some overlap between the business areas. However, consistent with their philosophy of decentralized management of operations, the planning and control system required the designated units to develop and implement their separate but co-ordinated plans within an integrated corporate framework.

These plans included assessments of:

☆ Consistency with approved strategic direction

☆ Balance between objectives sought and resources required

☆ Relationships to plans of other operating units

☆ Excellence in each functional area.

In addition, staff was required to write short critiques as to the strengths, weaknesses or risks associated with the individual plans.

Continuing and rapid change was recognised as inherent in IBM's business and the culture was dominated by this approach. In that respect IBM is somewhat similar to the way that some Japanese corporations operate. As a result New Ventures are implicit (at least for the time being — until the company becomes more 'mature') in the total corporate approach and a separate organization structure is not required or appropriate.

A different approach is taken by Norris,[99] who outlined the extensive programmes that Control Data once had to encourage New Ventures. He emphasized the key point that management was about managing innovation, and not about administrating the status quo. But the subsequent problems with Control Data's programme illustrate that positive innovation policy is not enough; it is essential that any such programme is effectively controlled and concerned with bottom-line results. Only a few companies can afford the luxury of ignoring the short-term in the interests of a ten year plus horizon.

An illuminating case study of the successful exploitation of a whole series of inventions over four decades around a central theme is that of Tetra Pak.[100] Here the key elements of success were found to be: first, market research, then in deciding how the resources can be utilized to achieve long term profitability and finally on the need to modify the product and production methods to preserve market lead. Tetra Pak is another example of growth through core business innovation, where a New Venture Strategy would not have been appropriate, although it could be argued that such an approach might be relevant today.

The use of some of the concepts of Strategic Business units is illustrated in the historical development of L.M. Ericsson, the Swedish manufacturer of telephone equipment.[101] It is also an example of the difficulties in achieving a successful corporate metamorphosis. As has been mentioned before, a successful metamorphosis is ultimately where the opportunities and structures for continuous evolution make innovation an integral part of corporate philosophy. Although there is some evidence to suggest that some companies can do this successfully for a reasonable period of time (and some companies can successfully undergo a quantum, rather than continuous, metamorphosis), there are very few (if any) organizations which can sustain the approach on a permanent basis. It is, however, to be hoped that a greater understanding of the whole process will increase the chances of success.

An alternative viewpoint is given by Lasserre,[102] who evaluated the resources of local and foreign partners required for an effective technology transfer strategy. He found the key factors in success were:

(1) Strategic vision.

(2) Strategic importance of the project.

(3) Assessment of technical and managerial resources.

(4) Commitment from top management.

Another example of the difficulties involved in the successful strategic management of technology is given by Lauglaung,[103] based on his experience at the Goodyear Tyre and Rubber Company. He developed the concept of a Techno Business portfolio which recognises that the 'technology portfolio can vary along a number of dimensions from offensive through divesture', and this was integrated into a Technology Resource Management System. He concluded that 'only through the integration of technology and business issues in developing strategy and a sharing of responsibilities in implementation will firms be able to succeed in globally competitive markets'. It is however, unfortunately, much easier to make statements of that kind than to implement them effectively in practice.

Another useful case study approach to the issues of diversification and expansion is provided by Eugster,[104] when he surveyed, 20 years ago, the situation in the Swiss Chemical Industry through the eyes of Ciba, Geigy, Roche and Sandoz.

In the final paper of this collection Fairtlough[105]★ discusses the overall issues related to innovation and planning for new technology. He evaluated the approach of Horwitch and emphasised the importance of linkage, particularly in the context of the Biotechnology example quoted in his appendix. It is also particularly relevant to highlight his quotation of Freeman when speaking about economic change resulting from technological innovation:

> However, it is essential not to under-estimate the vast scope of institutional change which is needed. It will involve enormous changes in the pattern of skills of the work-force and therefore in the education and training systems; in management and labour attitudes; the pattern of industrial relations and worker participation; in working arrangements; in the pattern of consumer demand; in the conceptual framework of economists, accountants and governments, and in social, political and legislative priorities.

As can be seen from the recent performance record of companies mentioned above, good intentions, and even short-term success, is no guarantee of long-term success. This conclusion was also found by those companies used as examples in *In Search of Excellence*. The successful management of change is much more difficult and risky than most people believe; although far less risky than doing nothing — that is an inevitable recipe for disaster! It is to be hoped that this discussion of the insights, experiences and mistakes of those who have tried to manage change, particularly within the New Venture concept, will enable readers to operate more successfully in this challenging and complex area.

To emphasise this point, it is worth finally quoting Turner's interview with Hayes, ICI's Chief Planner:[106]

> Someone came into his office recently and presented him with a check-list which, they said, he would have to satisfy himself about, if he were to recommend buying a particular business. 'Baloney', Hayes replied 'business deals are done from the guts, that's how people make millions.' 'ICI', he declared 'had got where it was by technical innovation and business creation and we have to have much more of that again'. The quantitative and analytical had given way somewhat to the critical business judgement, and that's what the executive directors expected of him in the brave new world.

The key to success in the long-run is not just correct analysis and judgement, but these need to be combined with an entrepreneural determination to make things happen. Nowhere is that combination more important than in Creating and Managing New Ventures.

Summary
Creating and Managing New Ventures has to be seen in the context of the overall need to manage change as well as plan for new product development, exploit R & D more effectively, develop strategies for diversification and to encourage links between large and small companies. The evidence on New Venture Departments suggests that success is far from easy and it is essential that companies learn from the mistakes of others. A number of suggestions and guidelines are made in this collection of papers and it should be emphasized that, although the papers primarily consider the experience of private corporations, the principles laid down are essentially the same irrespective of whether the organization is in the public or private sector. The issues are at the core of the critical management activity — *The Successful Management of Change and Innovation*.

References

All references are to articles from the *Long Range Planning* journal unless otherwise stated.

(1)   The Innovative Firm, Dr. H. Igor Ansoff, **1** (2), 26.

(2)   *Managing for Tomorrow — Managing in Turbulent Times*, P. Drucker, Harper and Row Publishers Inc. (1980).

(3)   Business Planning: The Gap Between Theory and Practice, John Martin, **12** (6), 2.

(4)   Managing Strategic Change: An Integrated Approach, Colin A. Carnall, **19** (6), 105.

(5)   Managing the Process of Corporate Development, Bernard Taylor, **9** (3), 81.

(5a) How to Assess the Strategic Value of a Capital Investment, John G. Wissema, **17** (6), 25.

(6)   A Practical Approach to Strategy Development, Markus Schwaninger, **20** (5), 74.

(7)   Who Influences Strategic Decisions?, W. Harvey Hegarty and Richard C. Hoffman, **20** (2), 61.

(8)   *Organizational Strategy, Structure and Process*, Raymond E. Miles and Charles C. Snow, McGraw Hill, New York (1978).

(9)   Helping Managers to Develop Strategies, M. D. Skipton, **18** (2), 56.

(10) Keeping Corporate Planning Relevant — A Key Task for the Planning Department, Blake Pinnell, **19** (1), 48.

(11) Planning for Changes in Stages of Corporate Development, Milton Leontiades, **12** (6), 74.

(12) Business Development Approach to Planning, Barrie Pearson, **9** (6), 54.

(13) Managing Diversity: Strategy and Control in Diversified British Companies, Michael Goold and Andrew Campbell, **20** (5), 42.

(14) Setting Corporate Objectives as a Basis for Action, G. J. Pearson, **12** (4), 13.

(15) Long-Range Strategic Planning: Is it for Everyone?, Thomas S. Carlson, **11** (3), 54.

(16) Paradoxes in Planning, John Robinson, **19** (6), 21.

(17) Planning for Flexibility, Briance Mascarenhas, **14** (5), 78.

(18) The Lost Art of Planning, T. J. Cartwright, **20** (2), 92.

(19) Turnaround — A Painful Learning Process, Frederick M. Zimmerman, **19** (4), 104.

(20) Turnaround and Recovery: What Strategy Do You Need? Hugh M. O'Neill, **19** (1), 80.

(21) Can Industries De-Mature: Applying New Technologies to Mature Industries, William L. Dowdy and Julian Nickolchev, **19** (2), 38.

(22) What is the Board of Directors Good For?, Dan Bavly, **19** (3), 20.

(23) The Bored Board, *Towards The Next Economics and other essays*, P. 107, P. Drucker, Heinemann (1981).

(24) The Role of the Board in Corporate Planning, Blake Pinnell, **19** (5), 27.

(25) Why Don't US Boards Get More Involved in Strategy, Joseph Rosenstein **20** (3), 30.

(26) The New Class of Chief Executive Officer, G. A. Steiner and Elsa Kunin, **14** (4), 10.

(27) Management in the Eighties: How is the Job Changing?, J. G. Wissema and J. M. M. van de Winkel, **14** (4), 21.

(28) How to Integrate Strategic Planning into your Management Process, Thomas H. Naylor, **14** (5), 56.

(29) How are Companies Planning Now? — A Survey, William R. Boulton, Stephen G. Franklin and Leslie W. Rue, **15** (1), 86.

(30) Corporate Culture and Strategy — The Problem of Strategic Fit, Christian Scholz, **20** (4), 78.

(31) Change in Management and the Management of Change, Robb. W. Wilmot, **20** (6), 23.

(32) Using Critical Success Factors in Planning, Per V. Jenster, **20** (4), 102.

(33) Strategy Consulting — A Shooting Star, Adrian Payne, **20** (3), 53.

(34) Planning vs Strategy: Which Will Win?, Michael A. Carpenter, **19** (6), 50.

(35) Strategic Planning — Which Style do you Need?, Bernard Taylor, **17** (3), 51.

(36) Corporate Planning for the 1990s: The New Frontiers, Bernard Taylor, **19** (6), 18.

(37) Strategies for New Product Development, Frederick D. Buggie, **15** (2), 22.

(38) How to get New Products to Market Quicker, G. B. M. Mathôt, **15** (6), 20.

(39) Product Planning — We're Still Getting It Upside Down, James Pilditch, **14** (5), 20.

(40) Key Strategic Issues for German Companies, Siegfried Höhn, **19** (6), 44.

(41) Competing with Japan — The Rules of the Game, Merlin Stone, **17** (2), 33.

(42) Strategies for Marketing New Computer Products, Merlin Stone, **18** (3), 41.

(43) A Model for New Product Planning, Americo Albala, **10** (6), 62.

(44) The Directional Policy Matrix-Tool for Strategic Planning, S. J. Q. Robinson, R. E. Hickens, D. P. Wade, **11** (3), 8.

(45) Portfolio Analysis and the Product Life Cycle, Hiram C. Barksdale and Clyde E. Harris Jr., **15** (6), 74.

(46) Risk Return Approach to Product Portfolio Strategy, Richard N. Cardozo, **18** (2), 77.

(47) The Theory of the Corporate Life Cycle, Barrie G. James, **7** (2), 49.

(48) Planning for Innovation, H. B. Locke, L. A. Wilson and K. Grossfield, **7** (2), 19.

(49) Resource Planning for Technology-Orientated Companies, J. S. Gansler, **6** (4), 17.

(50) Selecting R & D Projects for Development, Jackson E. Ramsey and James Madison, **14** (1), 83.

(51) Planning for Technological Innovation — Part 1, Investment in Technology, Joan G. Cox, **10** (6), 40.

(52) Credibility and the Assessment of R & D Projects, D. H. Allen, **5** (2), 53.

(53) Can Technology be Managed Strategically?, Narendra K. Sethi, Bert Movsesian and Kirk D. Hickey, **18** (4), 89.

(54) Co-ordinating Business Strategy & Technical Planning, Alan L. Frohman and Domenic Bitondo, **14** (6), 58.

(55) Competing with the Japanese Approach to Technology, John Prentice, **17** (2), 25.

(56) Innovation: The Way out of the Recession?, F. M. Smith, **15** (1), 19.

(57) Directing Technological Development — The Role of the Board, Simon Willder, **18** (4), 44.

(58) Planning for Technology as a Corporate Resource: A Strategic Classification, Lex. A. van Gunsteren, **20** (2), 51.

(59) Strategic Planning and Research and Development — Can we Integrate Them?, Giorgio Petroni, **16** (1), 15.

(60) Who Should Plan Technological Innovation?, Giorgio Petroni, **18** (5), 108.

(61) Focusing Innovative Effort through a Convergent Dialogue, E. P. Ward, **13** (6), 32.

(62) Strategies for Diversification, Bruno Hake, **5** (2), 69.

(63) A Systematic Approach to Diversification, E. G. Malmlow, **6** (4), 2.

(64) Assessing Opportunities for Diversification — An Analytical Approach, M. Younger, **17** (4), 10.

(65) Risk Analysis and the Formulation of Acquisition/ Diversification Strategies, H. Thomas, **16** (2), 28.

(66) Evaluating the Risks in Acquisition, David B. Hertz and Howard Thomas, **15** (6), 38.

(67) Acquisitions — Techniques for Measuring Strategic Fit, Christopher J. Clarke, **20** (3), 12.

(68) Planned Divestment — A Five-step Approach, Christopher J. Clarke & Francois Gall, **20** (1), 17.

(69) Management Buyouts in Britain — A Monograph, Mike Wright, John Coyne and Ken Robbie, **20** (4), 38.

(70) MBO: The Fad that Changed Management, Eugene J. Seyna, **19** (6), 116.

(71) Success and Failure in Management Buyouts, Sue Birley, **17** (3), 32.

(72) Alternatives to Merger — Joint Ventures and Other Strategies, Jeffrey S. Harrison, **20** (6), 78.

(73) The New Marketing — Developing Long-term Interactive Relationships, Evert Gummesson, **20** (4), 10.

(74) Trade Cycling in UK Industry, *Measurement and Control*, **8** (4) 152–156 (1975).

(75) Strategies for Declining Industrial Markets, S. J. Q. Robinson, **19** (2), 72.

(76) Diversification — The Key Factors for Success, Jean-Pierre Detrie and Bernard Ramanantsoa, **19** (1), 31.

(77) Japan's New Industrial Era — I. Restructuring Traditional Industries, Shuji Yamamoto, **19** (1), 61.

(78) The External Corporate Venture Capital Fund — A Valuable Vehicle for Growth, Knut Bleicher and Herbert Paul, **20** (6), 64.

(79) Strategic Management: New Ventures and Small Business, Arnold C. Cooper, **14** (5), 39.

(80) Alliance: The New Strategic Focus, Barrie G. James, **18** (3), 76.

(81) Five Stages of Growth in Small Business, Mel Scott and Richard Bruce, **20** (3), 45.

(82) How Entrepreneurs Manage Growth, Hugh M. O'Neill, **16** (1), 116.

(83) Business Strategies in Small High-Technology Companies, John Grieve Smith and Vivien Fleck, **20** (2), 61.

(84) Strategic Planning in Smaller Rapid Growth Companies, Jeffrey C. Shuman, John J. Shaw and Gerald Sussman, **18** (6), 48.

(85) How Large and Small Firms Can Grow Together, P. Wilson and P. Gorb, **16** (2), 19.

(86) *Corporate Entrepreneurship and Strategic Management, Insights from a Process Study*, Robert A. Burgelman (The Institute of Management Sciences), Volume 29, No. 12 December, 1983.

(87) *The Management of Innovation*. I. Burns and G. M. Stalker, Tavistock, 1966.

(88) Venture Management — Success or Failure?, B. C. Burrows, **15** (6), 84.

(89) The Delusion of Intrapreneurship, C. Wesley Morse, **19** (6), 92.

(90) Corporate Development — Preferred Strategies in UK Companies, D. A. Littler and R. C. Sweeting, **20** (2), 125.

(91) Organisation for Technological Change, E. P. Ward, **14** (4), 121.

(92) Piggybacking for Business and Non Profits: A Strategy for Hard Times, R. P. Neilsen, **17** (2), 96.

(93) New Venture Development at du Pont, A. B. Cohen, **2** (4) 7.

(94) *Business*, January 1988, p. 128.

(95) Regaining Your Competitive Edge — Michael E. Naylor, **18** (1), 30.

(96) New Venture Management in an Electric Utility, Gilbert D. Harrell and George O. Murray, **19** (2), 57.

(97) How Elf Aquitaine Provides Technological Assistance to Small Business, Jean-Pierre Turbil, **19** (3), 59.

(98) Planning in the IBM Corporation, Abraham Katz, **11** (3), 2.

(99) Developing Corporate Policies for Innovation: A Program of Action, W. C. Norris, **14** (4), 34.

(100) Tetra Pak — A Model for Successful Innovation, H. G. Jones, **15** (6), 31.

(101) A Complete Guide to Company Growth and Development, Christer Danielsson, **15** (6), 8.

(102) Selecting a Foreign Partner for Technology Transfer, Philippe Lasserre, **17** (6), 43.

(103) A Framework for the Strategic Management of Future Tyre Technology, Antonio S. Lauglaug, **20** (5), 21.

(104) Diversification in the Swiss Chemical Industry, Dr. C. Eugster, **2** (1), 42.

(105) Can we Plan for New Technology?, G. Fairtlough, **17** (3), 14.

(106) ICI Becomes Proactive, Graham Turner, **17** (6), 12.

PART ONE

New Thinking in Venture Management

Section One

The Strategic Management of Innovation

THE INNOVATIVE FIRM

Dr. H. Igor Ansoff
Dean of the Graduate School of Business,
Vanderbilt University, Nashville, Tennesee, U.S.A.

Dr. Ansoff, Dean of the Graduate School of Business, Vanderbilt University, was until recently Professor of Industrial Administration at Carnegie-Mellon University. He was at one time Chairman of the Advisory Council at the Stanford Research Institute (Long Range Planning Service) and is a former Vice-President—General Manager, Industrial Technology Division, Lockheed Electronics Company. He is author of the book "Corporate Strategy" (McGraw-Hill, 1965) and numerous articles on Corporate Planning.

THE PROBLEM OF INNOVATION IS OF much interest and concern to the business community. In observing the vast sums of money devoted to research and development in America, one might well suppose that American industry has successfully mastered the problem of innovation and that it provides an example for others to follow. The fact is that, while impressive progress has been made, many problems remain. The reasons for these can be inferred from a historical perspective.

As one looks at the early twentieth century, in the years between 1900 and the great crash in 1929, a typical method of growth was through annexation of markets in which demand had not been met previously. New products had relatively long life cycles. Periods of acquisition of new product-market positions, which were relatively brief, alternated with considerably longer periods of their exploitation.

An example of this behaviour is provided by the automotive industry. The early strategy was to maintain the same model for as long a period as there was demand for the car, as exemplified by Mr. Ford's introduction and perpetuation of the Model T. It was not until the middle thirties that the annual model change was first introduced.

The depression period, and the war time period, if anything, further accentuated the characteristics of 1900 to 1929. The pattern of stability of products and emphasis on exploitation of the profitability inherent in stable products was underlined during the war when emphasis was on volume production of military goods.

The post-war period brought with it a change in this pattern. The major forces which brought about the change were, on one hand, saturation of demand in some areas, and on the other hand, explosive impact of research and development.

The symptoms of the change were threefold:

1. An increasing rate of product replacements through improvement of products in order to keep up and stimulate demand in saturated areas.
2. A drastic shortening of many product life cycles through substitutes of new technologies. New technologies penetrated areas of established demand and provided new ways of satisfying consumer demand. Among examples are substitution of air transportation for the railroads, substitution of synthetic yarns for natural yarns, substitution of crystal and transistor technology for conventional tubes and components. One of the most interesting developments in the present time is the prospect of substitution of complex man/machine systems for the printed word.
3. An increasing recourse to creating demand through influencing consumer attitudes and wants.

A major result of these events has been a change from the previous cyclic business behaviour, in which relatively brief periods of annexation of new products and markets alternated with much longer periods of exploitation of the new product market positions. For many firms both periods became shorter and more equal in length. For an increasing number of firms cyclic behaviour disappeared: it became necessary to devote simultaneous attention to both activities. Thus from periodic innovative behaviour, business firms are moving toward what may be described as a continuous process of innovation. This transition to what might be called bi-modal business behaviour of simultaneous innovation and exploitation has been indeed difficult. There is evidence that even the most successful firms in the United States have not yet fully solved the problem. Thus, for example, IBM appears to have

This article originally appeared in "Enterprise" the house journal of the P-E Consulting Group, London.

E—C

> **Since the Second World War, changes in markets and technology have made it necessary for firms to organize for a "continuous process of innovation". Traditionally firms have been organized to exploit an established product/market position. The crux of the problem for senior management today is to design a "bi-modal" firm. Not a firm which is exclusively effective in exploiting a given market position, nor a firm which is successful in creating new product/market ideas, but lacks the capability of exploiting them profitably. The problem is to design a firm which is inventive and can exploit inventions, one that can deal with new products and new markets, and also maintain its position, with established products in traditional markets.**

had a very difficult time in making timely and appropriate decisions in replacing a previous product line.

Among the problems encountered by business firms are the following:

1. Perception and anticipation of the changes which are taking place, or are about to take place in the environment.
2. Within the firm, the problem of stimulating creative behaviour, as opposed to the more common attitude of promulgation and extension of previous modes of behaviour.
3. The problem of processing an invention from its inception through the various parts of the firm.
4. The problem of introducing new products alongside old and established products, and devoting an appropriate amount of management attention to each.
5. The problem of timing entry into the market, as has been exemplified, for example, by the development of colour television. Here RCA has been the firm which originally introduced and sustained public interest for many years, before colour television became a commercial reality. A question to be asked is whether the timing undertaken by RCA was more beneficial to the firm, than the timing of other firms which came in late, such as, say, Zenith or Magnavox.
6. A problem on the opposite side of the coin from innovation, that is, timely divestment of established products which are not unprofitable as yet, but which are facing a declining future.
7. Finally, the problem of resource budgeting: how much to budget for, for innovation, for capital assets, for investment in success of current operations, and for dividends to the shareholders.

The reason these problems arise is to be found in the fact that the pre-war firm was not basically structured for innovative behaviour. To illustrate this, one can consider the following typical features:

1. Information systems—which is really a modern word for what used to be known as accounting systems—characteristically dealt with data on past performance. They were inward-oriented by being more concerned with the data generated within the firm than the data generated by the environment surrounding the firm.
2. Capital investment decisions in business firms were characteristically predicated on the assumption of long economic life cycles and therefore were not responsive to conditions of rapid product market change.
3. The control systems were geared characteristically to past performance, to where the firm had been, as opposed to where the firm was going.
4. The incentive and compensation system in firms were geared to rewarding people on the basis of their past performance; they placed a premium on conformative behaviour rather than on unorthodoxy and inventiveness.
5. The organizational structure was not conducive to innovation; its response to new ideas was slow, their transfer from research and development to manufacturing and marketing was inefficient.

The previous discussion naturally raises the question whether the pre-war firm was very poorly designed to do business. The answer to this is no. One can assert that it was indeed very well designed, but in one of the two modes of behaviour mentioned above, specifically the mode of exploiting established product market positions. It was not equally well designed,

and ran into considerable difficulties when innovation and exploitation had to be accommodated side by side. The fact that this problem has not yet been solved is a testimony to the difficulty of transition to a new, more complex behaviour. The crux of the problem is to design what might be called a bi-modal firm. Not a firm which is exclusively successful in exploiting a given market position, nor a firm which is successful in creating new product market ideas but lacks the capability of exploiting them profitably.

While the problem has not been fully solved, progress has been made in new approaches to organizational design, to design of planning and control systems, to information systems, etc. There is an important anomaly in this progress. Modern management technology in some ways threatens to impede, rather than accelerate progress towards a fully bimodal, innovative firm. The reason is the fact that management scientists and computer salesmen, in their efforts to apply their ideas and sell the products to business firms, tend to take for granted the unimodal firm as it has existed and, by and large, still exists in the business community. As a result, they attempt to apply new technology to what is essentially an obsolete firm. Thus, for example, we find frequent applications of computer technology to information systems which are essentially already obsolete for management purposes.

In brief summary, the problem of the innovative firm is made complex by the presence of two conflicting design criteria. It is difficult enough to design a firm which is efficient in exploiting an established product-market position, or to design a firm which is inventive in creating new positions. It is doubly difficult to design a firm which can successfully perform both tasks. ■

Change in Management and the Management of Change

Robb W. Wilmot, CBE

The author believes that management by recipe and imitation are dead. That way, one is predictable and vulnerable to competitors. Management should create the changing environment, not merely respond to change. He advocates methodological approaches to innovation, value added dynamics and accelerated organizational change, with particular emphasis on realizing rapid competitive benefits from implementation of strategic information systems. He believes that accelerating the innovative use of information technology will have more impact on the performance of the European IT industry than any amount of subsidized R & D.

This decade has seen some remarkable changes for me. I left Texas Instruments in 1981, just as it was being featured by Tom Peters in his book '*In Search of Excellence*'. I was involved in many of TI's daring and successful ventures over a 16-year period but somehow the recipe that worked so well in the 1960s and 1970s failed to work in the 1980s. Why?

I moved on from TI, at the age of 36, to take on the rescue of ICL. Following years of 25 per cent p.a. growth to a billion dollars of sales, ICL had fallen apart in 1980, haemorrhaging cash and ending up with a \$40m market capitalization, 33,000 employees and essentially bankrupt. Why?

And why, only 4 years later was ICL among the highest return on capital companies in the world computer industry?

Why has the paragon of management excellence, IBM, fallen to number 7 in *Fortune* magazine's poll for best managed companies, after many years at number 1. Could it be that the good old recipe that worked wonders for IBM's shareholders and employees alike is no longer fit for purpose?

Dr Robb Wilmot is a prominent European entrepreneur. He was appointed Managing Director of Texas Instruments' U.K. subsidiary in 1978, at the age of 33. From 1981 to 1985 he was Chief Executive of ICL when he restructured the company and produced a dramatic improvement in profits. Since 1985 he has been involved in setting up new ventures such as European Silicon Structures (ES2), Octagon Investments, and Organisation and System Innovations Ltd (OASiS).

I believe that the answer to all these questions is that management by recipe is a dead end. This makes it somewhat difficult for me to structure this article on 'Change in Management and the Management of Change'.

Table 1. 'Changes in Management and the Management of Change'

- Management by recipe, and imitation are dead
- Create, not respond to change
- Culture perpetuates status quo, inhibits change
- Corporate value added; is the whole greater than the sum of the parts?
- Being big alone is no longer sufficient reason for existence
- Dismantle 'knowledge is power' hierarchic structures, make information a right not a privilege, mobilize total management population
- Risk capital process sets pace of innovation, provides 'quality control' on big companies
- Intellectual and information productivity—new competitive arena
- Investment in management and strategic information systems; best and worst practice 10:1 spread from industry average
- Organizations, their people and processes, are the essence of competition not products. Internalize competitivity
- Network experience acquisition to accelerate learning curve and stimulate innovation
- Externally facilitated issue-based intervention, build organizational capability roadmap
- Wilmot 80/20 (high/low value-added) rule of management

If you follow a recipe your actions are predictable and aggressive competitors with strategic intent to change the rules of the game can topple you just as in judo. You become transparent to your enemy.

Also you can never close a competitive gap by imitation, its like shooting at a moving target, and just is not a viable response. You will always be late, even if you pick the right competitors to imitate. For instance, in the 1970s, would you have picked Fairchild or NEC, Caterpillar or Komatsu, Massey Ferguson or Kubota, Grundig or Matsushita, Xerox or Canon, Leica or Minolta?

In each case, a new entrant entered relatively mature industries, and completely refuted learning curve theory, so popular in the 1970s by building a portfolio of competitive advantages over a 10- to 20-year period—taking on the No. 1 in the industry and living to talk about it.

At every major industry discontinuity, be it technology, marketing, quality or other innovations, waves of new competitors battle the encumbents. Some succeed. Some change the very structure of the industry. Many fail, but this nature of industry behaviour is now becoming universal, with new entrants invariably setting the pace for innovation, often fuelled by the risk capital process.

Change is everywhere but, like the term 'excellence', the word 'change' is both emotive and in danger of losing any serious meaning. In particular, it runs the risk of being completely externalized in many companies. There is too much pre-occupation with how one responds to change, rather than how one precipitates and leads change. Change has become associated with reactive rather than proactive behaviour, and this is completely inappropriate. It is viewed as miserable rather than exciting, depressing rather than exhilarating.

True entrepreneurs, be they in industry, charities, politics or academia are people that make things happen. They change things and understand which levers to pull to accomplish this. If there are no levers they build some.

Barriers to Change

There is a fascinating dichotomy surrounding change, and the role of corporate culture. Cultures, by definition, are about preserving the best of the past. Cultures exist specifically to prevent young hot shots, be they managers, prime ministers or archbishops, from changing everything. So using the word culture to describe an organization which has an appetite for change is an interesting paradox, but this is the challenge we face, and not just in industry, but across society in total. Perpetuating the status quo is also no longer an acceptable response, accelerating change is increasingly the only viable route forward for many organizations.

The alternatives are uncomfortable. Going bankrupt is not a recommended approach to culture change. Neither is being the victim of a corporate raider, but this is indeed the emerging solution for effecting management change, non-executive directors and institutional shareholders having apparently too often become part of the culture.

When a company is worth less than the sum of its parts, there is clearly an issue of the corporate value-added of senior management. When young managers have to 'spin out' to pursue their ambitions, it is clear that senior management has basically allowed a negative value-added event to occur.

This is a fundamental issue for senior management. To be honest with yourself and to ask the tough questions. Too often the actions of a charismatic or visionary leader can get confused with creation of genuine organizational capability and corporate value-added processes.

Too often corporate performance is deemed satisfactory if it is better than last year, with scant attention to what is possible with best practice, the urge to be better than the best simply is not there. Companies are increasingly being forced to justify their value-added both to the financial community and their own management communities, to be explicit about what they are good at, how they rejuvenate and how they avoid the fate of some of the former stars of 'In Search of Excellence'. In my experience, few large companies when pressed can do even a passable job of articulating their corporate value-added.

Being big alone is no longer an acceptable reason for existence, and we have seen several examples of this in the past year. Certainly size brings with it the capacity to produce change, yet size itself is often the principle barrier to change.

Mobilizing Management

In almost any underperforming large company, you will find that the younger managers, who of course represent probably 90 per cent of the management population, all know what the issues are and what ought to be done. They discuss it in the pub, or in the canteen but usually no one will tell the Emperor and his court that they have no clothes on. Yet it is these very managers, usually in their thirties and forties, who should be the agents of change. They do not yet know what is impossible. They are achievement oriented, with everything to play for. They have huge energy. Their companies have invested hundreds of thousands in them since they left college. They are the ones that can make change a reality.

This is the fundamental change that is occurring in management this decade—a mobilization of the critical mass of the management population, dismantling overpowering hierarchical organization structures built on the paradigm that knowledge is power, and replacing them with flatter structures where information flows are more horizontal than vertical and where the Emperor is *always* told he has no clothes on. This is the vital information invariably lost in yesterday's organization—swimming in its data reports and decision support systems.

Another change is the realization amongst such

managers that they must take their career into their own hands, to create their own opportunities. Most large companies have recruited far more potential managers than their structures will support, invariably leading to under-performance by individuals who rely too much on their environment to stretch them. In this sort of situation, it seems very difficult for a large company to be honest in its assessment of the individual, and increasingly managers are using external calibration of their competence, often via headhunters or venture capitalists with the inevitable results of losing the best.

Corporate Venturing

The more innovative companies, recognizing this as inevitable, are engaged in corporate venturing, turning a problem into a return on investment opportunity. They even encourage it as a mechanism to refresh their management structures. This approach, which is almost like running an open prison, puts tremendous pressure on the organization to keep its best people without the use of golden handcuffs, which is an interesting form of quality control on the organization.

It is vital that managers understand the risk capital process, how and why new high growth companies frequently set the pace of innovation for an entire industry sector, in the process stimulating the large companies, and keeping them honest, and also providing a significant portion of the wealth and employment creation in the economy. *This means going for 50 per cent plus rate of return, rather than the more normal corporate hurdle of 20 per cent.* It is how to get new products to market in half the time and quarter the cost—which is not untypical of a start-up compared to a big company project. How to kill sacred cows and avoid the president's pet project syndrome. Most large companies would add several points of profit if they developed these fairly unremarkable skills so common in the risk capital world. But stopping things is one of the most difficult tasks large companies ever have to do—it comes back to the culture issue again.

Investment in Management and Strategic Information Systems

Some large companies are developing assessment centres, where managers can get a clear picture of their capabilities and to determine if they are being adequately exploited and extended. These managers then put pressure on their companies to close the gap. It is almost like inverting human resource management, but it can unleash untapped potential. In parallel, the organization has an inventory of its management capacity and can mould and shape it by investment and recruiting policy to fit its long-term strategic intent. This concept of investment in management is rather new, but critical.

In industry after industry, we are seeing labour and overhead, in the traditional sense, dwindle, leaving cost of capital plus intellectual and information intensive activity as the principle constituents of value-added. But, as we have seen with the recent dramatic exchange rate realignments, cost of capital is becoming essentially a globalizing commodity —so competitive advantage and differentiation must increasingly derive from an organization's capacity to manage its intellectual and information resources. Competitive management ability and strategic information systems will become pivotal.

Strategic Information Systems are those that make a major competitive difference. They impact value-added rather than just contribute to ongoing cost reduction. The days when personnel directors and MIS directors were second-class citizens on the Board have gone forever, or arguably it may be inappropriate in many industries to even consider these as staff functions now, since frequently the product itself is the human resource or information.

Strategy is also moving out of the staff arena, where it disenfranchises 95 per cent of employees, and is increasingly becoming a process of capturing the entire collective knowledge of an organization, and of allocating intellectual and emotional energies, rather than just money. The new technology of knowledge engineering will have a seminal role in accelerating this trend.

Keeping score in this brave new world is not going to be easy. Even the basic accounting and legal processes are proving unfit for purpose as a company's principle asset becomes the know-how of its people together with its unique processes for managing these in ways that produce a result which is greater than the sum of the parts.

While investment in R & D and capital assets in most industries show a fairly close scatter around industry norms, investment in management and in strategic information systems is all over the map, with best and worst practice varying by as much as 10:1 from industry averages. Surely this is going to produce ongoing competitive turbulence for the rest of this century? (see Table 2).

Table 2. Best/worst practice investment spread

		Spread of best/worst practice to industry norms
Capital spending	% Sales	2:1
R & D	% Sales	2:1
Management	% Sales	10:1
Strategic information Systems	% Sales	10:1

Creating Competitive Advantage

So much for what is changing in management, but how do you go about managing change, and I mean *creating* it not reacting to it? How do you harness innovation and make competitiveness a personal issue for management, because, by and large, managers seem to have an amazing capacity to externalize competitive issues! If it is not lack of government R & D support, skills shortages from an inadequate education system, the short-term nature of the financial community, protectionism, or interest rates, it is something else.

Competitiveness and innovation have to be primarily an internal issue. It is about being able to say 'we have seen the enemy, and it is us' and knowing what to do about it. In most organizations today there is a serious investment gap in management. You cannot possibly catalyse change without investment in the management which has to lead the process—not just senior management, but *all* management—creating a language of change and the will and the skills to mobilize for change.

All other critical elements impacting competitiveness and innovation, such as increased skills training, industrial design, closer links with universities, R & D yield, total quality control, effective collaboration, excellence in customer service and so on would be being addressed by a competitive management.

The Myth of R & D Investment

It is critical that we separate cause from effect, because governments everywhere are being duped by industrialists into massive financial interventions to correct the symptoms with little chance of a return on investment unless the investment gap is closed in the pivotal area of management which, of course, is the cause. In any case, many of these interventions may well prove that the cure is worse than the disease.

Nowhere is this more evident than in the technology area, where the battle-cry of 'more R & D' is now heard loudly from both sides of the Atlantic. The 'more R & D' tribe is intent on persuading governments to pick winners and sponsor collaborative R & D, despite plenty of evidence that this has never been a recipe for accelerating anything especially in industries where speed is of the essence. *How can government sponsored projects which take over a year to meander through the machinery of picking winners make a difference in an industry where 6 months delay in getting a technology to market can cost a third to a half of life cycle profits?*

Becoming competitive involves getting honest with yourself. For instance, Europe already outspends Japan by 2:1 on R & D, and taxpayers' sponsorship of R & D in Europe is four times that of Japan.

Obviously the incremental spend represented by all the government measures together in the R & D area, no matter how desirable, is but a needle in a poorly performing R & D haystack, already totalling $100bn a year in Europe. More R & D, of a kind that already is not producing competitive results at the sharp end, is obviously not the solution. The core issue must be the overall yield and pace of all R & D and the associated innovation necessary to get this translated into competitive performance in the market-place. Clearly, this is a management challenge. *The investment gap is in management of innovation, not R & D.*

Improving Organizational Capability

What do I mean by investment in management? It is obviously more than an MBA or the odd short course in functional skills. It is about investing the time, and developing the techniques, to really understand what makes organizations successful, and passionately believing that it is organizations, their people and processes, that win competitive battles—not products, and that it is *my* problem and not someone else's. It's not just what strategy you adopt, but your capacity to execute it.

I call this organizational capability. It is the sum total of the organization's processes that make the whole greater than the sum of the parts. Traditionally, this has been an on-the-job learning process, but this is only viable as long as the company culture and its processes continue as a viable competitive option. The danger is that the nature of industry today, as we have seen, is that a company's organizational capability is likely to become obsolete within a 20-year period, or may be even less in the future, and that relying only on one's own experiences as a manager may not be enough to get up the learning curve fast enough, if competitors have mechanisms for accelerated learning and experience acquisition.

'Networking'

To spot emerging divergence between your own organizational capability and industry trends, and to network experience curves requires managers to invest a substantial portion of their time learning, firstly, about their own organization's capability, and secondly, by extensive interaction with customers, suppliers, competitors, academics and innovative high growth companies, to experience new cultures and organizational capabilities aimed at the 21st century.

In doing this, they do not just spot products, technology or sales opportunities but analyse various management and organizational competencies building a personal view of what works, does not work, and what is changing in an industry. *This process of networking is one of the most cost-effective and dynamic ways that exist of keeping change on the agenda and is a tremendous stimulus to innovation*. It is obviously limited to the present—even so, it prevents one living in the past.

Issue-oriented Research

To become 'futures-oriented' requires access to high quality issue-oriented research on the issues, with delivery to a critical mass of management via high quality pedagogy rather than by academic reports. This form of interaction, including scenario building, and case studies of other industries who are leading the global restructuring process, is best performed by external catalysts or facilitators who can energize group dynamics so that the amazing diversity of views about the future that usually exist in a management team can be powerfully focused onto an agenda for change and the production of an organizational capability 'road map' for the future.

These two processes, networking and external issue-focused intervention are becoming key for organizations determined to build cultures which drive rather than hinder change. They cost time and money. It is an investment issue.

Innovative Time Management

Let us take time first. I have yet to meet a group of senior managers who disagree with the Wilmot 80/20 rule of management, which is that 20 per cent of time is spent on high value-added activity, and 80 per cent on relatively low value-added activity, when the corporate machine somehow seems to take over.

It has never ceased to amaze me why managers, who of course are fully aware of this even if it is intuitive, so happily tolerate such a situation. It tells us something about the nature of big company corporate value-added. This led me to leave corporate life and found five new companies, with the intent to spend the right 20 per cent with each of them. My personal dream is a high value-added lifestyle. It is clear that innovative time management could allow most managers to carve out at least 10 per cent of the 80 per cent for the change agenda, that is typical best practice today for time investment.

Investment in Management

For investment in management, best practice, excluding opportunity cost, approaches 6 per cent of management payroll for organizations in the high tech or high change sector, which of course can and does include the public sector, finance and academia as well as the service and industrial sectors.

Managers do not have to wait for their companies to initiate this approach to competitive management, it can easily be a personal agenda for change. Investment in management is the gateway to change, which is the essential ingredient of competitiveness and innovation for both companies *and* individuals.

Investment in Strategic Information Systems

The second catalyst for change is investment in high quality strategic information systems and aligning these with the organizational processes and the strategic intent of the organization—and there is a great deal to play for here, by making information a right, rather than a privilege in the organization.

The gap between the value-added potential of IT, careering down its price/performance learning curve by an order of magnitude every 5 years, and its effective deployment in most organizations is staggering. *This is most apparent when observing the output per hour in the non-manufacturing sector of the U.S. economy, which now employs 80 per cent of the total work-force. It has been stagnant for 11 years. During this time investment in IT has doubled its share of non-consumer capital goods' spending, so something is desperately wrong* (see Figure 1). The seriousness of this issue is sharply displayed when you reflect that America's GDP growth of the last decade has been principally the result of putting 20 million more people to work, but with unemployment at 6.8 per cent, close to the theoretical minimum of 5·6 per cent there are clearly not another 20 million to support such growth in the next decade.

The essence of my argument is that investment in management and investment in strategic information systems are the central competencies underpinning the management of change and that whilst

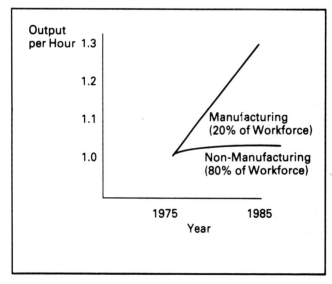

Source: National Bureau of Statistics.

Figure 1. U.S. productivity trends

R & D or capital spending as a per cent of sales are fairly closely clustered for any industry sector, these two new areas of organizational capability are not, giving tremendous opportunity for competitive differentiation and competitive innovation. It may just be that many of yesterday's star companies are coming to the end of their eras, that what they were good at may no longer be relevant. Their tremendous belief in *their* particular recipe may be *their* downfall and *your* opportunity.

Planning vs Strategy—Which Will Win?

Michael A. Carpenter

The author describes some of the changes that are taking place in strategic planning at General Electric—a company which is trying to be the most competitive enterprise in the world. He explains why these changes are necessary, the problems of implementation and how they are working out.

Corporate strategists are under fire today, just 10 years after strategic planning was touted as a panacea for all the ills of businesses. Top managers and management commentators are asking whether their commitment to strategic planning has paid off. Has it made existing businesses more successful than they otherwise would have been? Has it improved the effectiveness of resource allocation and identified and developed new opportunities? Has it helped avoid bad decisions on major investments or product line developments?

My answer to each of those questions is a *qualified* 'yes'. It has paid off to varying degrees, despite some unpleasant side effects. But it still has a long way to go to achieve its true potential for contributing to the success of our businesses. Improved analytical methodologies have resulted in a better understanding of the linkages between competitive advantage and profitability, and between competitive position, cash flow and resource allocation.

In turn, these analytical approaches have resulted in a more informed and intelligent dialogue between strategic business units and corporate management in multi-business corporations, a dialogue it has helped focus on the *real* strategy issues, rather than the numbers game that formerly was often the centre of attention. It has helped, as well, to encourage a thoughtful and disciplined approach to resource allocation in the business portfolio.

The author is Vice-President, Corporate Business Development and Planning at General Electric Company, Connecticut.
This article is based on an address to the Conference Board, New York, in March 1984.

Better decisions have been the result of the better processes engendered by the planning process. Today we see less pursuit of growth-for-growth's-sake strategies and more differentiation in the way the performance of individual businesses is measured, objectives are set, and performance is rewarded. Arbitrary edicts to the effect that each business must make 10 per cent return on sales and grow at 15 per cent a year have been largely abandoned.

But after placing these important contributions on the positive side of the ledger it must be said that the process of strategic planning that most companies use today is not responsive to the strategic management needs of today's business world.

Let's look back for a moment at an admittedly oversimplified history of strategic planning and how corporations embraced it.

The 1960s were characterized by long-range planning, a fancy term for 5-year forecasts and financial projections and objectives. During the late 1960s and early 1970s, the newly formed strategy-consulting boutiques developed a whole series of subsequently over-generalized concepts that led planners and chief executives away from extrapolation and forecasts, towards issues of business economics and competitive interaction. That was the beginning of the strategic planning era.

The corporate response in most companies, including General Electric, was to establish a strategic planning department with the mission of finding ways to institutionalize strategic thinking and analysis into the management process.

Systems arose that required the annual submission of a strategic plan document for each business, accompanied by a formal business strategy presentation during a predetermined plan review period. Discussions were channelled into set formats such as 'competitors', 'environmental trends' and the like.

As the process evolved, individual business financial forecasts were aggregated into a corporate plan, and an analysis was made of corporate portfolio evolution.

At General Electric the payoff from such a system was long lived and enormous in educating management to strategic thinking and planning, in raising the importance of focusing on strategy development, in forging a disciplined resource allocation process, and in making corporate portfolio decisions.

But, fundamentally, the whole idea of a ritualized process eventually becomes antithetical to what strategy is all about; namely, creativity and insight.

My exposure to strategic planning systems in 10 or 20 *Fortune* 500 companies leads me to conclude that today our strategic planning approaches have serious deficiencies and side effects, and that they are not sufficiently responsive in an increasingly fast-moving and competitively intense business environment.

These deficiencies merit examination, and I examine them here as they relate to individual businesses, not corporate strategy.

Issue number one is the side effects of the strategic planning processes.

Unfortunately, the strategic planning system at many companies took on a life of its own.

Managers substituted thick binders of data on the minutiae of their business for development of true insight and a rethinking of the basic assumptions of their strategy. A new bureaucracy took root, and with it came another control system that paralleled the financial one.

The general manager became preoccupied with tools and techniques rather than fundamental understandings, to the point where he would worry about his strategic plan presentation for the month or two prior to its delivery, and then run the business for the rest of the year without looking at it. As a result, planners began increasingly to communicate with other planners, and forms and formats began to stifle the creativity that is the essence of strategy.

The systems that helped introduce the discipline of strategic planning in the early 1970s are now getting in the way of effective strategic management in the second half of the 1980s.

Setting strategy is still one of the two most important functions of the general manager; the second being organizational and personnel management.

Every financially successful company has a sound strategy. It may not be explicit; it may be *implicit*. It may not be enshrined in handsome thick vinyl binders. But it *must* exist. How then do we modify our strategic planning approaches to develop and implement successful strategies without undesirable side effects?

The second issue, or problem, is the focus of the planning process. At the risk of being heretical, I would suggest that strategy and planning are two words that should not be juxtaposed. They refer to quite different activities, and the processes in place today focus on the latter, not on the former.

Strategy is concerned with the workings of a business and winning against one's competitors. The goal of business strategy is to secure an enduring competitive advantage that leads to a high ROI relative to the industry as a whole.

Planning, on the other hand, tends to focus on the development of specific, detailed programs for a product line, for facilities, for marketing, etc. that follow from the strategy.

Strategy development and planning are different activities requiring different skills, and our processes need to pay more attention to developing high-quality strategies.

The strategic development process must focus on making the strategy explicit, making the assumptions clear, and testing the strategy's validity.

It must try, as well, to answer these fundamental questions of strategy:

☆ How can competitive cost or price advantage be obtained?

☆ What are the structural shifts—technology, market or competitive—that are occurring in the environment and how can they be exploited?

☆ What are competitors' strategies and their implications?

☆ What do we have to do to win?

We must get back to basics in our strategic management by de-emphasizing the *process* and *bureaucracy* of strategic planning while re-emphasizing sound strategic thinking and effective implementation.

To increase the value-added of our profession, corporate planners must direct their activities towards strategic thinking and away from planning systems; towards vision and away from volume; towards insight and away from forms and formats; and towards creativity and away from control and bureaucracy.

Another issue is responsiveness. It will be an even

more important aspect of effective strategic management in the 1980s as we face an environment characterized by an accelerating rate of change. This change will manifest itself in technology, in structural shifts in markets, in environmental factors such as regulation and international business, and in dramatic competitive change of the type that has taken the personal computer industry from an embryonic stage to a brutal shakeout in just a few years. Competition of this type is now routinely global.

The implications for the adaptability of our strategic planning processes are profound. An annual planning cycle in the personal computer industry, for instance, would likely be a death warrant.

Let us now shift from selected observations on strategic planning to specific changes General Electric is effecting in its strategic management approach to deal with the issues that face it.

Some of the objectives we had for changing the process for managing and monitoring the strategies of our individual businesses in the late 1980s were: enhancing responsiveness to change while reducing ritual; focusing on the real gut issues facing each business; and reinforcing a general manager-to-general manager dialogue.

In doing this we wished to focus our efforts on businesses where there are real strategic uncertainties rather than wasting time on businesses where the strategy is agreed upon and implementation is proceeding smoothly. We are determined to make the strategic process a mechanism for pouncing on opportunities—rather than enshrining them in attractive vinyl-covered books. The goal is a creative process, not a bureaucratic one. And finally we have to focus on the external environment and our *competitors'* strategies, and not be deluded by the assumption that the competition will stand still while we cut costs or improve our products.

How then are these principles being implemented?

Strategic management in the future requires a rolling agenda capable of reacting to the strategic needs of the business as they evolve, rather than an annual process that takes place at a set time each year. This is done through a combination of full-day dialogues on the strategy of major businesses scheduled well in advance, and a monthly meeting set aside to review issues as they emerge and are resolved.

All of these interactions are general manager-to-general manager; they involve the three members of our chief executive office, business management and myself.

The strategic management process is differentiated, and to some degree exception-based. There are no full-scale strategy discussions for some businesses in 1986. Of course, we expect all our general managers to be continually monitoring the effectiveness of their strategies and updating their own plans whether or not they are reviewed by the CEO. Other businesses are reviewed more than once, where the strategy is not resolved or where the environment is turbulent.

Each business review has a well-defined purpose. In a few, the idea is to revisit basic strategy; in others, to monitor the effectiveness of strategy implementation and tactical programmes. In some cases, we address specific issues; and in others, we just kick the tires—or, on occasion, the drivers. In short, whatever is needed; whatever will be helpful.

Each session is issue-oriented. Agenda setting is a two-way street, determined after extensive discussions with corporate and business management to identify the right issues. The kinds of issues we might highlight include strategy overhauls, plant rationalizations, market share shifts, or the implications of a particular competitor's strategy, just to name a few.

With the issues changing continually and with no fixed formats, we preserve the creativity that is the essence of strategy.

Feedback is a very important aspect of the process. After each interaction, the business is given this feedback on the level of agreement and confidence in the strategy. It receives, as well, guidance on the issues to focus on in the coming months. But most important of all is the creation of an environment that is conducive to open dialogue on the real gut issues facing each business. The message is clear: it's better to be honest and say, 'I don't have a strategy', or, 'I'm not sure my strategy is appropriate', than try to cover up that lack of a correct business vision with 'wildest dream' projections. That admission of no strategy, or a shaky one, does not necessarily mean one is managing the business badly. Some of our businesses are so complex and changing so fast (factory automation, information services, semiconductors, for example) that it's extremely difficult to develop a long-standing, comprehensive strategy.

If the new process seems *ad hoc,* it is; if it seems dependent on openness and honesty, it is; if it seems dependent on both corporate and business management being both competent strategists and well informed, it is.

What we are trying to do at GE is right for us but not necessarily right for many other companies. Our ability to move in the direction I have described is heavily dependent on our historical commitment to a strategic planning process and the strong foundation that process gave us in terms of having a very high proportion of businesses with well-defined, successful strategies run by general managers with good strategy skills.

It also depends on the extensive knowledge of each of our businesses on the part of the members of the chief executive office, and the fact that the four members of the CEO are powerful strategic thinkers in their own right. They have helped create an environment where open and honest dialogue on strategic issues, however difficult and unresolved, is at a premium, and where covering up problems is the kiss of death.

Without these factors, we could not make the next evolutionary step: a new approach for the planning organization. These changes have had a profound impact on the role and staffing of corporate business development and planning.

For one, our role has shifted from one of corporate policeman to a value-added role in which we assist individual businesses with strategy development as well as concern ourselves with the overall management of the portfolio. As a result, the natural antagonisms between corporate planning and business management that are frequently the hallmark of strategic planning systems have dissipated in favor of a desire on the part of the businesses to work together with the planning organization.

Another effect on the planning department has been that the skill mix of our staff has had to change—towards strategic thinkers and doers with a general management perspective.

And finally, the time that used to be spent in managing 'the process' is now spent looking for acquisitions and creating new businesses for GE.

General Electric's commitment to quality strategic thinking and management is higher than ever. Our challenge at GE is to adapt our strategic management process to build on the investment of the past, while avoiding its historical pitfalls, and to respond to the accelerating demands of the future so that we can achieve our objective of being the most competitive company in the world.

Section Two

Developing New Products and Services

Strategies for New Product Development

Frederick D. Buggie, President, Strategic Innovations Incorporated

Guidelines are offered for following the tortuous trail of new-product development. To succeed, you must first accumulate many likely new-product concepts, rather than just one or two. They all should be subjected to preliminary market research at the same time that they are being investigated for their production feasibility. Feedback-loops must be built in to bridge and reflect results from these simultaneous processes, and the concepts themselves must be allowed to change and undergo a gradual metamorphosis . . . or they must be allowed to die painlessly at this early stage. Finally, the survivors will achieve commercial success only through the optimism and perseverance of their 'pilot'.

Part A—New-product Conception—Some New and Old Curves

A few years ago, a man named Jones graphically depicted the metamorphosis of a product in the market-place. It has since, been recognized as the standard, by professionals in the field of new-product conception and marketing strategy innovation.

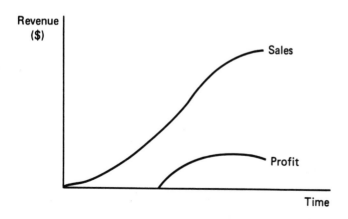

The product-life-cycle-curve, as it is called, applies across the board to any product line . . . any industry . . . any market. The graph simply asserts that a new product, upon introduction, starts from nothing . . . enters into an initial period of accelerating growth in revenues (impelled by the purchases of 'pioneers' and 'early adopters') . . . comes to a point of inflection of the curve, when sales grow at a constant rate—and then decreasing rate—and finally, sales begin to level off.

Beyond that point . . . who knows?! Your new product could meet the sudden demise of the Hula Hoop and the Nehru Jacket—precipitous decline!

It could follow Jell-O, or Shredded Wheat (which was first introduced on 1 March 1893)—fairly constant rate of continuing sales, at some level somewhat below its earlier peak . . . Ovaltine is forever! Or the product-life-cycle of your product line could follow that of the Duncan Company—which looks like a yo-yo over the long period.

I was in Santa Monica a while ago, and street skates had caught on with young people. I was in Marina Del Rey last week and saw a number of *adults* roller skating down the sidewalk. Who's going to bet on when street skates reach Kansas City, and how long the fad will last?

(A lot of opportunistic, profit-motivated entrepreneurs, that's who!)

Notwithstanding the best efforts of market researchers and professional planners, the dollar level of sales of any new product, and its longevity, are pretty hard to predict.

So, new products introduced by any individual firm tend to atrophy—their profit contribution disappears, over time: The fad passes . . . you're eaten up by new competitors . . . the market becomes saturated . . . Technology moves on (roller skate wheels have gone from metal to wood to

The author is President of Strategic Innovations Incorporated, 299 Old Westport Road, Wilton, Conn. 06897, U.S.A. The firm is represented in the U.K. at 66 Harpur Street, Bedford MK40 2RA.

plastic—is rubber next?) . . . Or any of a number of other reasons.

The *average* or *typical* rate of product obsolescence varies, from industry to industry. It is extraordinarily high in the electronics industry . . . toys and games live from Christmas to Christmas . . . 10 years ago, new food-product life cycles averaged 2–3 years—now they're down to about 6 months. On the other hand, the typical product life cycle in the machine-tool industry is relatively sluggish. Numerically-controlled machines are the first major innovation in that industry in 100 years.

But it's not safe to go by averages, and 'Industry' performance. The product-life-cycles for *individual* products, *within* an industry, exhibit greater variations than the difference *among* industries. Guitars are different from pianos (and so are the companies that make them) . . . We've already mentioned Shredded Wheat . . . Monopoly is a monopoly. The Chairman of Warner & Swasey told me, a few months ago, that he strolled outside and noticed that one out of every five trucks backed up his shipping platform was loaded with products that did not even exist 5 years ago! (That's conservative!)

If you extrapolate the past product-life-cycle experience of your industry . . . your company . . . your individual product lines . . . into the *future*—it is clear that you need to get cracking *now*, on bringing new products on stream, to supplant the income which will no longer be generated by your current products . . . 'sooner, or later'.

That's just to stay *even*! Now, if a *growth* imperative is imposed, in the face of the inevitable attrition resulting from the product-life-cycle, the planner faces a real *crisis*!

The 'crisis', caused by the product life cycle—combined with the growth required by management (and stockholders)—is compounded, by the current rate of inflation in our economy. What company is satisfied with 4 per cent simple annual growth, in the face of 12 per cent compound inflation?! 'CRISIS'?

The Chinese character for 'CRISIS' looks like this:

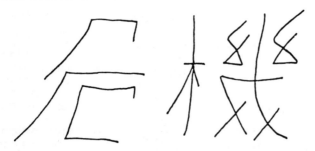

If you split it in two, you find that the character embodies the words for 'Danger' and 'Opportunity'.

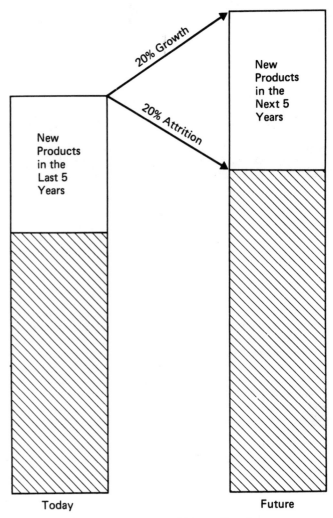

The Importance of New Products

Danger   Opportunity

Successful new product development is the solution to this particular crisis!

Fine!

Which particular 'new products' are you going to develop? Where do they come from? What are the *normal* sources of new-product ideas?

. . . The Director of New-product Development
(Of course!)

. . . The R & D Department . . . Engineering
(That's what they're paid for!)

. . . Technical literature
(Sometimes.)

. . . Your salesmen
(Hopefully.)

. . . Customers, direct
(Sure!)

. . . Independent inventors
('Over the transom'.)

... Competitors (me-too's)
        (Good luck!)

... Knock-off's (opportunistic shots)
        (Why not?)

... The Production Department
        (Once in a while.)

... The Chairman of the Board
        ('Monday-morning' ideas.)

... The Suggestion Box
        (Anyplace they come from!)

If that is where companies normally get their ideas for new products, how does it work out? How many of these ideas will succeed? What proportion will be launched in the marketplace ... and, of *them*, what percentage will ultimately return a profit, and *enjoy* a 'life-cycle'? What does the record show?

A couple of years ago, *The Journal of Marketing* reported that ...

> To produce a single successful new product, 80 ideas are required; seven-eighths of scientists' and engineers' development time is spent on products failing in introduction. Of every 10 products that emerge from R & D, half fail in product and market tests, and only two become commercial successes.

Bert Cross, the former Chairman of the 3M Company, commented that in his company ...

> Out of every 100 new-product concepts, 33 will prove technically feasible; and of these, three will become commercially successful in the market.

Another firm's experience ...

> Two out of 58 new-product concepts ultimately succeed.

Is your company's record better than 3–5 per cent? The rest of the world's record is not *that* good!

If this sort of a situation is what can reasonably be expected, ... and you recognize that your firm *does* need an additional new product line ... then the instant reaction might be to go and collect at least 50 new-product ideas, to be sure.

Such a brute force approach is impractical. To prove that, let's extrapolate back in time, from the starting point of our basic product life-cycle curve (Figure 1).

From the instant that a new-product idea is proposed, development effort, and money, begins to be spent on it. Small amounts at first—maybe just a drawing or concept statement—then, models, engineering drawings, market research, bench tests, redesign, pilot production, market testing. Increasing *incremental* investments, as each benchmark is passed, and as favorable evaluations are made by management.

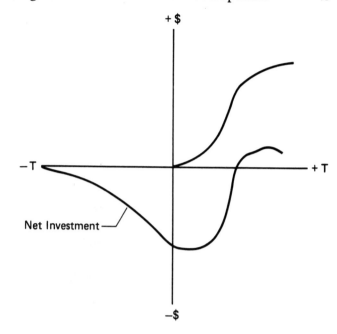

(Extrapolated *back*.)

Figure 1. The product life cycle curve—extrapolated backwards

The money and development effort expended on those that are *scrubbed* somewhere along the line is totally wasted. And lots of those, that survive the entire process, *still* fail at the end of the line (market introduction) after the really *big* investments are made.

As an example, General Foods' experience in a 'typical' 10-year period (Figure 2).

Our back-extrapolated graph only depicts the *successful* new products. It does not take into account the 95 per cent that are aborted sometime along the way. The earlier you kill those new products destined to fail, the more wasted money

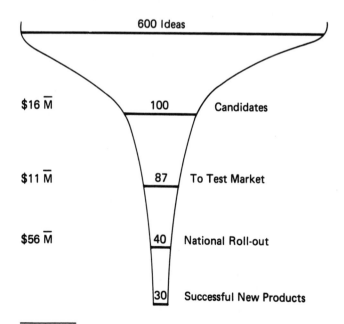

$243 Million, and 10 Years!

Figure 2. The selection of new product ideas

and development effort you will save, especially, since the *largest* amounts are required toward the *latter* stages! It costs the same, to develop a failure, as it does to develop a success.

Better yet—only develop the *successful* new-product ideas! But that is not possible, because the rousing successes . . . and the turkeys . . . look a lot alike during their early stages of development.

To improve the basic process of new-product development, perhaps, the new-product *idea* is not the place to *start*! Perhaps it is better to lay some groundwork, *first*, drawing up the 'specifications' of the ideal new product, abstractly; and *subsequently*, take the initiative in *generating* new-product concepts, to *conform* to the 'specs'.

The specifications, or criteria, for the 'perfect new product' can be developed by establishing the minimum objectives it must meet . . . and analyzing the strengths of your company which can be brought to bear on meeting those objectives. The following tool is useful in developing these criteria.

Of all possible markets that *could* be served, your company is a strong factor in *certain* segments—your current products are known . . . you enjoy an established reputation . . . you 'know your way around', in some markets.

Of all possible technologies and manufacturing capabilities, your company is knowledgeable, experienced, and possesses the capacity to operate certain production processes . . . better than anyone else.

The shaded area represents your *current* operations. Your *new* product will lie *outside* that area—how far outside, and which direction, i.e. along which axis, will be determined by your objectives, and your company's unique strengths. It makes sense to build on your competitive advantage.

Thus, if your long suit is the markets you serve, your successful next new product may lie at some distance away from home base along the horizontal axis; if your main expertise is in a particular technology or based on unique equipment, your ideal next new product will lie along the vertical axis, above the shaded area.

Once the groundwork is laid, and you have set the criteria for the new product, it is then possible to generate fitting new-product concepts.

It's time to look to the outside world—trends, changes, discontinuities . . . different perspectives . . . ingenious combinations . . . fresh insights—*relevant* to your new-product criteria.

But the business environment, within which your company operates today, has become awfully complex and diverse.

Figure 4 describes the growth of the world's population over the past 10,000 years. I submit, that the same Malthusian proliferation applies to technology, (and information, generally). There are now more than 100,000 technical journals published throughout the world; 72 billion new pieces of information came into the world last year. The total body of information is now doubling every 10 years. At that rate, 75 per cent of all mankind's knowledge has been developed in the last two decades. The National Science Foundation reports that the technical information received by a chemical engineer in the class of 1960 became essentially obsolete by 1965.

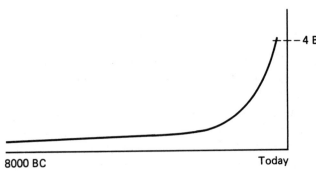

Figure 4. Growth of world population

Test this thesis against fields with which you're familiar, transportation, communication, medicine.

Under these circumstances, it is patently impossible for any single human being to possess all the information necessary to accomplish any task of significant breadth, such as the conception of potential new products as defined by your criteria.

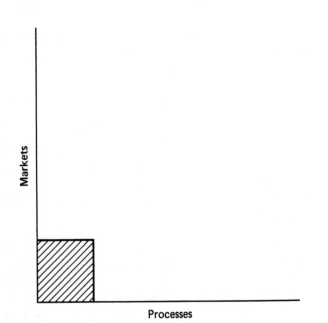

Figure 3. A process/market matrix

The solution to that problem is not to seek the omniscient, single human being who can come up with the perfect new product for your company, but rather, play the percentages! Draw together a *number* of forward-looking specialists, each having expertise in a different field relevant, somehow, to potential new products for your company . . . and lead them, stimulate them, encourage them, to generate a *number* of possible candidates, for an 'acceptable' new product for your company. (Acceptable, in terms of the minimum specifications you establish in the beginning.)

These individuals may come from inside or outside your company. Contribution to the success of current products or past products of your company, is not germane to the task—it is the capacity to contribute to the conception of possible *future* new products for your company, that's important. Get them from wherever they come from. Let them generate all the possibilities they can. Then, subsequently, feed these 'candidate' new-product concepts to a hand-picked team of the best specialists *within* the firm, who are responsible for the functions contributing to future profits. From their intimate knowledge of your company's main strengths, and your goals, they can be most effective in refining and selecting those new-product concepts bearing the highest potential for success.

In summary . . .

☆ Any firm, in any industry, needs a flow of new products to survive.

☆ It's not economically feasible to develop, and partially develop, a lot of new products in order to distill the few winners.

☆ The starting point should not be concepts themselves, but an abstract definition of the attributes of the ideal new product.

☆ A *future* orientation is essential.

☆ In the complex world of today, you've got to play the numbers game, many contributors, many possibilities.

☆ Once your best people have selected the candidates passing muster, your company can invest in the development of these new products, with a high expectation of success.

Part B—Strategies for New-product Development

The management sage, Peter Drucker, has said: 'Every great idea ultimately degenerates into hardware'. After you come up with all the great ideas you can, and after they are evaluated and the best of the lot are selected, finally the time comes when you have to stop studying and creating and planning—and go *do* something. Time for action!

Presumably, at this point, there are a number of potential new-product concepts at hand, any one of which may possess the potential to be a resounding success in the marketplace—and a magnificently profitable, future product line for your company. But it's a long way from here to there. The hard work is just starting. So who within your organization is to be responsible for bringing home the bacon? For shoe-horning one of these 'nothing' concepts through the thicket, to the end goal—a product that your company will ultimately manufacture and sell, profitably?

As the army is marvellously staffed, trained, and equipped to fight the *last* war, so your organization may be ideally equipped and staffed to develop your *last* new product. But what about your *next* winner? It is not going to be the same.

In his book, *On The Psychology Of Military Incompetence*, Norman Dixon argues that the very characteristics needed for successful leadership in war—the ability to tolerate uncertainty, spontaneity of thought and action, and open mind—are the very antithesis of personality traits that are needed to meet the requirements of military life, and attract recruits in the first place—obedience, orderliness, fear of failure, a need for approval. The system makes little allowance for innovation, initiative, and independent thought. Does that situation bear any resemblance to the capacity of your organization, as is, to develop your next new product?

Again, the main question is who, within your company will take the responsibility and do the job? Committees don't actually do anything—they review and approve (or, more likely, scrub) proposals. They are a convenient device for diluting or avoiding responsibility. We are looking for the *pilot*—the real-time, hands-on, decision-making, self-committing hero. You're seeking an individual, and a special kind of individual, at that.

You can recruit him from inside the organization, or outside the organization—those are the only two possible places he could come from.

In the latter case, you may opt for a heavyweight in the field you intend to penetrate. He really knows his way around in this market, which is alien to you, because you've never been there. Trouble is, he knows nothing about the policies and folkways of your particular company—you'll have to bring him up to speed and integrate him into your organization.

The other choice is to select an individual from within your organization, who is fully familiar with how to get things done internally, and in whom you have complete confidence—and he knows nothing, for starters, about the field you are about to enter.

I do not think there is a general answer. They both work. It depends on which is the more crucial to success—outside knowledge or inside knowledge.

In any case, you want an individual with a derring-do, entrepreneurial spirit. Avoid those made ordinary by having done the same thing repeatedly and reliably over a long period of time. Pass over the 'maintenance manager' who has earned a track record in a narrow discipline. Eliminate from consideration the stable conformist who never departed from convention, never shattered an icon. In the process of new-product development, you win no points for 'following standard procedures': losers as well as winners can follow all the rules!

Once you select your pilot, give him an airplane—a clear charter and a budget to get the job done. Next, remove the landing gear from his airplane so there's no way he can land, if his mission does not succeed.

A chicken and a pig were strolling by a diner one morning and the chicken smiled and said, 'Isn't that nice . . . doesn't that make you feel proud, that we are responsible, you and I, for enabling those humans to enjoy their breakfast?' The pig replied, 'That's easy for you to say. For you it's merely a contribution, for me it's total commitment'!

You have to put your pilot in the pig's position. Job on the line, no place to hide, do or die. New-product development is hard and dangerous work. It can't (or will not) be handled off the side of the desk of someone with other (safer) responsibilities. It requires total commitment. Reward for success, commensurate, of course. For high-rollers, it is a good, visible, fast route to the top.

The responsibility for success lies with the pilot. That responsibility has been assigned to him by the Chairman, or CEO, or whoever bears the ultimate responsibility for the future growth of the company. New product development is that important.

Problem is . . . the pilot will need a good deal of help and cooperation from others in the organization. Generally, within the typical corporation, the amount of 'help and cooperation' accorded an individual, is related to his perceived power, and there is a direct positive correlation between the two. The more power, the more cooperation. It is a fact of life, that an individual's 'natural' perceived power is a function of the size of his fiefdom, either in terms of the dollars accounted for by his unit, or the number of employees that have a solid-line, reporting relationship to him. And the pilot may have nothing but dotted lines beneath him and beside him . . . and he has authority over zero dollars of *current* income-producing activity.

Solution is . . . the CEO must *provide* the pilot with what is called 'nominal' power. That is, he must give him clear authority to command the kind of cooperation he needs, to get the job done. The CEO must support his new-product-development pilot, and must come out of the closet and give visibility to his support—wholehearted . . . staunch . . . unflagging . . . confident support. The pilot needs to be able, clearly to wield the power of the chief executive officer, in the eyes of those from whom he needs cooperation. That's the only way the job will get done!

What is this 'job'? It's very simple. It *should* be very simple. You've got to *keep* it simple. Otherwise, the corporation runs the risk of over-complicating, and over-spending on, what should be a quick-shot, 'fly-by', initially. You've got to stay light on your feet . . . follow trails . . . have a quick look-see . . . check it out.

There are only three things that must be done at this point . . . two, simultaneously . . . and one, thereafter. The first two are: check out the produceability by your company . . . and do the necessary market research. The third thing, that should be done next, is run the numbers.

Let me deal with the third thing first (figures!). A firm in Switzerland is anxious to know whether or not to manufacture and market in the United States, a new product they are considering. I just received a cable from them advising that they are at the point of doing an economic analysis, and asking us to supply them with information as to the price they should assume it can be sold at, and an estimate of volume of production. At this writing, I am still wrestling with what our response should be, inasmuch as the market research is only part-way completed at this point, and they do not as yet, therefore, have the feedback necessary to make decisions regarding the *design* to which they will produce the product, and *how* they will go to market.

They got one thing right, in their question, however: combining the subjects of price and volume. You can't really split the subjects. You can't ask a question about what price you should sell a new product for, without including an assumption as to volume; and you can't ask how many you can sell, without knowing what price you're talking about. Basic supply–demand economics dictates the relationship—the higher the price, the less you sell; the lower the price, the more you sell. Costs and production volume, face the same immutable relationship, for a different reason. (Of course there are aberrations such as perfume, where you can sell more if you raise the price. And one company I know of, manufactures products which have gained a reputation for being of higher quality than those of their competitors, experienced the same phenomenon—they raised the price of a new product, following introduction, and found that it sold much better!) But in any case, the principle stands—you have to consider price and quantity together.

The main point is that the financial analysis must come *after* the determination of the market for a new product (how sold, to whom, for what price) and *after* the determination of the design configuration and quality level to which it will be produced. Only then, can you grind in your discounted-cash-flow assumptions and begin playing what-if games.

Now for the first step—the produceability check and the market research, that needs to be performed at the same time on any and all of the potential new-product candidates you have at hand. It is well if you have several that you can start down the road at once. That way, you are sure to come up with a sure winner, or even a choice of winners, rather than keeping a turkey alive that should be killed, simply because you have nothing else to develop.

Figure 5 is the 'Landvater Snail' depicting the sequence of events in new-product concept check-out. It was published in *Planned Innovation* in the March/April 1980 issue, in an article reporting on a seminar John Landvater conducted in London, England.

I was with Mr. Landvater in May 1980 in Chicago and we discussed his 'Snail' at length. He agrees that the technical research, and market investigation, should proceed simultaneously. Pressed as to which should come first, if you have to make a choice (which you usually *don't*), we agreed that probably the market research should precede the technical investigation—so reverse, in your mind, 'Market' and 'Technical' in Figure 5. It is foolish to find a

great market for a product you cannot produce . . . but it's even *more* foolish to tie down all design tolerances for a product you'd love to manufacture, which does not happen to have a viable market— nobody wants to buy it! It reminds one a bit, of the time-honored question, which came first—the chicken or the egg. (The answer to that, of course, is that the egg came first—a chicken is simply the egg's way of making another egg!)

One major corporation in the health and beauty aid industry follows this basic procedure:

Concept Screening

☆ Product concepts would be developed for those ideas which appear to have high feasibility. These concepts would then be exposed to consumers in focus groups to determine the extent of interest. The most promising ideas would then proceed to quantified concept test (QCT).

☆ Detailed R & D evaluations would then be conducted for those ideas which perform well in QCT to determine costs and timing to bring a product to market.

☆ Development programs would be initiated for those product(s) which have the greatest potential for near-term development at a reasonable cost.

I asked one of their executives which they do first, as a rule. She replied that they always check the market first and then do the manufacturing feasibility investigation only on the survivors— 'except for a few notable exceptions'.

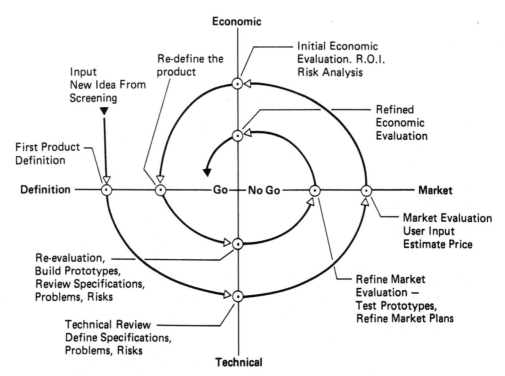

Figure 5. Sequence of procedures in carrying out a product feasibility study

That's to be expected of a cosmetic concern. They are especially market-oriented in their outlook. And the principal asset of these companies is their brand—their reputation in the marketplace. So if they discover a market need for a new product in the Health and Beauty Aid field that fits their name and position, they may well go ahead with it, regardless—even if they have to subcontract out its manufacture.

Another way to express this dual, simultaneous chore graphically, is by a PERT chart (Figure 6).

Such a schedule is appropriate to this activity, because it is a complex task requiring integration of many elements, and because the two streams—marketing and technical—must interact upon one another; and the new-product concept often changes or undergoes a metamorphosis as it goes down each stream. That is, you *expect* change, you *seek* to develop the new-product concept, as you examine its marketability, and as you investigate its produceability. And the changes and turns in one area will have impact on the other area.

Let us imagine you conceived a new gas-mixing/regulator device which may have application in the operating room, and in the welding shop. From the market, you discover, it 'wants' to be green. From the test lab you determine that it has a maximum-throughput capacity of 100 CFS. Now, you have to build in a feed-back loop, to see if the shop can make it green, and see if the market will tolerate a 100-CFS upper limit.

From this simple example, we draw three points:

Point 1. (again.) You ought to investigate market and produceability concurrently, not serially.

Point 2. Flexibility is the watchword. You don't earn any medals for coming back with the same concept you went out with. The concept you initially start with, should be looked on as a seed idea—a seed from which you hope to make something grow, even though you haven't the faintest idea what the flower will look like. It is most unlikely that the raw concept, in exactly its original form, will end up being the final version which will find its place in the market and be manufactured on the production floor. You are taking the concept out to allow the market place—and the test laboratory—to redesign your product for you. You are not asking the binary question, 'Will it or won't it?'' . . . 'Can I, or can't I?'. Rather, you are asking 'What?' and 'How?'.

Point 3. You've got to build in feedback loops between these concurrent activities: change-checkpoints, so that you can make progress, in developing a final product you can both make and sell.

One advantage of using a PERT chart is that it will clearly show the dependency relationships among 'events'. That is, it will force you to await the result of one activity, prior to proceeding with another activity which should reflect that result and be built upon it.

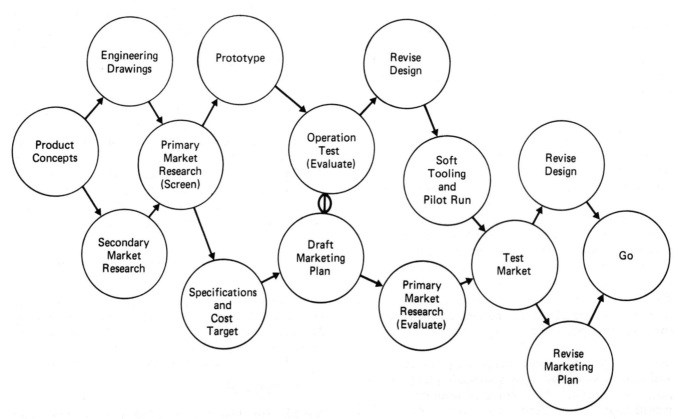

Figure 6. A PERT chart for product development

The other main advantage of the PERT chart is that it nails down the schedule for each event, in advance. That prevents a new-product concept from languishing in the research department being tinkered with *ad infinitum*.

One must recognize that the 'technical investigative unit' of the organization is always, and will always be, 100 per cent loaded with work. Whether, in your company, it's called the 'Research Department', the 'Research and Development Division' the 'Test Lab', that group was completely, totally busy, the day it was formed, and has been ever since. And as soon as a new scientist or development engineer comes on board, he will have no 'time available', from the day he reports to work. It is a classic exhibition of Parkinson's First.

There is a company in the Midwest which manufactures small kitchen appliances. The tempo of their new-product development activity is very high, understandably. They've had some winners and some losers. I asked why they did not develop a hot-air popcorn popper. The president replied that their R & D department was completely loaded at the time. I did not pursue the question. You have to wonder if they were busy developing some products that were less successful than the popcorn popper that Christmas.

The point is that top management must constantly review *what* is being worked on, and *how long* each project is being worked on in the research lab. There is a natural tendency to work on any existing project in process, in favor of a new one—regardless of the relative objective benefit, of doing *more* development, as contrasted with *initiating* development, in any situation requiring the establishment of priorities. Top management (to whom the marketing department also reports) must continually review priorities for R & D effort.

So much for 'Technical'. Now a word on the 'Market'—the watchwords are, *Optimism* and *Perseverance*. You have to go out with a positive, optimistic attitude, convinced that you can carve out a niche, somewhere, for your new-product concept. Anybody who has ever had a new idea, was always, in the beginning, a minority of one. And he faces a world full of people with vested interests: pride in their current position in their market: desire for the security of the *status quo*: and Machiavellian hostility toward anything new. Fortunately, the market researcher can also find people who are alert, perceptive, aggressive, and open to new possibilities.

With a negative attitude it is easy to collect reasons and build a case, that any new idea is bad. With a positive attitude, you can force your new idea into a world that had no ready-made place for it. You must project potential markets, in situations where there is no direct base of comparison (because your new-product concept is, after all, new).

Perseverance. The answers rarely fall into your lap—but sometimes it is even worse than that. In some cases I have talked to a lot of people in an industry and obtained nothing but general, conflicting, 'mushy' opinions and information which somehow did not seem to be on the mark—until finally we stumbled onto an obscure subsegment of the industry where, at last, everything fell into place.

In another specific instance I recall, we talked to the Chief Engineer in every leading firm in the industry and could not succeed in raising even a glimmer of interest. Finally, as we dropped to second and third tier below the leaders, we contacted a hard-charging Vice President of Engineering in a small but aggressive firm in that industry. He seized upon the new product concept and agreed to run with it (contract to purchase the initial quantity), in order to achieve an edge on his laconic, conservative, old competitors. We have about concluded that there is no such thing as an 'industry'—only a number of firms doing roughly the same thing in different ways, and with different positions and different philosophies of doing business. So you can use SIC codes to start, but never forget that they were devised originally by the federal government to keep records of past events. You have got to keep digging, in any field where you think there might be pay dirt!

Finally, there is a limit. There comes a time, for some new-product concepts, when the cord should be pulled. They have had their chance and they just cannot make it. If a new-product concept begins to trot like a turkey, gobble like a turkey, and look like a turkey—it may be a turkey! Killing turkeys is top management's job.

That's the beauty of starting out with multiple new-product concepts, for the first-round 'fly-by' on the Landvater Snail. You can kill a lot of turkeys and prevent the company from spending *real* money, half-developing them, and, at the same time, obtaining insurance on the survivors. When the time comes to invest in them, you can have confidence that they are sure winners.

Acknowledgments—This article is an extract from *New Product Development Strategies* by Frederick Buggie, published by AMACOM, a Division of the American Management Association, in September 1981, and distributed in the U.K. by Business Books, Ltd., 17 Conway Street, London.

Appendix A

A small, relatively-new company had been formed to exploit certain high-technology devices that had been developed by

National Aeronautics and Space Agency during the U.S. space program. Their first product was an electronic system designed to aid ophthalmologists in diagnosing vision defects. Their system cost $30,000. And they were very good at selling it. As a matter of fact, within a few years, they had succeeded in selling a $30,000 system to just about every ophthalmologist in the U.S. that could ever be sold.

At that point, management realized they were facing a serious problem: their one-product company had saturated their market. Their system didn't wear out in just a few years. There were not that many new ophthalmologists graduating and setting up practice each year. What were they to do? They had to take fast action to assure the continuity of their company, which in a few short years had established an excellent reputation in the health-care industry.

Management decided to follow a dual approach to the problem, simultaneously. First, they set up a network of representatives in Europe to sell their system to European ophthalmologists, thus starting a new product-life-cycle in that new area. And second, they launched an all-out effort to come up with complementary new product lines to sell within their current health-care markets. I conducted that program, personally, utilizing the brain-power of 17 outside experts.

The result was some 70 new product possibilities in all, one of which, the client implemented by acquisition even before the program was concluded. They acquired a company that sold micro-surgical instruments.

Now, to appreciate the beauty of that move, you have to know that 'micro-surgery' simply deals with eyes, hands and brains. So by this action, the company extended its field from eyes alone, to include hands and brains as well; and at the same time they broadened their interests from just diagnosis, to diagnosis plus surgery to correct defects.

Appendix B

We recently completed an assignment for a large international computer manufacturer. The STRATEGIC INNO-VATION System was used by their Research & Development Division to identify new potential software products, warranting intensive development efforts, based upon verified needs in the current marketplace for 'actionable data'.

Over the course of 6 months, we established the criteria for the ideal R & D subject (software product to be developed) from their own standpoint: developed the strategy for generating likely possibilities (looking for easier, more versatile, more adaptable, 'user-friendly' systems to be developed); and, with the help of 20 diverse experts from our Brain-Bank (see representative profiles), produced 37 new software system concepts. Of these concepts (reviewed, refined and evaluated by the team of internal experts within the computer manufacturer's own research and development organization) 10 were selected for feasibility investigation. (Naturally, they are highly confidential.)

That is where the matter stands now. It is expected that several of these systems will provide the base for expanded growth and profitability of their computer business in the future.

Appendix C

A major chemical company undertook the development of a new composite material to meet rigid performance specifications. They succeeded: they utilized graphite fiber reinforcement in an epoxy resin matrix. But then they discovered that the total market consisted of three antennae on some planet other than earth—which was definitely not their idea of a smashing commercial product.

So the company's marketing executives stepped back and took a look at the material developed by their laboratory and said to themselves: 'With this interesting combination of unique properties, that material just has to be good for something else!'

Sporting goods had already occurred to them, so on their own they started developing golf club shafts and tennis racquet frames. In the hope of finding other applications, they placed advertisement in popular science magazines, running a contest, and offering a prize. That turned up a lot of impractical junk.

Then they came to a STRATEGIC INNOVATION Program. We established the criteria defining the minimum objectives that a new product application had to meet. Then we developed a strategy. What was stopping them was their knowledge that the composite material currently cost $200 per pound to produce, which was intimidating! So we figured that the only way they could actually sell the material at this point was to mold key components of large expensive systems, which would enable superior performance of the entire system, thus leveraging its value.

We drafted a briefing document, describing the properties of the composite material, offering some possible applications as 'seed ideas', and categorically stating that this new material only cost $2.00 per pound.

We recruited, altogether, 21 diverse experts from various fields to participate in a series of innovation sessions. The result was 106 possible applications for the material. The big winners were: textile machinery components (picker-sticks, shuttle arms, etc.), computer peripheral equipment components (for parts requiring low mass and good lubricity because they have to start and stop very quickly), and believe it or not, musical instrument structural components (such as the spline that supports the neck of a guitar and must resist very high torque forces).

In the course of performing the final market research, I personally borrowed the guitar that belonged to the vice president of a large manufacturer of guitars and delivered it to our client's project leader. I emphasized that the guitar manufacturing vice president wanted his guitar back. So an early meeting was arranged and incidentally a contract was negotiated for the supply of the graphite composite material for guitar necks.

Sometimes things go that way.

How to Get New Products to Market Quicker

The Systematic Development of New Products, Markets and Production
Methods so that The Concern Can Operate Successfully

G. B. M. Mathôt, *Consultant for Innovation, Amsterdam*

*Innovation encompasses a number of activities within a
concern that lead to successful introduction of new products,
gaining new markets and/or the introduction of new production methods. The basis for these activities is the combined
creative capacity of management and employees. By forming
an Innovation Group from suitable concern functionaries, new
products, markets and production methods can be effectively
developed that will not only suit the available external
opportunities but also conform to internal strengths, so that
the potential of the concern can be optimally used.*

Productive Creativity

Every innovation springs from an original idea. And indeed, many a director
sighs 'if I only had a good idea' or 'if only
my employees were a little more
creative'.

A strong feeling that creativity is essentially unintelligible brings many to wait
in tension on the 'divine spark', the genial
idea that has such inner power, that it can
allow the innovation process to go on on
its own.

Such a spark is often awaited in vain, so
that years go by without taking the
necessary steps.

Contrary to what one tends to accept in
such a situation, creativity can be consciously introduced using, for instance,
brainstorming. The *probability* that such
an idea will grow into a successful concern
activity is, however, extremely *small*.[6] To
develop one single success-product (the
so-called 'bread earner') one must consider 50 product ideas: The development
of the 49 other ideas takes just as much
time (and money) but does not lead to the
desired result.

Still, the effectiveness of the existing
creativity techniques can be appreciably
increased. But only on condition that one
gets more insight into the functioning of
human consciousness.[5,12,14]

Following the theory of Freud, we can in human
consciousness distinguish between conscious, sub-
conscious and pre-conscious. The function of the
pre-conscious is especially important for innovation. It is a kind of store in which a number of
programmes are kept with which we can process
information.

A problem perceived in consciousness is conducted
to our pre-consciousness for processing, after which
the result of this processing—in the form of a
solution to the problem—is led back to the
conscious level. During this process the passage of
information between consciousness and pre-
consciousness is of prime importance. The choice of
which information is put through to the pre-
consciousness, which programme is used to process
it, and which solution is returned to consciousness,
is done by a 'mechanism' called *censor*.[5]

Ir. G. B. M. Mathôt is a consultant for Innovation, Diversification and
Concern Strategy with Bakkenist Management Consultants, 3
Emmaplein, 1075 AW Amsterdam, The Netherlands. He is preparing a
Ph.D. thesis on New Businesses with Professor Eekels of the School of
Industrial Design Engineering at Delft University of Technology.

The censor is a screen formed by influences of education experience and environment, and screens out everything that does not conform to the accepted standards.

A thought pattern dominated by the censor we call *convergent*.

Some typical expressions of this convergent thought pattern are the following:

☆ my five-, ten-, fifteen-, ... year experience teaches me that this cannot be done;

☆ practice has shown that this product does not suit our business;

☆ we tried this once already and it failed then too.

Figure 1 illustrates this convergent thinking with a dotted line.

To get innovation we have to break out of this convergent thinking. Characteristic for innovation is originality, the leap which is made ahead of the known technique, the present market or the existing product design.[7,15] We call original thinking, unhampered by the censor, divergent (in (Figure 1 indicated by a full line).

To think creatively we have to consciously switch off the censor. This can be done with the help of a *creativity technique*. But the stream of unrestrained creativity that emerges, just like strictly logical (convergent) thinking, cannot on its own lead to new products, markets and production methods. In order to be able to use the creativity techniques productively, they should be preceded by an *analysis* to determine precisely what the right problem is, and be followed by a phase in which the original ideas (the result of divergent thinking) are checked with the help of an *evaluation procedure* (a convergent thought operation) for their prospec-

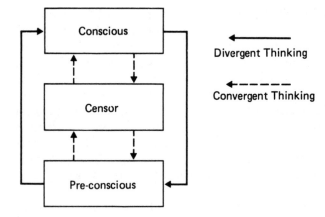

Figure 1. Schematic illustration of convergent and divergent thinking

tive value for the concern. Convergent and divergent thinking in innovation must therefore be thought of not as being *opposed*, but rather as *complementary*,[5,2] thought processes. The point in innovation is to recognize both sorts of thought process and to apply them *consciously*. We illustrate the conscious application of convergent and divergent thought techniques in innovation in Figure 2.

Innovation begins with the analysis of the innovation problem. Through interviews, collection of written information, analysis of bottlenecks and the like, the innovation problem originally stated in global terms is explained in terms of the *heart of the matter* and *a number of criteria against which possible solutions must in principle be judged*.

The analysis of an innovation problem is carried out using convergent (critical, logical) thought techniques and a specific divergent thought technique: progressive abstraction.

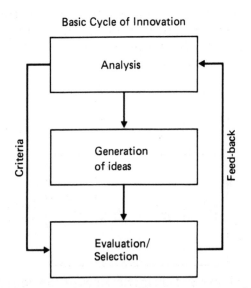

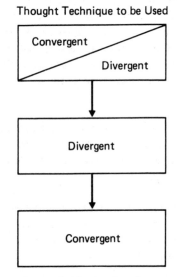

Figure 2. Conscious application of convergent and divergent thought techniques in the innovation process

When the heart of the innovation problem has been discovered, a number of *original solutions* (ideas) have to be generated.[5,15] To generate these ideas, divergent thought techniques such as morphology, method 635 and synectics can be used. The divergent thought process is very inefficient. Only 2 per cent of the ideas generated have the potential to effectively solve the given problem. The point is then to find out which idea gives greater prospects for the concern. For *evaluation and selection* of ideas convergent thought techniques are used.[7]

It is not enough to carry out the operations: analysis of the innovation problem, generation of original ideas and evaluation of original solutions, *only once*. Often, only after the evaluation is the real problem discovered! In such circumstances the innovation analysis is continued (using the newly acquired knowledge) more intensively, so that for the 'changed problem' new original solutions are conceived that are checked against the (newly formulated) criteria, and so on until an acceptable solution is found.

In practice the conscious application of logical (convergent) and creative (divergent) techniques is not so easy.

The following section indicates the organizational measures that have to be taken in order to be able to use these techniques.

Organization

In a concern, conscious use of convergent and divergent thought techniques is mostly hampered by the normal concern activities such as keeping production going, acquisition of orders and control of costs. A condition then for innovation is that besides the time necessary for the normal concern operations, *time has to be set aside for the development of new concern activities*. While the concern functionaries could take the development of new activities (each in his own field) upon themselves, practice has shown that it is *more effective* to carry out part of the work together.[11]

The problems of innovation (these are multidisciplinary by definition) can be more quickly and effectively discovered by a multidisciplinary *Innovation Group*.

Such an innovation group can moreover effectively collect the informal business data important for innovation, and process it into a form suitable for use by the concern.

It can also effectively investigate the advantages and disadvantages of the various propositions for the concern and make them *decision mature*, so that Top Management can take the innovation decision.

Since the members of a multidisciplinary Innovation Group all speak their own language, working together can sometimes be difficult.

It is therefore necessary that the group develop *a common language* through which the various functionaries can 'understand each other'. This common language necessary for innovation we indicate schematically in Figure 3.

A good organization of the activities of the group is crucially important for successful innovation.[7] The main ingredients are:

☆ right mix and size of the Innovation Group;

☆ 'hard' agreements on frequency and duration of meetings;

☆ efficient discussion technique;

☆ planning the innovation activities.

As innovation is one of the *basic functions of the concern*, the Innovation Group should be recruited from Top Management. The chairman of the Group should be the Managing Director. He is the one to take the *innovative decision* eventually and he must bear the attached *risk*. At least the Production Manager, the Marketing Manager, the R & D Manager and the Financial Manager should also be in the Innovation Group. If the concern product is service-intensive, then it may be wise to have the head of the Service Department also in the group, and so on.

To avoid normal business operations squeezing out the strategic innovation activities, a *tight consultation programme* is necessary. 'Running around in circles' by the Innovation Group is avoided by *efficient consultation technique*.

And to keep the activities from getting bogged-down the Innovation Group must have a clear *activity plan* which describes the *strategic activities* in *operational terms*.

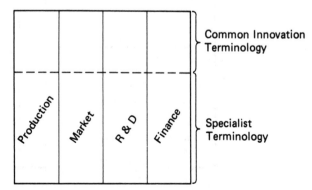

Figure 3. Schematic view of the common language and specialist terminology necessary for innovation

One Innovation Group is not enough for a large concern with a complex package of activities.

An electro-technical company with 900 employees and four product groups (with largely differing markets and technologies) should, for instance, have one innovation policy steering committee and four innovation workgroups.

With such an organizational forum the innovation policy group decides on the total innovation policy of the concern while the innovation workgroups do the more detailed work such as development assistance.

Innovation Systematique

The Innovation Systematique consists of a number of connected *methods* by which with a large change of success, new products, markets and production techniques can be developed.[2,13] As shown in Figure 2, analytical idea generation and evaluation/selection methods are used consecutively. All innovation activities from the determination of the innovation need up to and including introduction, is divided into a number of *phases*.[11,13] In this way a product innovation process consists of:

☆ determining the innovation need;

☆ generation and evaluation of areas of search;

☆ generation and evaluation of product ideas;

☆ setting-up Business Innovation Plans;

☆ design of new products;

☆ introduction of new products.

In the following pages some of the specific innovation methods per phase will be illustrated with examples.

To make the chance of success as great as possible, the following *aspects* should be considered in each phase of the innovation process (in as far as they are applicable):

☆ procurement;

☆ production;

☆ sales/marketing;

☆ service/maintenance;

☆ research and development;

☆ personnel;

☆ finances.

The knowledge and experience of the concern with respect to these aspects is operationalized by involving the functionaries with the specific know-how in the innovation activities. The main part of the work is, however, done by the members of the Innovation Group(s) as already indicated under Organization.

The mutual relations between, on the one hand, the phases of the product-innovation process and on the other the aspects that appear in every phase are schematically indicated in Figure 4.

Similar matrices exist for market and production innovation and combinations such as product *and* production innovation.

Innovation Need

The first task facing the innovation group is to

Phases / Aspects	Determine Innovation Need	Generation/ Evaluation Fields of Search	Generation/ Evaluation Product Ideas	Setting-up Business Innovation Plan	Design New Products	Introduction of New Products
Procurement						
Production						
Sales/Marketing						
Service/ Maintenance						
R & D						
Personnel						
Finances						

Figure 4. Schematic indication of the relation between the phases and aspects of the product-innovation process

determine the innovation need.[1,7] To do this the existing concern activities are so grouped into Product–Market–Production (PMP) combinations that the effects of trends and decisions can be realistically estimated. Following this, an investigation is made of which internal and external trends are important so that an estimate can be made of the development of the PMP combinations when policy remains unchanged. By then estimating the effects of suggested policy decisions, the probable development of the individual PMP combinations can be determined. By comparing the sum of these probable developments with the desired targets the *innovation need* of the enterprise can be determined. The innovation need so determined shows what the *size* of innovation effort must be in order to meet concern targets in terms of turn-over, profit and employment figures.

We shall illustrate the determination of the innovation need by means of a simple calculation example. (See Figure 5.)

Suppose a concern with a yearly turn-over of £5,000,000 has 3PMP combinations PMP1, PMP2 and PMP3 with turn-overs £2,000,000, £2,000,000 and £1,000,000 respectively. PMP1 is in the decaying stage. The expectation is that its turn-over will gradually decline as shown by the lowest line in Figure 5.

Despite heavy competition it is expected that PMP2 can hold its ground in the coming years. (The yearly turn-over of PMP2 at £2,000,000 is superimposed on that of PMP1 in Figure 5.) PMP3 is in the growth phase. It has been decided to make use of this growth potential and it is expected to double the turn-over of this PMP in the coming 5 years.

When this expected turn-over is superimposed on that of PMP2 then one finds the probable turn-over

development of the concern when no innovation takes place (shown by line 1).

If we take it that in the sector in which the concern works the productivity will increase by 4 per cent per year and it has been decided to stabilize personnel requirements, then as a result of this trend and the policy decision the turn-over should increase by 20 per cent in the coming 5 years.

This desired growth in turn-over is shown in Figure 5 by line 2. When we compare the probable turn-over growth (line 1) with that desired (line 2) we can conclude that this concern must attain £2,000,000 extra turn-over with 1 (or at most 2) new PMP combination(s) in order to meet its concern targets.

Besides *turn-over*, the innovation need can be expressed in profit development. If the concern is in danger of becoming vulnerable because of dependence on a certain export market or a specific production technique, then the innovation need may be expressed in terms of the necessary *diversification* of the activities of the concern, etc. In practice these methods are very often used complementary to one another, so that one gets a balanced view on the real innovation need of the concern. Determining the innovation need is a convergent thought process at a rather high level of abstraction. This process mostly requires outside assistance.

Search Areas

After having found the size of the innovation need, a start must be made in searching for the new concern activities that will lead to *closing* the *gap* between probable and desired development. Since the *possibilities* are, in principle, *unlimited* there is a great danger than the innovation process will

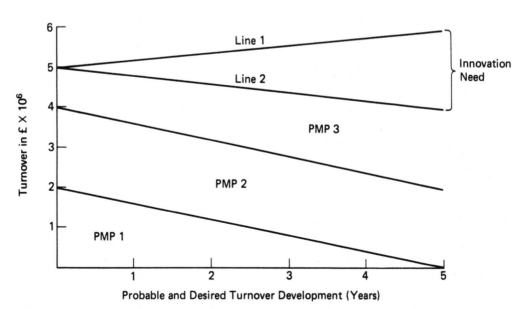

Figure 5. Schematic innovation need determination

founder in the great number of innovation suggestions. To be able to develop the necessary new activities within the stated time (laid down in determining the innovation need!) it is necessary to work *systematically* in the search for new products, markets and production methods.

The first step in this systematic search process is to determine the *field of search*.[13] In doing this a field is set out based on the present concern activities within which it is probable that many innovation ideas exist that 'suit' both the *opportunities* of the market and the *strong points* of the concern which allow these opportunities to be used to advantage.

A method applicable in practice to generate attractive search areas for the concern, is one using a search-area matrix. (See Figure 6.)

Firstly the internal investigation (started by discovering the internal trends) is continued until the results can be expressed in terms of a number of strong and weak points of the concern. The *strong points* are noted in the search-area matrix where the numbers 1–7 are.

Then the *opportunities* formulated as a result of the external investigation are noted where the letters A–E are. By combining a strong point (indicated in Figure 6 with a number) with an opportunity (shown as a letter) a search field can be generated that suits both the *external* opportunity and the *internal* strong point (the combination 4B is shown in the search-area matrix with a cross).

Now the fields of search are tested for attractiveness for the concern using a number of *quantified policy criteria* so that top management can decide to *concentrate* the search activities on one or a few areas that are rich in opportunity for the concern. Analysing internal/external trends and formulating strong points and opportunities is a convergent thought operation. Generation of search fields on the other hand is a divergent process, while the selection of search fields again is carried out using convergent techniques.

Just as for generating the innovation need, the generation and selection of search fields is a process on a high level of abstraction. Employees who have difficulty operating at this level should only be involved in a later (more concrete) phase of innovation activities.

Product Ideas

In selecting fields of search the question as to which innovation direction (product, market, production) is more attractive for the concern will have been considered. Depending on the answer the process of generating ideas will be directed towards either product, market or production ideas.

In further describing the innovation process we shall give special attention to product innovation.

The generation and selection of product ideas begins with the analysis of the field of search. Here both *innovation problems* within the area are sought out and *criteria* determined to which possible solutions for these problems (product ideas) must conform in principle.[7,15] In analysing the field of search both convergent critical–logical thinking potential and progressive abstraction, a divergent technique, are used. (See Figure 2.)

Abstraction is understood to be the making of a problem or situation more general. When we use this technique more than once on the same problem we speak of progressive abstraction.

In this way a bicycle can be abstractively described as: a road vehicle. As we have omitted one characteristic of the bicycle in this description (i.e. that it is passenger propelled), a *trailer* (that is pulled) among others and a *car* (self propelled) are included under the term *road vehicle*. Going on from road vehicle we can abstract further. Under the term vehicle come also rail and air vehicles. The method of progressive abstraction is shown schematically in Figure 7.

Strong Points / Opportunities	1	2	3	4	5	6	7
A							
B				X			
C							
D							
E							

Figure 6. Search-area matrix for generating fields of search

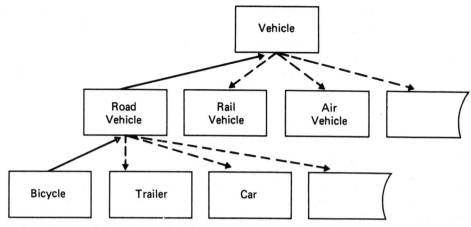

Figure 7. Progressive abstraction schematically

Progressive abstraction has proved its value especially in analysing innovation problems. Using this method, complex problems can be separated into main and secondary aspects. Also, with its help, insight into the innovation problem can be extended, so that bit by bit original solutions mature that were not obvious at first sight and that would have previously been considered impossible.

After the problems within the area of search have become sufficiently clear, *potential solutions* (product ideas) can be effectively generated. In doing this both *existing* product ideas and totally *new ones* can be explored.

To collect the ideas the concern has both internal and external sources. The more important internal source is one's own employees. The product ideas they *live* with are mostly laid aside prematurely in the usual business situation. To break out of this convergent thought pattern, one has first to create a *channel* through which the product ideas of the employees reach the right place. By getting every product idea onto a form and sending these forms *directly* to a given number of the Innovation Group, these ideas can be effectively collected. Besides one's own employees other internal sources can be consulted. Old market study reports, existing R & D memoranda, technological surveys and suchlike can give important *indications* for new products.

The number of external sources for new product ideas is practically unlimited. At first sight this seems rather pleasant. In practice, however, it is not at all probable that the concern will *draw* in the great number of product ideas.

Again the value of the search-area concept is proved when consulting the external sources of ideas. Search activities are *limited* to the areas of *rich opportunity* for the concern and an *effective* and *efficient* search process is made possible. Important external sources for product ideas are among others: *data banks, patents office, comparative market research, customers/users/consumers, existing needs an-alyses, opinion journals, Technological and other Universities, Research Institutes, Chambers of Commerce and Factories, Public Reports, Government Papers, scientific publications, subject bibliography, catalogi, shows/exhibitions, lectures/congresses, scouting trips, etc.*

As well as collecting existing product-ideas, totally new ones can be generated.[7,12,14] For this divergent techniques such as the following can be used:

☆ systematic analytical techniques;

☆ associative techniques;

☆ analogy techniques.

These techniques can be used both by the members of an innovation group and by other *employees, customers, customer panels* and *the like*. To apply these techniques effectively among other things a short and clear description of the innovation problem is necessary.

In the *systematic analytical* techniques the innovation problem is split-up into *parts*. For each *part* a number of independent *partial solutions* are sought that afterwards, in combination, lead to the generation of a number of *original solutions* of the problem formulated.[16]

A well known example of this systematic analytical technique is Morphological Analysis.

Original product ideas can also be generated using *associative technique*. The most original associative technique is brainstorming. In brainstorming the participants are encouraged to give their thoughts free rein (divergent thinking) on a clear problem formulation (the result of analysis'. Brainstorming is both the more *universally used* and *least effective* of divergent techniques.[5] The effectiveness can, however, be greatly improved by *regulating* the divergent thought process. This can be achieved by using for instance Method 635, a divergent technique quite applicable in practice.

Method 635 is a written pre-programmed brainstorming based on the fact that brainstorming becomes effective *if an idea of one of the participants is picked up by other participants who go on developing it rigorously* (which seldom occurs in traditional brainstorming).

In Method 635, 6 persons give 3 solutions for a given problem in 5 minutes (hence the name 635). Then the participants pass their sheets to their neighbour, who, based on the solutions already found, thinks of a further three solutions. This process is continued until all six participants have gone through each sheet once. The solution sheet looks like Figure 8.

Product ideas can also be generated using *analogical techniques*. This involves seeing how certain *problems* in *other sectors* have been solved. Very fruitful here is the comparison between technical problems and analogical problems (and solutions!) in nature. One of the more advanced analogy techniques for producing product ideas is Synectics.[3]

In selecting product ideas financial-economic criteria might be thought of first. The problem, however, with this is that the information necessary to calculate the profitability, for example, is not available at this stage in the innovation process. In fact, it cannot possibly be known!

What we can do is check the measure in which *product ideas* satisfy the *product criteria*[4,7,8] formulated in the analysis of the search area. By consequently *comparing* the product ideas so evaluated *with each other*, a judgment can be formed of the *chance of success* of these ideas.

With these converging thought operations we can distinguish three types of technique:

(evaluation by means of)

☆ number weighting methods;

☆ line profiles;

☆ block profiles.

By evaluation using the *number weighting method* a product idea is given a number relating to the measure in which it satisfies a product criterion. By summation of the values given for all criteria the value of a product idea is expressed in a *final number*.

Insight into the required innovation decision can be deepened by using *line profiles*.[8] In this method a product idea is also evaluated on the basis of a number of product criteria. A check is made of how the product idea satisfies each criterion. By allocating, after averaging, these scores to a related group of criteria, factors like marketing, production and R & D for instance, the result can be visually presented in a *line profile*.

In evaluating product ideas using *block profiles*,[4] the relevant criteria are described in very concrete terms following a thorough analysis of the search area, for instance as follows:

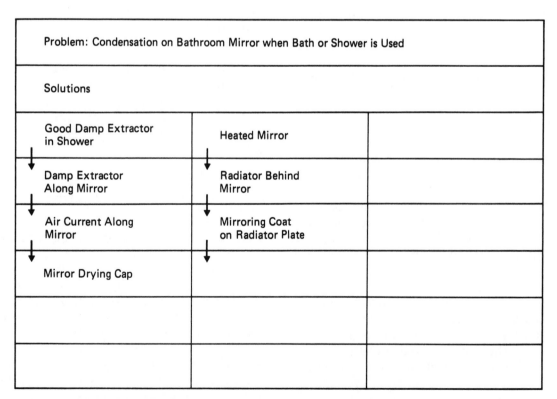

Figure 8. Solution sheet Method 635

Yearly turnover in £1m

between 10 and 20	+2
between 5 and 10	+1
between 1 and 5	−1
under 1, above 20	−2

Each product idea is then evaluated by the *innovation group* using these criteria. *Mutually consulted estimates* of the degree of satisfaction of the *criterion* in question are made. The result of each separate estimate is indicated by colouring-in one or two blocks left or right of a division line (Figure 9). The various estimates are indicated in this *block profile*, (temporarily) *independently* of the importance of the product criterion.

Business Innovation Plan

Even in the case of the product idea with most chance of success, we do not know more than that it satisfies, in principle, a number of criteria formulated as a result of the analysis of the search area. Before putting such a potentially successful product idea into development, its chance of success must be *tested*. The testing is carried out on the basis of the results of a so-called *feasibility study*, in which all factors which are thought to be important for the *success* of the potential new product are investigated.[2]

As we possess a concrete product idea in this phase of the product innovation process, the necessary internal and external investigation can be carried out very efficiently. In this way not only can we *increase immensely the chance of success* by working systematically but also *keep the level of costs to the strictly necessary*.

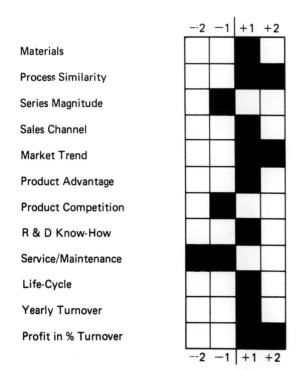

Figure 9. A block profile of a product idea

E—E

In the feasibility study in principle the following subjects must be treated:

The product, among other things:
Required function, product characteristics necessary for functioning, raw materials/components from which the product is made, possible alternatives/patents/licences.

Product development, among other things:
Existing know-how/patents, expected development problems, duration of product development, costs (development budget).

The market, among other things:
Total market size, present and future competition, price situation, possible selling price, possible volume of demand, costs of additional market research.

Marketing, among other things:
Target groups/geographical sales area; product name/trade name, supply form (among other things, packing), selling channels, selling methods, alternative selling channels, costs of marketing efforts.

Production, among other things:
Means of production to be used/bought, production development, minimum production quantity, cost price of the new product, alternative production methods, environmental problems, costs.

Organization, among other things:
Management, executive personnel, organizational structure/teamwork relationships, infrastructure, training, costs.

Finance, among other things:
Selling price, cost price, volume, investments, rendement, financing.

After all these points have been studied sufficiently, a well thought out Business Innovation Plan can be formulated using the resulting data. It is on the basis of this plan that *Top Management* can *decide* to set the development of the new product in motion.

Product Design

Design of the new product begins by formulating a Programme of Requirements and Limitations. This means in first instance translating the Business Innovation Plan into *design terms*,[10,15] that is to say: into a *design problem* and a number of *design criteria* solutions to the design problem must in principle satisfy. (See Figure 10.)

The formulation of the Programme of Requirements and Limitations is a convergent thought operation to be carried out by the Innovation Group as a whole.

After having formulated the Programme of

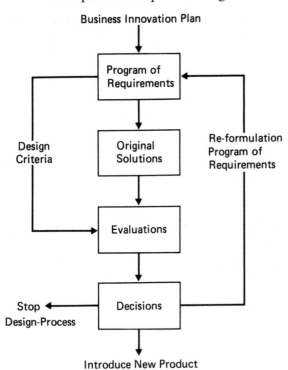

Figure 10. Scheme of product design

☆ introduce the new product;

☆ go through the design process again;

☆ stop the design process.

Evaluation is done by the *Innovation Group*, *decisions* are taken by *Top Management*.

Introduction

After finishing design work the new product is *introduced*. It is in this introduction/pioneering phase that the new product has to be built out into a *successful concern activity* by the procurement, production, marketing and service departments.[13] Only when introduced will it be known whether the new product satisfies, whether the customers are willing to pay the selling price fixed, whether the concern can make the new product for the calculated costprice, etc.

A recently introduced new product is seldom immediately a success. The task of the Innovation Group is to *discover disturbances* systematically and take such *measures* that the new product be *adjusted* to the *market requirements* and the *possibilities of one's own enterprise*.

We can summarize the whole of the activities of the Innovation Group in the pioneering phase under the concept *product monitoring* (see Figure 11).

The basis for product monitoring is the *Introduction Plan*. In this way discrepancies between *plan* and *reality* can be signalled. *Prudence* is required. Communication channels must remain open or be opened.

By *analysing* (convergent thinking) discrepancies insight can be attained into where 'the shoe pinches'. By thinking up *original solutions* (divergent thinking' for the problems met and *judging* (convergent thinking) their effects, effective readjustments can be advocated.

Requirements and Limitations, a design of the new product can be made.[9,10,15] *Product Design* is a divergent thought process carried out by properly trained design engineers. If the R & D/Development department of the concern has enough capacity the design activities can be done 'in house'. If the concern has no development department or if the capacity is insufficient, then the design of the new product can be ordered from an external party; for instance a Design Consultant.

In evaluating (convergent thinking) the first designs it will often appear that none of these designs satisfy, that the requirements and/or limitations are contradictory. In such situations the evaluation results should be accurately stated and *new requirements and limitations* should be drawn up within the context of the Business Innovation Plan. Then the design process begins anew. Following every evaluation the possibility exists to:

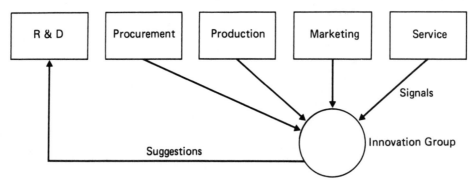

Figure 11. Product monitoring

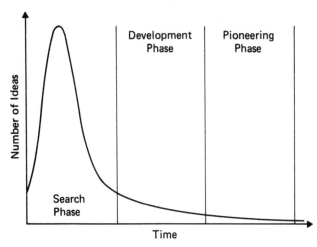

Figure 12. Mortality of innovation ideas

	Time %	Investment %
Search	15	15
Development	40	25
Pioneering	45	60

Figure 13. Division of time and investment over the innovation phases

It is through this process of analysis, generation and evaluation that new products can be *made* a success.

Mortality Curve

The chance of an idea growing out to be a successful concern activity is 1 in 50.[6] A systematic approach can increase this chance to 1 in 5. The 'life span' of a number of ideas is shown in the mortality curve (Figure 12).

Time spent on innovation and money invested are spread out over these phases as follows (Figure 13).

When one compares Figures 12 and 13 it can be concluded that the effectivity of the innovation effort is greatly improved by doing the *search phase* (15 per cent of time and costs) really well, so that the development phase is entered with an idea with a much greater chance of success (1 in 5 instead of 1 in 50).

Increasing the innovation effort of the concern should then, in general, not be sought first by increasing R & D budgets but in setting up an effective *search process*;[2,13] determining the innovation need, generating and selecting the fields of search, generating and selecting product ideas and making Business Innovation Plans. Tracking the design (in the developing phase) and monitoring the product (in the pioneering phase) form together the final key piece of a systematic innovation process that leads from idea to realization.

References

(1) H. I. Ansoff, *Corporate Strategy*, New York (1965).

(2) J. Eekels, *Industriële Doelontwikkeling* (with English summary), Assen (1973).

(3) W. J. Gordon, *Synectics*, New York (1961).

(4) John S. Harris, *New Product Profile Chart, Chemical and Engineering News*, 17 April (1961).

(5) K. Linneweh, *Kreatives Denken, Techniken und Organisation produktiver Kreativität*, Karlsruhe (1978).

(6) *Management of New Products*, Booz, Allen and Hamilton Inc. (1960).

(7) G. B. M. Mathôt, *Innoveren is te leren, creativiteitstechnieken in het innovatieprocess, Intermediair*, 16e jaargang 36, 5 September (1980).

(8) T. T. Miller, Projecting the profitability of New Products, *Eng. Progr.*, Vol. 54 (1958).

(9) Abraham, A. Moles, *La Creation Scientifiques*, Paris (1956).

(10) G. Nadler, An investigation of design methodology, *Management Science*, Vol. 13, No. 10, June (1967).

(11) E. B. Roberts and A. R. Fusfeld, Staffing the innovative technology—based organization, *Sloan Management Review*, Spring (1981).

(12) C. Spearman, *Creative Mind*, London (1930).

(13) Verein Deutscher Ingenieure: Systematische Produktplanung, ein Mittel zur Unternehmenssicherung, Dusseldorf (1976).

(14) M. Wertheimer, *Productive Thinking*, New York (1959).

(15) Ira G. Wilson and Marthann E. Wilson, *From Idea to Working Model*, New York (1970).

(16) J. G. Wissema, *Morphological Analysis Futures*, April (1978).

Competing with Japan—The Rules of the Game

Merlin Stone, The Management College, Henley

This paper explains that, to deal with the Japanese challenge, it is important to understand the comprehensive nature of that challenge. The challenge covers every function and every phase of the product development and marketing cycle. Therefore, solutions must not be piecemeal. In writing this paper, the author draws extensively on his working and consulting experience.

Introduction

In early 1983, the EEC asked Japan to restrain her exports of video tape recorders (VTRs), light vans, fork-lift trucks, cars, motorcycles, quartz watches, hi-fi, machine tools, colour TV tubes and TV sets. Following closely upon the 'Poitiers episode', in which France dictated that all Japanese VTR imports to France should pass via Poitiers, this request showed the depth of feeling in Europe and the significance of the Japanese impact in these markets. In products where European industry was not traditionally strong (e.g. facsimile machines, small plain paper copiers, electronic calculators, SLR cameras), Japanese producers already dominated the European market, with shares of 70 per cent plus. In other products (e.g. electronic typewriters, telephone sets, small telephone exchanges, floppy disc drives, small computer printers, small computers, integrated circuits), a similar process was at work.

The request by the EEC smacked of desperation. The message to Japan seemed to be to restrain exports of anything they produced and marketed efficiently. Why did a mighty industrial bloc have to make such a request of a state which not so long before had the reputation of producing low quality goods?

Merlin Stone was until 1983 a business planning manager at the International HQ of Rank Xerox. He teaches marketing at Henley—The Management College, Greenlands, Henley-on-Thames, Oxon RG9 3AU, and is a founding partner of MIDAS Consultants, a management consulting firm specializing in operations management.

The Conventional Story

Conventional explanations of the problem are often in terms of technology and culture. After years of importing Western technology, and learning the best technical (research, development and production) management practices from the West (and discarding the worst), Japan's technical act came together in the 1970s, to good effect. MITI's strategies for industrial development involve the formation of consortia to develop key technologies, often backed by government investment. This is supported by the large groupings of companies (Zaibatsu), using an extensive worldwide technical and commercial intelligence network to provide the information needed to formulate and implement strategy. In addition, cross-licensing and other forms of co-operation between otherwise competing companies is common. These and other factors, combined with a high level of technical literacy, ensure that the technical requirements for world-wide success are present. But this is only part of the story.

The True Story

The real story is one of manufacturing and marketing strategy, bolted on to a firm technological base. Without the three working together in an integrated fashion, Japan's success story would have been fiction. Until the West understands the nature of this three-pronged attack, its capacity to deal with it will be minimal. This paper concentrates on manufacturing and marketing strategies, and on their integration with technological strategy. But first, we need to introduce a term, which, in the English-language Japanese press represents part of that story. It is the term 'mechatronics'.

Definition of 'Mechatronics'

'Mechatronics' refers to certain volume-produced engineering products. They range from those which are principally electronic (e.g. computers, facsimile, telephone sets, small telephone exchanges, calculators, digital watches, hi-fi, video tape recorders) to those which are principally mechanical (e.g. photocopiers, cameras, typewriters, printers, machine tools). The term also applies to some components used in the manufacture of or connection between such items (e.g. integrated circuits, optical fibre cable). Mechatronic markets are durable goods markets, and display classic features of such markets. Some features (product design and cost, feasibility of high volume production) are affected by rapid progress in electronics. Western companies may find it hard to deal with Japanese competition here partly because of an apparent strong Japanese concensus on how to handle such markets.

Aim of this Paper

This paper aims to explain the Japanese view of manufacturing and marketing strategies for success in these markets, show how this view gives Japanese industries (but not necessarily all Japanese firms—often more fiercely competing with each other than with Western firms) an advantage over Western firms, and suggest how Western firms must change in order to deal more successfully with the continuing Japanese challenge in mechatronics. This paper draws upon the author's own experience of working in and consulting with Western companies affected by Japanese competition, and upon published data. Because of the sensitive nature of this work, names of companies are not used in examples, unless the information happens to be in the public domain. In some cases, it has been necessary not to mention the product.

The Behaviour of Mechatronic Markets

The behaviour of a mechatronic market can be explained by a simple paradigm, varying slightly between products. This paradigm consists of a cycle, which is a combination of some or all of the following: a diffusion process; several product life cycles; recurring product, component and production innovation; competitive entry; after-market development; distribution channel evolution; joint-venture development, production or marketing; and overseas assembly. The variety of processes may be responsible for the difficulty some Western firms have in dealing with mechatronic markets. The cycle is characterized by a number of phases. The phases may not be sequential (some phases overlap in time, or may encompass other phases). The phases are as follows:

Phase 1: Recognition of opportunity.
Phase 2: Product design to meet the gap.
Phase 3: Establishing production capacity to seize the opportunity.
Phase 4: Rapid production build-up.
Phase 5: Marketing high output volumes.
Phase 6: Developing the after-market.
Phase 7: Overseas manufacture.
Phase 8: Further market development.
Phase 9: Moving on to the next market.

Phase 1: Opportunity Recognition

The cycle starts with recognition of an opportunity. It may be a widespread need, which is being met either by complex and expensive mechanical means, or by electronic means sold only in premium markets, or not at all, because no products meet the need. For calculators, the need was met by products that were too costly to meet mass needs; in typewriters, by electro-mechanical and expensive electronic means. Sometimes, an opportunity is created by Western industry with a perfectly adequate technology creaming the market (e.g. photocopiers). The opportunity may be recognized by an individual firm, or through interpretation of a MITI strategy (e.g. drive into office automation).

Little Role for Market Research
Opportunity recognition rarely occurs through using detailed, specially commissioned, market research to identify user needs. One reason for this is that successful market development will, via much lower prices or greatly improved performance, take the product to users who never considered buying it before. Highly specific market research is not a good basis for predicting demand in this case. The need is more likely to be identified by gap analysis, based on analysis of more general market statistics (e.g. sales figures for different products) combined with creative understanding of customers' general needs. For example, Sony's personal stereo, the Walkman, was designed by a research team and piloted on the instructions of Sony's managing director, because he felt it would be good at relieving travellers' boredom. Market research conclusions may also be misleading because mechatronic markets are often supply-driven, with very strong force-feeding of or discounting into distribution channels to achieve widespread product awareness, coupled with very strong advertizing. In other words, the forces operating on the buyer change substantially as the market starts to move.

Size of Opportunity: Breadth of Gap vs Volume of Gap
Opportunity recognition consists of identifying a gap. It may be broad (i.e. a whole range of needs may be unsatisfactorily fulfilled) as well as high volume (i.e. many potential users' needs are unsatisfied). For example, in office automation, most offices have many needs that are unsatisfactorily dealt with by existing hardware, and there are many potential office customers.

The difference between the typical Western and Japanese view of the gap can be illustrated in a simple diagram (Figure 1). Here, the example of VTRs in a developed economy is used. The Japanese view would be that a high proportion of potential users would become actual users quickly if the price could be cut deeply, and if distribution channels were available to get the product to the market (User Base Path 1). The Western view would be that product diffusion would be slow and steady, with price falling more gently and distribution channels adapting to the product more slowly (User Base Path 2).

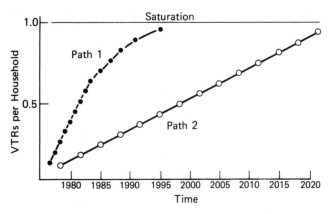

Figure 1. Japanese vs Western interpretation of market potential

Phase 2: Design of a Product Range to Fill the Gap

Impact of Product Design on this Process
In many Japanese companies, the lack of acute divide between production and design engineering ensures that design and production decisions are usually taken together, by engineers and managers working on a single site. Products are designed for high volume manufacturability. This affects both component standardization and ease of assembly by workers or robots. Some engineers will normally have experience in a commercial department in the company, and understand the marketing implications of design. Single-site design is also faster. In one case, the multi-site, highly functionalized design process of the leading Western firm doubled the period to commercialization, and trebled or quadrupled the staff involved, relative to Japanese producers. This could be seen in as basic a measure as the number of drawings per part.

New Materials: Parts and Cost Reduction, Increased Performance
One aspect of design for manufacturability is the stress on cutting the number of parts in a given product. This increase manufacturability and reliability (much unreliability is due to connections or interaction between parts). In doing this, Japanese companies actively explore substitutes for

metal, such as ceramics and plastics, which require less machining or assembly to produce a complex part. The search for new uses for certain materials is also driven by the need to cut cost and increase performance. Among the leaders here are companies like Kyoto Ceramic and Mitsubishi Chemical, who originally specialized in particular materials, and now work closely with mechatronic companies to develop material substitutes. An example of this is thin film technology, which is finding applications in a number of mechatronic industries. In mid-1983, Casio announced a new ultra-thin calculator, in which the circuits were printed on nine thin films laminated together.[1]

Featured vs Basic Models
While the Western producer goes for a basic model, with more features available only at a price (and with a high margin on the feature), Japanese producers usually build as many features as commercially practicable into the basic product. This undermines the Western approach, which is often to assume (usually wrong) that there is a distinct market for the 'base product'. This is the classic trap of defining the market by the product. Western companies may misinterpret market research to show that people who have never bought a product with a particular feature will not buy it if the feature actually becomes part of the specification of the product. In fact, the all-featured product sells very well against the unfeatured product of the same price!

Search for Standardization
In the later stages of market development, a search for standardization may emerge, particularly for products with a high electronics element or ones with substantial supplies after-market (e.g. video tapes, floppy discs, software). It is rare for one standard to emerge, as the video tape recorder market has shown. The loss to a major supplier of failing to have his standard adopted is very heavy, so coalitions of companies (often including foreign companies) tend to emerge around the major suppliers, with other companies supporting both standards. A good example of this was the 1983 battle between proponents of the 3 in. and $3\frac{1}{2}$ in. floppy disk drives.[2] Such battles usually end up with 2 or 3 standards being adopted.

Design to Cost Limits
Product costings take into account expected declines in price and components cost levels over the product life. Lately, as fluctuations in exchange rates have increased, some companies started adding an additional margin of safety by planning on a yen exchange rate against the U.S.$ 10–15 per cent stronger than forecast, implying much more aggressive attempts at cost reduction. Ironically, Reagan's economic policy completely reversed the expected trend by pushing the dollar high. An immediate consequence of this was extra high profits for Japanese companies on sales in the U.S.

which in some cases allowed Japanese companies to cross-subsidize sales into Europe.

Phase 3: Establishing Production Capacity to Meet Opportunity

Public Announcement of Capacity Additions

Recognition of mechatronic opportunities is rarely a secret. Opportunities may be publicly signalled by MITI. Even if they are not, public announcement by companies of their plans to build new plants or add production capacity make intentions clear. These announcements serve various purposes. They are confirmation to component suppliers of the market potential for their own products, and therefore help to ensure a robust state of component supply. They signal to local and international distributors the kind of trade volumes that are being looked for. They indicate to investors the confidence the company has in the future of its new products and also indicate how funds which are being borrowed to finance the expansion are being used. The company workforce also understands the efforts being made to ensure their own future.

Validity of Capacity Numbers

Announcements are not attempts to bluff competitors. Tracking of announcements against production for appropriate periods shows a good correlation, with departure from expected production usually due to unforeseen product or trading problems. A prime driver of rapid capacity growth is competition between Japanese firms. With an opportunity publicly signalled, the hunt is on. Firms failing to add capacity may be left out of the market altogether.

Some Western companies doubt the validity of capacity announcements, holding that it is not certain what is being committed. Factory space and tooling are committed, but the arrangement is flexible enough to allow quite rapid switching between products if the market turns out to be overestimated or if a product range or a distribution arrangement turns out to be unviable.

Manufacturing Flexibility

Many companies are introducing flexible manufacturing systems, allowing production to vary at short notice between variants of a product. They work by programming parts delivery to workstations and programming machine tools to change activities according to the variant being produced. This is only possible if the components are available for variants.

Response to Shortages

If shortages emerge before capacity comes on stream, companies may contract manufacture to other firms. Companies entering a new line of business may seek supplies from another company already in business. These may be within the same industrial grouping, but in some cases are effectively competitors. This is a good way of learning about the production or marketing of new products.

Components Availability

Component availability for a new product is helped by high parts commonality, between products of the same company and between competing companies' products (with components usually sourced from one of the larger suppliers, such as Alps Electric for electrical, Asahi Glass for optical, and all the major electronics manufacturers themselves for semiconductors). This reduces the proportion of special parts for each variant, and cuts the unit cost of parts and the size of inventory that needs to be held.

Role of Component Suppliers

The role of component suppliers in facilitating the build up of production is crucial. They must be as fleet-footed as the end-product manufacturers. For example, as the audio equipment boom petered out, Alps Electric's proportion of turnover accounted for by audio parts fell from 50 to 20 per cent in the 3 years 1980–1983. VTR parts also fell sharply in the latter part of the period, while parts for information technology equipment rose to 40 per cent by 1983. A good example of this was floppy disc drives. Alps was shipping 50,000 of these a month in Autumn 1982, principally under OEM arrangements to U.S. microcomputer manufacturers. By May 1983, the total was nearly 300,000 units a month. The U.S. microcomputer boom was clearly having a dramatic impact. In addition, the explosion in demand for electronic parts for cars was expected to have a similar effect. The company's R & D spending was soaring, in an attempt to keep pace with developments in user industries.[3]

Semiconductor Industry Impact

The key role of component suppliers has been demonstrated best in semiconductors, principally memory chips (the Japanese were at the time of writing still massive importers of U.S.-made microprocessors). In 1983, the nine major semiconductor makers (NEC, Hitachi, Fujitsu, Toshiba, Mitsubishi Electric, Matsushita, Sharp, Oki and Sanyo) were expected to spend 240bn yen in 1983 on investment in semiconductor plant and equipment, over 36 per cent more than in 1982. This reflected a large increase in 1982–1983 in the proportion of investment spent by diversified mechatronic manufacturers on semiconductor manufacturer (e.g. from 34 per cent to 44 per cent for Toshiba, from 41 per cent to 53 per cent for Mitsubishi Electric). Twenty-five billion yen of Mitsubishi Electric's 33bn yen semiconductor investment was scheduled for their new Saijo plant, which would have a monthly capacity of 3 million 64K dynamic RAM chips when ready in Spring 1984. Sharp announced in May 1983 that they would be building a second LSI plant, planned to go into operation in April 1985, at an initial production level of 3 million chips per month, rising to 6 million after a year. Much of this surge in investment is in preparation for the next generation of RAM chips, i.e. 256K. The ferocity of inter-Japanese competition in each stage of this component market easily equals that of the end-user mechatronic markets.[4]

This expansion caused problems, with new generations of semiconductors being produced in high volumes when there was still a large tail of older products, whose volumes were declining slowly. Since a production line for VLSI semiconductors cost around 20–30bn yen, and had a life of around 3–4 years, failure to depreciate it rapidly led to severe financial problems. The chance of failure is increased by too wide a variety of products, particularly older products produced in smaller volumes and at lower margins. For this reason, Oki announced in March 1983 their intention of subcontracting the manufacture of 'twilight' semiconductor products, on an OEM basis, to concentrate on products with large and rapidly growing production volumes.[5]

Importance of Speed in Raising Volumes

The need to depreciate R & D and plant investment rapidly was well illustrated by Sanyo's decision in March 1983 to use communications satellites to transmit programmes for microprocessors and mask read-only memories from its affiliate in New Jersey to its HQ in Japan. This would enable Sanyo to shorten the delivery of sample products by 7–10 days.

Impact on U.S. Plants in Japan

In addition to the inter-Japanese competition, U.S.-owned semiconductor plants in Japan were going through the same process. Over the period 1983–1984, Texas Instrument's was expected to double the production capacity of its Miho plant, which in early 1983 had a production capacity of 3 million chips a month, mostly for shipment to the U.S. This plant was reckoned to be one of TI's most efficient plants worldwide. Once again, the move was partly related to expected 256K RAM production.[6]

Without this surge in production of semiconductors, many end-user mechatronic products would have been short of components. This semiconductor investment was in turn conditional on makers of semiconductor manufacturing equipment responding to the surge in their demand during 1982–1983. The strength of the components industry is making it more attractive as a source for U.S. producers. Data General announced in early 1983 that it was opening a procurement office in its Japanese subsidiary, Nippon Data General, for this purpose.[7]

Optical Fibre

Another quasi-component where similar moves are taking place is optical fibre, expected to be a prime component of a variety of information systems (e.g. local and wide area networks) in the next few years. In March 1983, Sumitomo Electric announced its plan to double capacity within a year to 20,000 km per month, to outdistance its two main rivals, Furukawa Electric Company (which was producing 10,000 km per month) and Fujikura Ltd. (8000). This was despite the fact that at the time, supply exceeded demand (which came principally from Nippon Telegraph & Telephone's construction of a nationwide fibre-optic cable network). Sumitomo's aim was to dominate the industry. Corning Glass were reported to be 'concerned' by the development, since Sumitomo is one of the few Japanese producers not to use Corning's patented production process.[8]

Size of Capacity Additions

In some mechatronic markets, addition to industry capacity is at a rate which alarms most Western companies. This is partly because the latter usually operate on a judgment of market size conditioned by User Base Path 2. If worldwide sales are X, it is not unusual for capacity additions over a year to be equal to 1·5–2X. In the late 1970s and early 1980s, this was so for plain paper copiers, electronic calculators and VTRs. The typical growth path for capacity and production was as in Figure 2. Capacity additions raise the stakes in an already high-stake game. Companies with too low capacities may end up with low market shares and uncompetitive production costs. Given the common understanding that there appears to be concerning production processes (partly due to common equipment sourcing), it is not surprising that at any one time there seems to be a concensus on plant scale. However, this consensus may be broken by quantum leaps by companies attempting to dominate the market (as in the Sumitomo Electric case above).

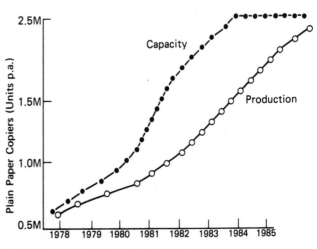

Figure 2. Capacity vs production

Financing of Capacity Additions

There was once a myth that this whole process was made easier by Japanese access to cheap capital. But the lower money interest rates paid usually reflected lower inflation. Further, the interest rates paid often did not reflect the sole financial cost to the company—many other payments to banks financing loans go through the accounts as financial costs, as part of a package deal with the banks. Confirmation of these points comes from the large borrowings made throughout 1981–1983, denominated in various foreign currencies and sold in a variety of bond markets, including Japan, partly to finance successive 'bursts' of investment. A major reason for the issue of these bonds was the restrictive conditions imposed on the issue of bonds in the Japanese market (they were being relaxed by mid-1983). Bond issuers in 1981–1982 included Fujitsu, NEC, Minolta, Konishiroku, Sanyo and Canon. In March 1983, Sanyo was expected to float SwFr300m of bonds, partly to finance an industrial robot plant. Others (e.g. Fujitsu, Sharp, Mitsubishi) were expected to follow.[9]

Surge in Foreign Purchases of Japanese Electronics Equity

The marketability of Japanese electronics companies' paper was boosted by foreign purchases. Foreign shareholdings in Alps Electric went up from 5·7 to 17·9 per cent in 6 months to the end of April 1983. Chase Manhattan was in May 1983 the sixth largest shareholder in Fujitsu. These figures are significant, given that the interlocking shareholdings by financial intermediaries, banks, etc., in Japan, make large changes of this kind difficult without institutional consent.[10]

Phase 4: Rapid Production Build-up

Capacity is built up rapidly because achieving the rapid market growth path is conditional on reaching high production volumes. High volumes drive prices down, through the economies of scale in assembly and in component manufacture. The slower the market is expanded, the lower the maximum production rate. In other words, the stock of an item of mechatronic equipment is cheaper if built more quickly. Because its relative cheapness broadens its market, the stock is also larger. Finally, the more rapid the build-up, the greater the advantage of the Japanese producer vs Western producers, or (where relevant) vs the equipment being replaced by the mechatronic item.

In integrated circuits, the surge was very noticeable in 1983. Japan's exports to the U.S. in the first four months of 1983 were up to 70·7 per cent in value over the same period in the previous year, despite large price falls. They rose 64 per cent in 1982 over 1981. The importance of Japanese capacity investments here is shown by shortages in some U.S.-made ICs, resulting in U.S. mechatronic manufacturers turning to Japanese sources for supplies. At the individual level, this is expected to produce massive volume increases for most Japanese IC manufacturers. For example, Toshiba was expecting to increase its monthly production of microprocessors (mostly made under licence from Zilog) from 3 million in March 1983 to 5 million by the end of 1983.[11] Manufacturers of most computers and other electronic parts experienced similar surges in production.

Production of industrial electronic equipment (including computers), was up in value by 14 per cent in 1982. In VTRs, production volumes rose 38 per cent in 1982 over 1981, and shipments by 46·5 per cent (representing a slight run down in the large inventories of 1981). In value terms, production was up 19 per cent to 1291bn yen. The Japanese market for VTRs was far from saturated in this period, as domestic shipments rose by 51 per cent in the same period.[12] But for some of 1983, VTR exports fluctuated under the impact of export and import restrictions.

Phase 5: Marketing the Output

This phase coincides with (and may pre-date) the production build-up phase. Typically, Japanese mechatronic companies will be aiming to fully employ new capacity 1–1½ years after commissioning. This implies that a great surge of production has to be disposed of in markets relatively quickly.

Importance of Domestic Market

When Japanese companies were new in world markets, a new product would usually go first to the home market (where distribution was well understood), followed 2 or 3 years later by volume exports. Now, many firms (especially those with long export experience, whether in their own right or through OEM deals) export high volumes immediately. But the domestic market is still a vital laboratory for most Japanese mechatronic companies. In many cases, the 'youth market' provides the necessary dynamism to sustain growth. A survey carried out in mid-1983 by Tokai bank among young Japanese up to university age showed that 85 per cent had digital game watches. One quarter of boys interviewed and 16 per cent of all those interviewed named personal computers as their most wanted item. This was ahead of VTRs (14 per cent) and stereo sets (11 per cent).[13]

Importance of Distribution Channels

To export high volumes, distribution channels must be in place. This often means using dealers, retailers, etc., but may not involve national third party distributors. Sometimes, joint ventures are used, but they are normally terminated after a certain time, while distributors may be taken over. To recruit the (normally) large number of outlets required to sell the rapidly rising export volume, the Japanese company needs to offer the trade a good 'business opportunities package', as follows:

(1) Heavy advertising, where appropriate, to create buyer brand awareness (either in general or as applied to the specific product) and sometimes to generate a high volume of customer enquiries. This advertising takes a number of forms. Awareness creation advertising often uses sporting sponsorship or displays at sporting events. Lead generation activity normally appears in the appropriate trade, professional or consumer press. Only for the highest volume consumer products is television used.

(2) Favourable terms, such as high gross margins, substantial discounts, extended credit, and (in some cases) help with training.

(3) High availability of stock, to guarantee fulfilment of orders.

This package is offered to the trade in a number of ways, depending on the product and on the planned speed of launch. Trade exhibitions are a favourite, as they allow the Japanese company access to large numbers of potential trade customers in a short time, increasing the speed of recruitment. Some companies have recruited as many trade outlets as their largest Western competitor in the first year of operation, and then doubled or trebled the number within 2–3 years. Another approach is to go for big regional or national chains.

Leaving Segmentation to the Distributors and Subsidiaries
In many markets, a volume strategy is followed. That is not to say that no market segmentation takes place. What tends to happen is that subsidiaries, distributors and dealers carry out their own segmentation, since the products normally have enough features to permit this (segmentation often involves exploiting one feature more than another). Careful segmentation at the international level rarely pays in a rapidly changing market. Segmentation may involve substantial data collection, and time to interpret data to find appropriate segments, to develop policies to deal with segments, and to test those policies.

Efficiency in the Marketing Process
To offer good margins to the trade, everything possible is done to cut other costs in the marketing process, except the all important advertising. Shipment is usually in bulk from Japan to Europe, for the very largest companies in a dedicated freighter. Japanese companies rarely have a sizeable European HQ, preferring (except perhaps in the early set-up period) to deal direct with each national market. But European distribution centres are quite common.

Staffing and Controlling Marketing Subsidiaries
National operating companies are leanly staffed, with manpower stretched, and concentrating on the tasks of getting business, developing programmes to get more business and supporting trade outlets. Financial control is often exercised by a Japanese Controller. Little is spent on excess middle management, devoted to reporting back to Japan or to supervising operations. Authority may be delegated to a low level, with (strict) control on one or two key variables only (e.g. profit or non-loss and units sold). Top management are increasingly Japanese, not European. This may reflect two factors:

(1) The difficulty some Europeans have in adjusting to the Japanese way of doing business.

(2) Problems in adjusting to the personal style of Japanese management.

In 1981–1983, some European Managing Directors of Japanese subsidiaries were replaced by Japanese, to facilitate communication and management. For example, Akai decided in February 1983 to change the top executives of its five overseas subsidiaries to Japanese. Such moves may become more common as more Japanese companies set up production or assembly facilities overseas. These are nearly always headed by Japanese, with a strong Japanese team on site, in which case the liaison between manufacturing and marketing operation may be facilitated by the marketing subsidiary being run by Japanese. In addition, most Japanese subsidiaries use the services of the banks in their associated domestic groups (zaibatsu). The overseas branches of these banks are well staffed with Japanese, who usually understand their business needs well.[14]

Financing Overseas Subsidiaries
Some overseas subsidiaries are kept lean by being set high transfer prices, and being required to break even, with profit taken in Japan. There is no 'fund of profits' on which to draw for excess expenditure. More expenditure can only be financed by more gross margin, i.e more business. Transfer prices into overseas subsidiaries are often denominated in yen, causing profit problems for the subsidiary in times of yen strength. This is changing, with more frequent price adjustment to take into account fluctuations in the rate. In addition, a number of Japanese companies are restructuring the capital base of their overseas subsidiaries, to reduce interest liabilities.

Marketing subsidiaries are often the main location of inventory, providing a strong incentive to avoid stock pile-ups by marketing actions. But pile-ups do occur, resulting in intense local price cutting and consequential losses for subsidiaries, particularly during recession. This occurs not only for products which are being overproduced on a world scale, but also for products where demand temporarily sags in the export market. This approach ensures that when the local market weakens, the Japanese will intensify their marketing effort until excess inventory is reduced, albeit at a cost. If the market recovers, Japanese companies are in a correspondingly good position.

Attacking Western Competitors

In attacking Western competitors, Japanese companies use all the elements of the marketing mix. Price if often lower, but true dumping is rare. Low Japanese subsidiary profits are often due to high transfer prices. Losses in subsidiaries tend to be confined to the early years of operation, reflecting marketing investment to build up sales (which is what any Western company following the same worldwide strategy would do). The low price usually reflects genuinely lower manufacturing costs.

Advertising is central to strategy. Because Japanese firms are typically competing with well-known Western brand names, this is a vital investment. Many mechatronic products are seen by buyers to be potentially unreliable, so it is important to ensure that buyers are wooed from the brands that they know and trust, often by promised reliability.

Japanese companies have the advantage of any new entrant, in that they see the market with fresh eyes. Western companies may segment the market in one way (the above example of base vs featured is a case in point). Japanese companies may try different ways of segmenting, different target customers, different distribution channels, different advertising approaches, etc. This makes response more difficult for Western companies, saddled with a particular interpretation of the market and of how to deal with it. In reprographics, Japanese companies attempted to destroy the Western interpretation, based on a close connection between copy volume, speed and sophistication of machine.

Phase 6: Developing the After Market

Many mechatronic products have an after market, i.e. revenue arising from the customer following the initial sale of the product, excluding rental revenue. Sources include after-sales service (labour, parts, etc.), consumables (e.g. toner and paper for copiers, tapes for VTRs), software, add-on hardware (e.g. computer peripherals). It may arise from replacement and upgrade demand, i.e. identical or more advanced substitutes for the original equipment. After market revenue does not always go to the supplier of the original equipment. This depends on technical factors specific to each after market, as well as on marketing factors such as brand loyalty or multi-product marketing by the supplier. For supplies, the link between original equipment manufacturer and supplier manufacturer may be weak or non-existent. Magnetic

media manufacturers (floppy discs, video tape) are benefitting immensely at the moment from the explosion in the machine base. For example, Fuji Photo Film was expecting record profits in 1983, not just due to continued success against Kodak, but also because of its activities in magnetic media, sales of which rose 58 per cent by value in the year to October 1982, and were expected to rise a further 45 per cent in the year to October 1983, taking the ratio of non-film products to 16 per cent a figure which is expected to grow to 20 per cent by 1985–1986, for the same reason.[15]

In after sales service, the user will tend to go to the distributors of the equipment. If that distributor uses parts supplied by the manufacturer, then the latter derives after market revenue. For add-on hardware, much depends upon the product range of the manufacturer and on whether there is widespread compatibility between hardware of different manufacturers.

Cross-Subsidization Between Initial Sale and After Market

After market revenue to the manufacturer over the life of the product is often larger than the original sales value. The cost to suppliers of market access to the existing customer is low (relative to the new customer). Brand loyalty (or inability to obtain service or compatible parts or products) is likely to be higher than for the new customer (allowing a higher price to be charged). So profit margins on the after-market are often much higher than on initial equipment sale. Japanese and Western companies often develop strategies to exploit this (e.g. substantial profit mark-up on service parts). But Japanese product design and the growth profile of the stock of equipment generated by the Japanese companies' production and marketing policy combine to make Japanese after-market profits particularly high (though these profits are more likely to be shared with distributors than in the case of Western companies).

Design for Life Cycle Performance and Obsolescence

There is sometimes a difference in design philosophy between Western and Japanese companies. Suppose that the Western product is designed to last for 10 years, at a reasonable level of reliability (sometimes improving, due to the application of 'field fixing'). The equivalent Japanese product may be designed to last for 5 years, at an initially high level of reliability, but with a relatively high degree of failure in the last year or so of life. Japanese choice of length of life is normally determined by the period after which the average buyer would want to replace his product, given that technical progress will have made it obsolescent. There is no point in designing a product to last for 10 years if it will be obsolescent within 5 (see Figure 3). This is partly a reflection of the domestic Japanese tendency for rapid product replacement. Designing for limited but reliable life length should produce a

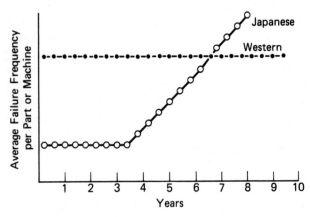

Figure 3. Failure frequency

cheaper product. The number of spare parts used over the product's life is normally lower, as is repair frequency, particularly if the Japanese supplier has succeeded in reducing the number of parts relative to the Western supplier. Operating in a market with Western reliability profiles (effectively leading to frequent replacement with cheaper parts), it becomes more possible to charge a high parts mark-up on parts. Customers often relate to the total service bill, not individual parts prices. When the 5 years (of the above example) is up, the assumption is that reliability will be a less relevant consideration in replacement than technical modernity. This reliability profile, and its associated cost and price advantages, make it crucial to ensure customers do replace equipment more often. This is done by ensuring that the latest technical developments are incorporated in all new products, rather than introducing them slowly at premium prices (a Western habit), and that products are as fully featured as possible.

Impact of Design, Marketing and Production Policy
Japanese policies lead to a particular age profile of stock. Their new products are introduced frequently, build up to peak stock very quickly, and the stock then declines rapidly. The equivalent Western product will build up more slowly to peak stock, which will then decline less rapidly (due to much greater variability of scrappage time around the expected life of the product). However, in order to keep up with market development, the Western company may have to introduce new products nearly as frequently. This tends to leave Western companies with a more varied and older machine stock. This makes for a more complex and costly after-market (carrying parts, training service engineers, designing software, designing up-grades or add-on products to be compatible with as many existing machines as possible). It may leave the door more open to third party after-market suppliers, who rely on a long tail of equipment to address. Parts piracy is discouraged by lack of a substantial and enduring stock of older, less reliable equipment.

Important of Parts After-Market to Japanese
One sign of the importance of this market is the

investments made by many Japanese companies in developing a reliable and efficient parts logistics system. Ricoh, the plain paper copier company with the largest installed base amongst the Japanese companies (but still a smaller company by Western standards), developed and implemented a satellite controlled international logistics network. The four principal Japanese motorcycle manufacturers (Kawasaki, Honda, Suzuki and Yamaha), now in intense competition with each other in world markets, freely admit to selling motorcycles at or near break-even, with most profit taken on well-organized parts supply. The high level of service delivered from stock also reduces the incentive to piracy. The profit from the after-market makes all the more feasible the policy of discounting the initial product sale to capture market share. Furthermore, the very rapid initial build-up of installed base means that the after market grows to peak size earlier than in the Western interpretation of the market. This means that the optimum sized after-market operation can be developed at an early stage.

Phase 7: Overseas Assembly and Manufacture

Overseas assembly seems to be undertaken for three reasons, as follows:

(1) Political/economic risk avoidance.

(2) Genuine savings in transport and/or manufacturing costs.

(3) Need for closer link with overseas markets.

Political/Economic Risk Avoidance
VTR and TV plants in developed economies usually belong to the first category. The production volumes and degree of automation in overseas plants rarely permit matching of cost levels achieved in Japan. But political and economic (in particular, foreign exchange risk) is reduced. Given this reason for plant location, Japanese companies try to ensure that the investment pays off in market domination and profit, even if the plant is a joint venture with a local company. There are signs that earlier investments made abroad are beginning to pay off, to the extent of having a noticeable impact on the Japanese invisible balance of payments.[16]

Political pressure usually occurs when there is a domestic industry of some size. Even then, it is dependent on industrialists and politicians seeing what is happening (e.g. the U.S. calculator industry's loss of most of the market to Casio and Sharp). As Japanese companies tend to move on from market to market, the window that is provided by Western political processes before 'damage' is proven is all the Japanese companies need. Political pressure in one market may only divert output to another. In April 1983, shipments of VTRs to the EEC fell 35·3 per cent to 259,000 units, as voluntary export restrictions took effect. In the same month, shipments to the U.S. more than doubled, to reach 419,000.

An example of political manufacture is Sanyo's expected second VTR plant in Europe, announced shortly after their voluntary restriction of exports. If political pressure increases, Sanyo will be able to increase sales via local manufacture. At some stage, 'political' plants may become economically justified, as the market reaches maturity, and plants in Japan move on to the next generation of products. For example, Sony (U.K.)'s plant expanded its production of colour TV tubes in 1983 by 50 per cent to 180,000 tubes a year.[17]

Economic risk avoidance is now less important to Japanese companies, with the yen increasingly being used to denominate Japanese trade. The proportion of Japanese export contracts denominated in yen rose from 32·7 per cent in January 1981, when MITI first compiled this statistic, to 40·5 per cent in February 1983. This is a rapid change in a statistic of such magnitude, and partly reflects the increasing strength of Japan as a supplier in world markets.[18]

Economic Justification
Savings in transport and/or manufacturing costs characterize some plants in developing countries, and manufacture of certain 'cabinet' products, such as loudspeakers and electronic organs, in developed economies. For example, in April 1983, Pioneer received French government approval to build a plant to produce 220,000 loudspeakers a year, rising to 330,000, with 90 workers. Half the output would be exported to other EEC countries.[19]

Some products go through a different cycle, where overseas manufacture (e.g. south east Asia) is viable prior to complete automation, to save labour costs. Once automation occurs, labour content collapses, and it is economic to relocate production to Japan, the source of most components. But the cycle may reverse again as local component manufacture by Japanese companies extends.

Need for Close Links
The need for close links particularly characterizes components manufacture. Overseas Japanese IC manufacture at an early stage in the cycle is aimed at domination of the overseas component market. This market requires close technical contact with customers at the beginning of each new cycle of development. Plants are therefore close to customers (Silicon Valley, Silicon Glen, and similar Pacific Basin areas). By the end of 1982, NEC, Hitachi and Fujitsu had plants in Europe, and Toshiba had announced that it would join them in 1983, with a plant in West Germany, with monthly production of 1 million chips, to be doubled in 3 years. The payroll would be 50, rising to 300 in 5

years. At first, the plant would assemble chips from Japanese components. It would be Toshiba's fifth overseas semiconductor plant (after the U.S., Mexico, South Korea and Malaysia).[20] In 1982, Hitachi began memory chip production at its Malaysian plant, expected to be producing 1 million chips per month by the end of 1983, compared with the end-1982 monthly production rate of 0·5 million in its other overseas plants (U.S. and West Germany).

Phase 8: Developing the Market

As the market saturates, the sales that can be sustained with the original product concept fall to straight replacement demand. This is unlikely to sustain most of the original companies in the business at volumes near their average production during the period of market growth. If we assume that the rapid growth period of the market (when most of the installed base was built up) lasted 3–4 years, during which Japanese companies increased their output two- or three-fold, production in the last year of this period may be equal to 35 per cent of final stock. If so, with the product on average lasting 5–7 years, replacement will be around 14–20 per cent of final stock, not enough to fill capacity. Sometimes (particularly the more mechanical and therefore usually less reliable products), the after-market is strong enough to substitute (in profit terms) for the initial market. In other cases, technical progress may be fast enough to render earlier products technically obsolescent well before the end of physical product life. The major TV makers in Japan are currently trying to bring forward scrapping of serviceable sets by the introduction of additional electronic features. Rendering obsolescent the existing installed base is not usually undertaken in a negative sense. It reflects the speed of technical progress. This may be through size reduction, to increase portability. An example of this is the development of the ultra-compact video tape recorder and the single unit VTR system.[21]

Phase 9: Moving onto the Next Market

If Japanese companies succeed in developing a market as above, they have to look to other markets when the original market reaches saturation in all respects, including after-market, upgrades, etc. The typical company then moves on to the 'next' market. Sharp's sequence included calculators, microcomputers, photocopiers and electronic typewriters, with (at the time of writing) home computers next on the list. Surplus workers from the fully automated calculator plant were moved into copier production. Hitachi switched some of its domestic electrical appliance factories into office automation and personal computer production.

The sequence of cycles for an individual company is normally similar across several companies, due to the concensus on opportunities. But individual companies respond to those parts of the concensus that best suit their own particular skills. Communications companies (e.g. Fujitsu and NEC) are responding to office automation primarily via systems based on digital exchanges and networks (although they do market stand-alone products with great success). In communications, products awaiting massive expansion are fibre-optic systems, satellite broadcast receiving equipment, mobile telephone and radio and cable TV. Casio, an expert in the high volume, low unit cost production, is moving from calculators, where production has topped out, to pocket-sized TV sets. Kyoto Ceramic, which acquired Yashica cameras in 1983, moved from ceramics, into electronic components and finally whole mechatronic products (personal computers).

Success Involves Structural Change

Most large Japanese companies recognize that success involves structural change.[22] Firms failing to change suffer declining output and profitability. Moving onto the next market does not necessarily imply explosive expansion. The 'twilight' products may be a problem. In some cases, exports to the developing world allows for smooth transition. In the watch industry, mechanical watches are now sold almost entirely to these markets, still accounting in 1982 for one third of the Japanese industry's unit output.

Part 3: Success and Failure

Companies succeed by riding the technical, production and marketing phases of a succession of product cycles. Each cycle produces ripples of product line extensions and new applications, and reinforces the worldwide marketing strength of the company, as the goodwill built up via advertising, trading relationships and distribution channel presence increases. Despite worldwide recession, 1981–1983 produced good results for companies which succeeded in riding a number of cycles. Hitachi's 1982–1983 pre-tax recurring profits were up 12 per cent, Mitsubishi Electric up 6 per cent, Sharp's up 17 per cent, Kyoto Ceramic's up 29 per cent, Canon's up 33 per cent and NEC's up 19.7 per cent. This took place despite heavy investment in plant and R & D, and prior to any impact of the worldwide economic recovery.

The Consequences of Failure

Failure can come at most phases of the cycle. It may be in product development (e.g. Ricoh's failure to develop a reliable medium speed photocopier early enough). It may be in market development (e.g. Ricoh's failure to develop its photocopier distribution network fast enough, once it had ended—

before reverting to it—its agreement with Savin in North America and with Nashua and Kalle (Hoechst) in Europe). It may be through overcalling the market size. Pioneer's 1982–1983 loss was caused by pile-up of hi-fi inventory. Similar problems occurred in SLR cameras (e.g. Canon, Nikon and Olympus Optical), VTRs and digital watches at the same time. Certain companies, such as Sony in 1982–1983, had problems with over-optimism over a range of products, requiring general inventory reduction. Yaskawa Electric's 37 per cent fall in profits was due to intense price cutting in industrial robots, with discounts of 30–40 per cent.[23] Many of these problems were temporary, caused by over-anticipation of a product boom. The renewed growth of world audio and VTR markets in 1983 is expected to produce substantial profits for companies that had difficulties in 1982.

Failure or substantial under-target profit produces rapid response. Pioneer had a fire-sale of inventories, switched emphasis to other products, such as video disc machines (manufacturing flexibility pays well here), and was expected to be back into reasonable profit the year after its loss. Rapid recovery like this is explained by the Japanese bamboo analogy—it springs forward with more force, the further back it is bent. Ricoh's efforts went more strongly into semiconductor development and computer printers, and Canon's into copiers and other office automation equipment (from SLR cameras). Sony's reaction was also rapid inventory reduction, lower fixed investment, and reduced employment and expenses. But R & D expenditure was maintained, as the key to the next generation of products. The company also planned to raise its proportion of non-consumer electronics equipment from 12 per cent to 25 per cent.[24]

Importance of Permanent Employment

Company commitment to employment continuity (whether it is sustainable in the economy as a whole is another matter) is a key factor. The work force is a company asset. Lack of skilled labour or research staff impedes expansion, even in Japan. Workers are retained by increased automation and higher output, generating the increased productivity necessary to make it worth employing a worker. Labour productivity in the electric machinery sector rose by 7.9 per cent in 1982, in contrast with manufacturing as a whole, where the figure was 1.5 per cent.

Government Help With Restructuring

Provisions exist for restructuring industries which have failed to ride a continuing boom. In 1983, the

Temporary Law for Structural Improvement of Specific Industries was used by MITI to restructure parts of the chemical industry, impacted by worldwide recession and over-capacity. Seventeen PVC makers were grouped into four marketing groups, with each group to scrap surplus capacity, aiming to cut capacity overall by 24 per cent. Eight other petrochemical and fertiliser products were also under consideration by MITI for the same treatment. Oil refinery realignment was also under consideration by MITI, for the same reasons.[25] Mechatronics manufacturers aim to avoid such treatment!

Inherent Riskiness of Japanese Approach

The Japanese approach is inherently risky. This is the essence of the Japanese challenge—to take risks, but to make sure that everything that is necessary to make the risk work is done. If failure occurs, it is rarely by shooting too low and being overtaken by competition. Rather, it is by shooting too high.

Part 4: The Western Response to the Challenge

Given the Japanese record of success in mechatronic markets, what can Western companies do to meet the Japanese challenge, and what impediments are there to successful response? There are two broad kinds of response to the challenge in a given product market, as follows:

(a) Go for a volume strategy similar to the Japanese.

(b) Segment the market, and defend a small customer base by serving it better than anyone else.

There is also a choice of responses to the rate of movement between product cycles:

(c) Speed up the rate of internal new product development and introduce more flexible manufacturing and marketing procedures.

(d) Forge links with other companies to create multiple cross-sourcing.

Volume Strategy

Before considering how this might be approached by Western companies, note that there are three positive reasons for going for this strategy, as follows:

(1) Under the impact of Japanese competition, markets become less stable. Japanese companies, in intense competition with each other, continue trying to win each others' customers.

With brand loyalty continuously under attack, and with whole product ranges becoming obsolescent every few years, it is never too late to come back into the market.

(2) There has been a substantial increase in the world wide availability of high quality electronic components produced by Japanese plants in Japan or abroad. Western firms can now obtain them more readily, removing one of the obstacles to being competitive.

(3) The high quality volume manufacturing tradition (which after all is very recent in Japan) is now much better understood by Western management.

Large vs Small Companies
To succeed with a volume strategy, a high degree of risk taking and commitment is necessary. Normally, the scale of risk involved puts volume success out of reach of small companies, set up with venture capital. Note that none of the Japanese companies mentioned above are new companies— they are all mature electronics or precision engineering companies, and none of them are small. Though the cost of a production line to produce a new mechatronic product may be high, it is financeable by issuing bonds, borrowing from the banks, and using accumulated profits. Though Western new venture companies in mechatronics may be very profitable, their impact on the competitiveness of a whole industry is, with one or two exceptions, likely to be small.

Change in Attitude to Investment
The above suggests that change is needed in Western mechatronic companies' attitude to investment, involving viewing all investment as high risk with high potential gain, with the chance that perhaps only half of major research or plant investment will yield good profit. It also involves seeing the company as dedicated to destroying today's products as rapidly as possible (or someone else will). Banks and shareholders must also become accustomed to the investment and profit profile generated by companies competing in this mode.

Fallacy of Short Term Profit
It has been argued that frequent (in the U.S. quarterly) financial reporting of Western companies and its impact on share values prevents companies taking the longer view, because of the need to maximize short term profits. This is a poor excuse. It assumes that all that changes is the amount of investment needed to execute a volume strategy. In fact, lower marketing and management costs per unit output implicit in volume strategies and simpler activities downstream from manufacturing should result in as much profit, and almost as early. But Western companies often only look at one side of the picture—the manufacturing and marketing costs, rather than the benefits.

Cash Flow Impact

The tight cash flows of recent years may seem a serious barrier to adopting a volume strategy. Though the 'lump sums' involved in investing for a volume strategy may seem large (plant investment, initial inventory build-up, advertising, distribution channel credit), the volume production and marketing process is geared to depreciating or liquidating these investments quickly, through high production volumes, which are sold quickly. Though the downside cash risk may be high, the expected cash flow is not weak. Indeed, Japanese companies depend upon it for financing further research. It is important for Western financial institutions and company financial managers to understand these points. Note in particular that cash flow is not (as often in Western companies) tied up in financing stock of obsolescent products or parts, overpaid management hierarchies, and leasing of large business facilities. It is important for would be pursuers of volume strategies to understand that there is no reason why finance should be forthcoming for the investment required if only some of the required changes are made.

Requirements for Success in a Volume Strategy

The story that emerges above indicates that in pursuing a volume strategy in competition with Japanese companies, each part of the company must run in a particular way. The story is not a story that applies to particular functions, but to the whole company. It is the responsibility of general management, and planning departments, to work towards the creation of new ways of doing business in the company. This means creating a 'vision' of what an efficient, dedicated, integrated and fast-moving company will look like, and implementing that vision. It does not mean copying the Japanese in every respect. It does mean removing the obstacles to efficiency, dedication, integration and speed. The history of Western enterprise is characterized by willingness to learn, once the problem has been identified.

Has the Volume Lesson Been Learnt?

Some Western firms are well placed to deal with Japanese challenges in their sector. IBM invested heavily in improving manufacturing efficiency, reduced the prices of many of its product lines, and adopted a volume strategy with its personal computer (as have some minicomputer suppliers).[26] Some telecommunications firms (e.g. Ericsson, Alcatel) adopted similar strategies with some products. But U.K. firms pursuing such strategies are rare, with a glowing exception in Ferranti's domination of the uncommitted logic array chip market.

Segmentation Strategy

The Western view is often that highest profits are made by picking off high-margin, specialist segments of volume markets (e.g. the 3M strategy). This assumes a high availability of segments for companies to specialize in. It also assumes that segments are always defensible against volume strategies.

The Wheel of Segmentation

There is a 'wheel of segmentation', similar to the more well-known 'wheel of retailing'. In this wheel, a company starts by serving the needs of a well-defined segment of the market better than anyone else, with a marketing stance (hardware, software, sales strategy, etc.) closely attuned to the needs of that segment. Other companies, often new entrants into the industry, adopt a different stance. They pick out elements that are common to many segments, and design a marketing stance to satisfy these elements. They may not satisfy them quite so well as segmenting suppliers, but find other ways of compensating for this (price, inventory availability, etc.). In the mechatronics market, specialist applications become standardized, or dealt with by distributors or local manufacturing subsidiaries customizing highly featured hardware, via other elements of the marketing stance (software, sales strategy, different combinations of hardware). The segmenting company may then move on to another segment, or undermine the volume strategy by further segmentation (creating a yet closer fit between their marketing stance and the needs of the segment). Note that the optimum strategy in such circumstances may be to take the volume approach with respect to some elements of the marketing stance, the segmented approach with respect to others. In the computing market, most of the major U.S. corporations have announced policies along these lines, based upon major software investments to adapt standard hardware to the needs of key segments (e.g. manufacturing and office automation).

A whole economy cannot easily opt out of a volume strategy, at least with respect to manufacturing, in mechatronic markets, if it wishes to have a viable mechatronic sector. For an economy to meet competition of the kind described above, it needs to have companies pursuing both volume and segmented approaches. It helps if companies are always seeking to turn segmented into volume strategy. Volume and segmenting strategies are appropriate at different times, depending on the nature of buyer needs and the state of production and product technology. But, in competition with a large number of companies following volume strategies, at least one volume strategy should be open. The strategic risk of not doing so is complete exclusion from the market.

Accelerated Product Development Plus Manufacturing Flexibility

A central problem of some Western mechatronic

companies has been failure to match the pace of Japanese new product development and marketing. This requires improving the process of designing and developing new products to replace the previous generation of products, and moving quickly to high manufacturing and marketing volumes. The difficulties Western companies have in achieving this are often due to structural and organizational factors—the system is not designed to work at the appropriate pace, nor are there many incentives to do so. This applies to factory lay-outs, management structures and decision processes, depreciation rules, marketing practices, workforce attitudes to change and so on. These problems are not insuperable. They are more likely to be successfully dealt with by companies which realise that they are dealing with a challenge which is a total system challenge, covering all functional areas and general management. Programmes adopted by a number of large U.S. corporations (e.g. the Ford 'after-Japan' programme), have had some success.

Links with other Companies for Cross Sourcing

The early 1980s were characterized by a plethora of announcements by mechatronic companies concerning links with other companies (e.g. AT & T and Philips, IBM with Rolm and Intel, Amdahl and Sperry). Computers, telecommunications, office equipment and component companies were the main parties involved. The links covered anything from joint research, through product development, to marketing. The links were of a variety of forms, from shareholdings through to contractual arrangements and agreements in principle. Although some of these links ran into trouble (e.g. IBM and Mitel, Olivetti and Savin), most of them seemed to be durable. If they succeed, they will enhance the ability of the companies concerned to add to their product lines rapidly, and also to exit from old products more quickly. These moves, which are as much a response to market opportunity as to the Japanese challenge, will put the companies in a better position to deal with the challenge.[27]

Part 5: The Future

In one market, home computers, the U.K. led the world at the time of writing. Japanese firms (particularly Sharp, Sord and National Panasonic) were launching their own home computers. Their were signs, despite the success of the Sinclair and other machines, that the opportunity was not fully recognized. While penetration of U.K. households in early 1983 was around 3 per cent, Western suppliers were expecting that this might 'shoot up' to 10 per cent by 1985 (with the limit expected to be the 60 per cent of households with people under 55 years old). But, 4 years after the launch Sinclair's first product, there were still signs of a shortage of home computers, with several large retailers on allocation. The response was a big increase in volume on the part of Sinclair (whose manufacturing was subcontracted to other, larger electronics companies) and the entry of many small U.K. suppliers, often with venture capital backing, sometimes assembling components from abroad. But this was not really enough to meet demand, even taking into account the inflow of imports (Texas Instruments, Atari) or the increased local manufacture (Commodore) of U.S. companies. Japanese producers are known to be aiming to sell as many home computers as there are households with TV sets or telephones, as a first step in home automation. This was a classic scenario for Japanese entry. At the time of writing, it was on the horizon. It will be interesting to see the result. But meanwhile, one wonders why no major established U.K. electronics manufacturers took the opportunity.

References

(1) Casio produces credit card-like calculator, *Japan Economic Journal*, p. 11, 3 May (1983).

(2) Sony will commercialise 3·5-inch FD in summer, *Japan Economic Journal*, p. 12, 31 May (1983); 14 more makers back 3-inch floppy disc, *Japan Economic Journal*, p. 13, 1 March (1983).

(3) Corporations in the news/Alps Electric, *Japan Economic Journal*, p. 21, 17 May (1983).

(4) Big semiconductor makers boost capital expenditure, and Mitsubishi Electric plans investment of 62 billion yen, *Japan Economic Journal*, p. 17, 26 April (1983); Sharp will build 2nd LSI plant in Hiroshima, *Japan Economic Journal*, p. 11, 10 May (1983).

(5) Oki will consign output of 'twilight' items to others, *Japan Economic Journal*, p. 15, 29 March (1983).

(6) TI will double capacity of semiconductor plant at Miho, *Japan Economic Journal*, p. 18, 26 April (1983).

(7) Data General Corp. plans procuring more parts, components from Japan, *Japan Economic Journal*, p. 11, 8 March (1983).

(8) Sumitomo eyes doubling fiber optics cables, *Japan Economic Journal*, p. 15, 29 March (1983).

(9) Sanyo Electric envisages flotation of Swiss Franc convertible bonds, *Japan Economic Journal*, p. 16, 8 March (1983); Electronics firms eye convertible bond insurances for capital expenditures, *Japan Economic Journal*, p. 10, 22 February (1983).

(10) Foreign holdings in Japanese companies are on the rise, *Japan Economic Journal*, p. 1, 31 May (1983).

(11) IC exports to the U.S. are rising at fast pace, *Japan Economic Journal*, p. 1, 14 June (1983); News briefs—more microprocessors, *Japan Economic Journal*, p. 11, 1 March (1983).

(12) Home video tape recorder production tops color TVs, *Japan Economic Journal*, p. 14, 1 March (1983).

(13) Personal computers, VTRs, stereos are items most coveted by youths, *Japan Economic Journal*, p. 4, 7 June (1983).

(14) Export-oriented companies boost foreign subsidiaries, *Japan Economic Journal*, p. 3, 24 March (1983); Japanese companies buy into Europe, *Fortune*, p. 146, 16 May (1983); Does Japanese management work in Britain, Malcolm Trevor, *Journal of General Management*, **8**(4), 28–43, Summer (1983).

(15) Corporations in the news/Fuji Photo Film, *Japan Economic Journal*, p. 17, 10 May (1983).

(16) Japanese investments overseas reach stage of yielding returns, *Japan Economic Journal*, p. 7, 29 March (1983); Returns from investments overseas set new record, *Japan Economic Journal*, p. 1, 17 May (1983).

(17) Sanyo will locate VTR plant in W. Germany, *Japan Economic Journal*, p. 15, 14 June (1983); Sony will boost pix tube output in U.K., *Japan Economic Journal*, p. 15, 14 June (1983).

(18) Ratio of yen-denominated dealings in exports surpasses 40%, *Japan Economic Journal*, p. 5, 29 March (1983).

(19) France okays Pioneer bid to set up plant, *Japan Economic Journal*, p. 17, 26 April (1983).

(20) Toshiba will build large LSI assembly plant in W. Germany, *Japan Economic Journal*, p. 15, 14 December (1983).

(21) Sanyo Electric will market ultra compact type of VTR, *Japan Economic Journal*, p. 15, 14 December (1983); Sony will start sales of single unit VTR system, *Japan Economic Journal*, p. 15, 17 May (1983).

(22) Profit gap among major firms grows as industrial structure changes, *Japan Economic Journal*, p. 7, 7 June (1983).

(23) Cut-rate robot sales plague Yaskawa, *Japan Economic Journal*, p. 20, 14 June (1983).

(24) Pioneer's status is improving, *Japan Economic Journal*, p. 20, 17 May (1983); Corporations in the news/Sony Corp., *Japan Economic Journal*, p. 17, 22 March (1983).

(25) PVC manufacturers agree to cut production capacity by 24%, *Japan Economic Journal*, p. 16, 14 June (1983); 14–38% capacity cut eyed for nine chemical products, *Japan Economic Journal*, p. 1, 7 June (1983); Oil refiners agree to 16·3% cut in capacity; still face realignment, *Japan Economic Journal*, p. 9, 7 June (1983); See also: How Japan manages declining industries, *Fortune*, p. 34, 10 January (1983).

(26) The lean, mean, new IBM, *Fortune*, p. 69, 13 June (1983).

(27) Suddenly U.S. companies are teaming up, *Business Week*, p. 48, 11 July (1983); A new weapon against Japan: R & D partnerships, *Business Week*, p. 62, 8 August (1983).

Section Three

Strategic Planning for Research and Development

Directing Technological Development—The Role of the Board

Simon Willder, Executive Chairman and Managing Director, STC Technology Ltd., London, U.K.

Market pull will always be present in businesses based on technology. This article is concerned with the other force: technology push. However, the two are naturally inter-related and management of the technological development involved in satisfying market pull can be viewed as a part of that which is involved in a technology push. The author discusses how a successful market change can be brought about by technology push, through innovation, and by carefully planning the cultivation of the right environment.

Introduction

Two major forces act on a technology-based business (Figure 1): firstly, the pull of a relatively-known market place whose requirements a business endeavours to satisfy; secondly, the push which the development of more advanced technology creates to meet requirements not necessarily extant in the existing market.

The telephone is an example of technology push. Man needs to communicate, but nobody conceived of the ability to talk remotely with someone else before Alexander Graham Bell invented the telephone. Now the telephone has become an essential part of our everyday lives. The next major step in telecommunications is an example of technology pull—Strowger's invention of the automatic telephone exchange.

Almon P. Strowger was an undertaker. He found himself losing business to a competitor who had suborned the exchange operator into eavesdropping on Strowger's conversations with customers and passing on the information. His answer was to design an automatic telephone exchange. Today, almost 100 years later, Strowger's invention is still in use in about 90 per cent of the world's telephone exchanges.

What are the elements of a successful market change brought about by technology push? Obviously an element of fundamental technological innovation is involved. Careful planning of the product or service development is essential. And there must be the right environment within the organization to enable its exploitation.

Technology push starts with research. In business this is usually applied research, undertaken in the company's own laboratories. It is arguably the most difficult part of technological development to relate to successful business exploitation. Studying the feasibility of business exploitation follows once technical feasibility is proven. This is a more formalized process, of analysing the market for the novel product or service by comparison with its realization from the research work undertaken.

The two processes which follow, of detailed product specification and design, then need to be iterative, converging towards an optimum solution from a business point of view. Having produced the ultimate specification from a marketeer's point of

Figure 1

Dr. Simon Willder is Executive Chairman and Managing Director of STC Technology Ltd., STC House, 190 Strand, London WC2R 1DU.

view, one often, in designing it, finds that something slightly different is cheaper or more suitable. This iteration needs to be recognized and allowed for. If the specification is too restrictive, the end-product may be uncompetitive.

The design is then taken by development teams and engineered into a product ready to be manufactured and launched into the market place.

Many organizations do not view these last three activities (manufacturing, launching and supporting the product in the market place) as part of the technological development of a novel product. It is, however, most important to remember that product development does not end with the transfer to manufacture, and development management must remain actively involved and responsible for the product into manufacturing and then into the field.

Research

The principal objective of research is to provide a technology base for the business. All good research laboratories are populated by staff who are highly intelligent and usually academically orientated. To obtain optimum output they must be supported by a good administrative organization, and they must be rewarded both financially and with recognition.

From the business point of view there are certain research management activities which have to be undertaken with great diligence. Skills must be developed progressively and not be allowed to rest on current technology and past achievements. Another important facet of research is programme continuity. It is very tempting to see an area where research may yield exploitable business and undertake that research work; then, when times are hard, curtail or reduce that work. Research is not amenable to a stop–go policy. This can only result in demotivation and inefficiency. An administrative structure which allocates firmly, on a long-term continuous basis, money for properly directed research is therefore essential.

The cost of high technology research is, these days, increasing enormously, certainly in the case of information technology (IT). Shortage of expertise in the field pushes up salaries. The equipment and tools needed to support state-of-the-art research are expensive. Technological innovation requires an expensive laboratory; an increasing portion of the revenue from selling products and services must be used to support it. It is important to get value for money from research facilities, by conducting regular and proper management reviews of its activities. It is therefore equally important to ensure that technically competent people flourish in the upper echelons of corporations based on technology, because the future of those corporations is dependent upon successful innovation and exploitation as never before.

Research Management Reviews

Management reviews of research activities should have the following objectives:

- To define programmes in the first instance, specify their scope and chart progress.

- To ensure that all programmes have an identified sponsor, preferably from among the business divisions, charged with the responsibility for subsequent exploitation and sales.

The basic task of the reviewing body is to assess the relevance of the programmes; to initiate relevant programmes quickly, in order to obtain maximum potential for exploitation; and to terminate irrelevant programmes ruthlessly, even though they may be of great academic interest within the laboratory. Once a potential innovative product or service has been identified, the next step is to analyse its business feasibility.

Business Feasibility

This process consists of taking a specification conceived by the marketing function, which gives information on the product functions and facilities, its performance, its appearance, the standards to which it must conform, its cost targets, the market window which it has to satisfy and its product life; taking all these and comparing them with the feasibility of developing, from our technology base, a product to satisfy those requirements.

It is necessary to identify technological grey areas which require more research or investigation. In the IT industry an important and frequently omitted aspect is the dimensioning of the critical parameters of a product. Most large, complex, computer-based systems have had problems of speed or capacity during their development, due to inadequate understanding of the requirements and of how to implement the required performance at an early part of the system development cycle.

During the feasibility study, cost estimates are needed for the product, for its development and for its subsequent support—the so-called life cycle costs. We also need to plan not only the subsequent development phase but also the build-up to manufacturing. When the business feasibility study is complete then we have reached the critical go/no-go decision point, where the Board must exercise its authority and responsibilities before major business expenditure.

The Development Process

Specification
We now move to formal specification of the

product by the development team. This combines the outcome of the feasibility study and the resolution of the technological grey areas identified during that study. It specifies the functions and facilities of the product, its performance and capacities, and includes as an important item the user interface (for example, the screen and keyboard interface to an operator of, say, a word processor). It should also specify the standards to which the product will conform in both operation and manufacture, expected costs (or cost targets), time scales for development, the constraints under which the development shall occur, such as in collaboration with an overseas partner who will subsequently market the product in his own country and finally, what the product will look like.

Design

As mentioned previously, the specification process is iterative with the design. There are many different definitions of design, but from the management point of view, a useful one is:

> Design is the successive partitioning or functional decomposition of the chosen architecture of the product, until each part thereby defined can be developed by one person in an acceptable time.

That is, one has broken down the complexity of the overall product into elements which individual human beings can deal with.

Design is an exercise in documentation. It must be stated *why* it was done this way and *what* the resultant structure is. A clear description of the overall design of the product is essential. For instance, in large, real-time computer system development, it has usually been impossible to get hold of a clear overall description of the technical design of the total system, unless a particular person or group has been specifically given the responsibility of documenting the work. Documentation, then, is the outcome of the design process: a description of the design accompanied by drawings, flow charts, circuit diagrams, layouts of the equipment, parts lists, artist's impressions, and the quantitative performance parameters so often neglected.

At the end of the design process, all the interfaces between the partitions should be specified in detail and thereafter rigorously controlled. Subsequently the design should not be changed without a formal review and consequent configuration control change.

In addition, it is necessary to design or specify the development and manufacturing environments in which the product is to be developed and made, as well as the tools which are to be used. These are further activities often omitted as part of the formal design process.

Feasibility studies, specification and design are often under-emphasized during the process of technological development. By the end of the design stage, before any development begins we should have spent at least 15 per cent of our total development budget; yet all there is to see is documentation and probably a few feasibility models from the laboratories.

Development

We now move to the development of a real product, when we form teams to develop the parts determined by the design process. The structure of each team should reflect the functional breakdown of the product design. Individual development team managers will be responsible for the development and testing of the parts of the overall design which are their discrete functional entities or system components. The largest part of the development task is the rigorous testing of the product as it is progressively built up, a process which itself needs to be designed and planned. We need to design and provide test harnesses to do the job thoroughly at every stage.

We must write comprehensive test specifications. And, finally, we must perform the component integration and testing of our product, as it increasingly approaches the end realization, under quality controlled conditions.

Note the emphasis on careful and comprehensive integration and testing at each stage— this is fundamental to the successful development of a quality product. There should be a separate test team to undertake this task, acting independently of the development teams charged with realization of the component parts. In most product developments, something in excess of 50 per cent of all the effort and cost should go into testing.

Finally, throughout the development phase one must remember the great importance of efficiency. This will enable us to obtain a product as quickly as possible and at the lowest possible development cost. For this reason we need to use the most up-to-date development tools available.

Manufacture

Products must be designed with manufacturing in mind. The product must be capable of being manufactured in the most economic way. Specification or design of the manufacturing facility in which the product will be produced must be part of the design process itself. This is particularly important with innovative products, because they usually require some new manufacturing technology. Thus one has to undertake design trade-offs between specification of the product and its manufacturability. An example of this is a new production line which STC has recently put into its Northern Ireland factory, for the manufacture of transceivers for telephones. This automatic production line was designed in parallel with the transceiver itself, resulting in the optimum product capable of being manufactured by the latest machinery. In fact, the only way of making this product is on this automated production line.

The output of development is a comprehensive package of manufacturing information, covering all aspects of the product manufacture, including purchasing, assembly and test. It is essential to avoid finalizing the development on the shop floor. Launching a partially developed product into early manufacture does not save time—it is more expensive and time-consuming to correct faults on the production line than in the development laboratories. In fact, particularly for novel products, it is worth finding time for a prototype run of a small volume, prior to main production, so as to de-bug the manufacturing process itself.

The sales department, eager to satisfy customers at the earliest opportunity, will argue differently; but it can sometimes be attractive for customers to know that there will be a limited first batch from which, if they order quickly, they can have samples prior to quantity procurement.

In order for businesses to be competitive, manufacturing costs must be kept as low as possible. Automation is always desirable. A new product provides an opportunity to implement the most modern automation facilities; in fact, history has shown that it can be a mistake to introduce an innovative product into an old manufacturing environment. If an old site and facilities have to be used, then a new environment must be created for innovative product manufacture. But even so, new ventures are best started on new sites.

Product Launch
Introducing an innovative product into the market place requires more than usual emphasis on the proper technological launch and subsequent support activities. It is essential to set up a multi-disciplinary team to support the launch of a novel product in order that salesmen can be assisted with demonstrations, customers' questions can be answered and their problems solved. The multi-disciplinary team also provides a quick feedback loop to the specification of the product, its design, its testing, and actual manufacture.

The multi-disciplinary launch team, for which the development organization should be responsible, in the long term, shrinks to a field support team for problem-solving. the subsequent evolution of the product is then beneficially influenced by this team, by their involvement in the definition of the Mark 2 product.

Management Organization

Addressing now the organization and management of these development processes (Figure 2), one can view the formalized task of specification, through design, development, testing and launch, as the responsibility of a development organization managed by a person who is best referred to as the Product Champion. This organization is the core for the realization of the product. Choosing the proper Product Champion therefore is an important issue for the Board. He or she must be an individual who is convinced, by logical analysis, of the worth of the product to the business, and has the stamina and personality to bring about its successful implementation. The Product Champion and the engineering teams must rigorously follow the engineering discipline described above, with the necessary planning and administration support being provided by a dedicated support activity.

Having appointed the Product Champion, the Board needs to establish an environment in which he can operate. This environment can be described as a 'Greenhouse' (Figure 3), where the novel and

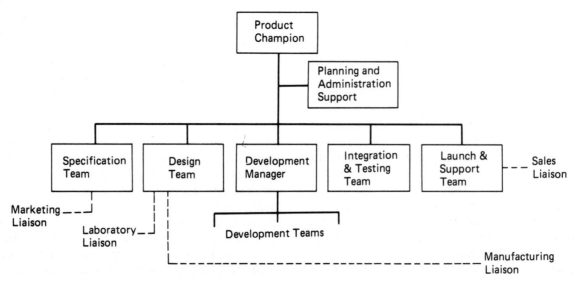

Figure 2. Technological development organization

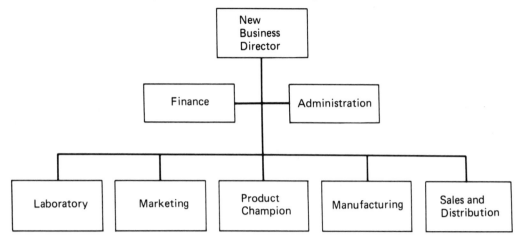

Figure 3. 'The Greenhouse'—the environment for the Product Champion

innovative product, or rather series of products, can be nurtured before subsequent planting into the garden. The Board should include a specific New Business Director who is responsible for generating new business derived from technology. He has his Product Champion, perhaps many of them, responsible for the development of the product. He has the ability to manufacture that product, through an organization which may not report directly to him but over which he needs adequate authority. Initially, the marketing of the product is his dominant responsibility, and he needs to support this task by market research, a strategy formulation staff, pricing, distribution and direct sales activities.

Marketing strategy should be kept separate from sales, because marketing is essentially an extrapolation of the New Business Director's own responsibility for the overall activity, whereas sales is strictly operational. The laboratory should also be part of his remit, so that he is directly looking for the exploitation potential from it.

The New Business Director will need supporting financial services, orientated towards business evaluation, and an administrative arm to ensure that exactly the right people are selected for this very people-sensitive environment. This latter function is also needed to provide the organizational and administrative support to the operation—aiming at maximum flexibility, to enable new business activities to be established speedily, under Product Champions, in order to take advantage quickly of the technological opportunities offered. An important aspect of the Greenhouse is that it enables subsequent planting out into the garden. Thus it should be the responsibility of the New Business Director to re-parent new business activities elsewhere in the corporation, once they have reached satisfactory viability. If this is not done, then the Greenhouse will become filled with mature plants, which will demand an increasing amount of senior manage-

ment attention, to the detriment of the real purpose of the Greenhouse—starting new businesses out of technology. Thus we have determined that exploitation of new business is of sufficient importance to merit a place on the Board of our company.

The Role of the Board

One sees, therefore, a possible Board structure somewhat like that shown in Figure 4: a chairman, supported by specialist executive directors in the financial, technical, legal and administrative (or personnel) areas. Of particular importance in fostering the right overall company environment for new business based on technology is an executive director responsible for the overall corporate strategy, in terms of the products and services offered by the company, and the way in which the company operates based on these offerings. He is, therefore, also an overall corporate focus for the company's marketing activity.

Our ideal company would then have a seat on the Board for the New Business Director and, of course, other directors who are operating existing established businesses within the total corporate entity. Advice would also normally be available from a number of non-executive directors, who generally represent the independent interests of the shareholders.

The role of the Board, with regard to new businesses based on technology, must be basically supervisory; this means regularly reviewing their progress and making decisions associated with the establishment and curtailment of new ventures. It is most important that this happens at Board level because new ventures change the direction of the overall business. The Board must be enthusiastic about and encourage the exploitation of new technology. The best inspiration is that which comes from the top downwards. Leadership,

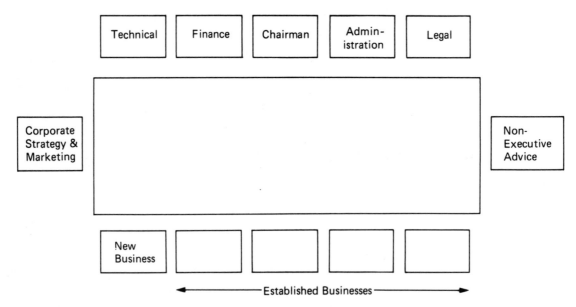

Figure 4. The Board

coupled with encouragement to exploit novel technology, makes an enormous difference to the attitude of the staff involved and thus the success of new ventures.

The most important job of the Board is to choose. It has to choose which new technologies it is going to support. It must set up the Greenhouse for careful and logical development and analysis of business potential from new technology. It must ensure the integrity of those analyses and receive presentations from the New Business Director on his future proposals.

The proper time for the Board to make its choice is at the end of the business feasibility study, before most of the real money has been spent.

Presentations given at this stage must cover the customer requirement, how much he is willing to pay, how the product is sold and distributed, how it is manufactured, how it is developed, what other risks are associated with the total process, how much investment is necessary, and, of course, what the eventual return is expected to be. The choice must be a corporate one, with the whole business backing the new venture.

The balance to this encouragement from the Board is the corporate conscience, which must be satisfied by thorough and systematic reviews. It is essential for maximum exploitation of technology that the Board be positively involved—we should not leave it to the backroom boys to cook up an idea then try and make a go of it on a shoestring.

Finally, within this context, what are the roles of the individual Board members? The Chairman must be given adequate information if he is to have a proper understanding of the proposals. If the choice is positive, he must lead and stimulate enthusiastic support for the new venture, but retain the authority to cancel it if necessary. Finally, he must be involved in the external projection of the new business and identify himself with the resultant change in direction of his company. Taking their lead from the Chairman, the other directors need to be enthusiastic in their own areas.

The Finance Director should be involved in obtaining funds for new business ventures, because of the implications on shareholders' equity, and he must monitor carefully the financial performance of the ventures, where major swings in fortune are possible. The Technical Director must carefully review, from an independent position, the technological cases made, and then be involved in progressing the development of the product or service. The Legal Director must review the commercial environment in which the new product or service is offered because it may well be novel to that particular company.

The Marketing Director needs to understand the *corporate* implications of entering the new markets, and needs to obtain or give advice on the marketing strategy involved. The Administration or Personnel Director needs to be particularly sensitive to the appointments made and responsibilities given to people in the development of new business because new and rapidly changing situations are involved. He needs to ensure also that the total corporate organization is appropriate to and supportive of the venture.

And finally, the New Business Director must be a strong creator of the Greenhouse environment, be able to analyse and present the cases carefully and well, and be prepared to re-parent his successful ventures into other parts of the company.

Section Four

Strategies for Diversification

Diversification—The Key Factors for Success

Jean-Pierre Detrie and Bernard Ramanantsoa, CESA, Jouy-en-Josas, France

This paper describes research aimed at finding the key factors for success and failure of diversification decisions. A survey of a sample of 200 French medium size companies was conducted through a mailed questionnaire. Further interviews were made in 20 firms which recently diversified their activities.

We consider that a corporation which diversifies is one which acquires a skill likely to change radically the characteristics of its business. In contrast, a firm which starts a new production operation by using the skills it already has does not diversify but increases its *specialization* along a new axis. One cannot call 'a strategy' diversification when it is based on the use of distinctive skills already existing in the company.

Having the necessary competence is certainly necessary but it is not enough by itself. The management must know how to combine and organize the required resources which is sometimes difficult.

Diversification vs Specialization: A Strategic Dilemma

Why diversification?
A study of the development of corporate strategy clearly indicates that the choice of diversification should be the last step of a logical and progressive strategy. In general the development strategies adopted by firms consist of a number of steps.

As long as the traditional market is growing, firms devote most of their resources to it. The financial

Jean-Pierre Detrie and Bernard Ramanantsoa are Professors of Business Policy at HEC. and ISA. at Jouy-en-Josas near Paris. They are doing research into strategy formulation and implementation especially on the diversification processes. Their book *Stratégie de l'Entreprise et Diversification*, Nathan 1983, Paris, received the 1984 award of the French Academy of Commercial Sciences.

needs are such that they do not allow much thinking about diversification. The usual managerial reason for not considering diversification is that there is still a lot to do in the firm's present area of activity. They mean in fact that it is possible for the firm to increase its share of the market and to break new ground.

The stagnation of the traditional market leads the firm to expand geographically on a regional, and then, on an international basis. Once the internationalization process is over, new complementary products are made.

Finally, when the market has reached its peak and is about to decline, and the firm cannot conquer any further territories nor develop complementary products, a diversification strategy is called for. It will involve either launching new products on the original market or moving into totally different activities.

Thus, there is a chronology which leads to diversification in four progressive steps:

(1) market penetration,

(2) geographical expansion,

(3) development of complementary products,

(4) entry in to new fields of activity,

which is, strictly speaking, what diversification is all about. Of course, it may happen that a firm is faced with a very attractive opportunity which will make it pass directly from step 2 to step 4. It is also possible that going through step 2 is not possible either for financial or for political reasons, a protectionist environment, for example. Except for these two cases, the development scheme is valid. When following such an approach, managers must face two issues:

☆ will the firm benefit from the diversification?

☆ are the necessary resources available?

A Strategic Analysis of Diversification Policies

The answer to the first question must be given in relation to a strategy of specialization. It results from a two-fold analysis of the appeal of the present business (growth potential, present and future competitive structure, profit estimates) and of the present and future competitive position of the firm (i.e. its capacity to control the key factors of success within its resource allocation scheme). This typical strategic analysis makes it possible to determine the priorities strategic direction, that is to say those markets which give the best chances of development and high return given a certain level of risk.* The financial assessment (profitability and financial requirements) of these strategies determines the financial balance, considering the financial strengths and structure of the firm. The need for and the objectives of any diversification strategy must then be weighed against these strategic and financial analyses.

It is clear then, that the decision to diversify has to be taken with caution. Two major elements have to be examined carefully:

(1) The Urgency. The degree of urgency as far as it can be assessed from the point of view of the firm. The stronger the competitive position is, the less necessary the diversification appears to be for the development and the survival of the firm.

(2) The Resources. The resources available to achieve diversification and the level of risk which it involves. The better the competitive position is, the greater the chances are for the company to build up financial surpluses and the wider are the opportunities for diversification. Also the better the starting position, the less risk will be encountered.

This analysis leads us to conclude that a diversification strategy is easier for the corporation which does not really need it and vice versa. Diversification is indeed a strategic step which should be recommended only to companies which can produce good credentials and have firm strongholds in their original activities.

Four Types of Diversification

Diversification strategies have different objectives. Indeed, each objective corresponds to a specific strategic position.

As with business portfolio analysis it is possible to classify the different diversification projects according to two criteria: the *Competitive Position* and *Maturity* of the original business. These two criteria describe the strategic and financial situation of the firm.

Each period of the product life cycle requires a different strategy orientation. Two of these phases have to be given careful attention by the manager and raise directly the question of diversification: Maturity and Decline. In the Start Up or Growth phase, a diversification strategy may also be necessary if the firm is in a poor competitive situation.

On the other hand, a firm which has a dominant market share, should avoid diversification providing the business is growing, because in a highly competitive situation, the competitive structure of an industry is fluid when the market is growing rapidly. In such a situation, high investment is important to secure the firm's strategic position. In a market reaching maturity a strong competitive position is likely to generate a great amount of cash which will allow diversification. On the contrary a bad competitive position is often accompanied by financial difficulties and low profitability. In terms of objectives the differences in competitiveness produce important differences between firms. Four major types of diversification can be observed (see Figure 1).

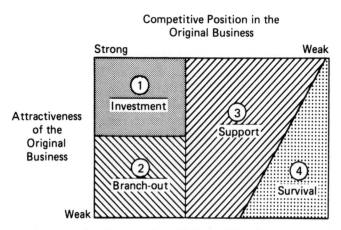

Figure 1. The four types of diversification

Type 1. Investment Diversification

Only firms with a good market position are concerned with investment diversification. If the original business remains attractive it will be necessary to make further investments to maintain a leading position. In that case it will reduce the financial resources available for diversification. The risk of diversification, at the stage when the growth of the business and securing a leading position still requires increasing investment, lies in dissipating financial resources which might be required to support the firm's competitive position in its original business.

The range of diversification varies according to the importance of the financial surplus. If it is massive, the firm has as its disposal sufficient resources to acquire a whole set of new skills. Investment is the only way to fill in the gap of competence between the company and its competitors. However, if the firm has limited financial surpluses the management will find it advantageous to aim at a sector in which its original distinctive competence can be used. The initial investment to achieve the required level of competence will not be so high. A firm's financial strength increases the number of opportunities available to it. Having the ability to invest in any business the corporation will be able to aim for the most profitable activities. The internal return on investment is indeed the first criterion which is taken into account in this kind of diversification. The profit rate must obviously be higher than what it would be if the firm decided to reinvest in its traditional activity.

One technical aspect must now be examined. It concerns the legal form of the investment. Most of the time the firm will look for a majority or a minority interest. Other approaches are of course possible, such as the creation of an affiliate company. But the problem is to distinguish between an industrial investment and a financial investment. In our analysis, a financial investment, especially if it takes the form of a minority interest, is considered as part of a diversification policy only if the firm has access to new skills, that is, only if it becomes a partner in an industrial joint-venture. That kind of decision is irreversible in the sense that it would be extremely expensive for the firm to pull out. From a legal point of view the investment participation must be sufficiently important to enable the investing company to control the decision process.*

Type 2. Branching Out Diversification

'Branching out' diversification is an interesting strategy for companies operating in businesses which are approaching maturity. Diversification, in this case, is a substitute for growth because the original activity of the firm is entering its decline phase. 'Branching out' diversification is then part of a medium- and long-term development plan. The choice of the activities will take into account mainly their growth rate potential rather than their immediate profit return. Depending on the time horizon, within which the new business portfolio will be operating, synergy between the original activity and the new one will more or less important. Because of rapid environmental changes, firms tend more and more to try to turn their existing capabilities into profits straight away.

Mostly this type of diversification is achieved through operations with majority of minority interest. Such a participation is essentially technical. It means that whether majority or minority, the financial interest must enable the management of the firm to control the decision process. Control is vital for the success of the diversification. When branching out is the objective management should always keep in mind that the firm hopes to find a 'cash cow' in this new activity, which means in the long term a higher growth and return than with the traditional activity.

Type 3. Support Diversification

The principal objective of 'support' diversification is to protect the existing activities. The firms concerned are those which have an average competitive position and which are not likely to improve it by investment. By adding a new business to its portfolio the firm tries to enlarge its competitive position. This strategy is similar to product diversification, and does not necessarily imply a change in skills.

The choice of the new activity lies essentially in the efficiency of the synergy between the traditional and the new business. In this situation the question of synergy is vital. Indeed, because of its mediocre competitive position, the firm cannot produce a large financial surplus. Consequently it is necessary to take into account as much as possible the firm's own experience and try to reduce the need for external skills. The use of internal synergy is the only way to satisfy these limitations. What is important in the choice of activity is, once again, the immediate return but the profitability of the new business portfolio, considered as a whole. By choosing such a strategy, the firm hopes to compensate for the lack of experience it faces relatively to its competitors and to improve its overall profitability more than if it decided to increase its specialization. Politics of vertical integration are a good example of support diversification.

Type 4. Survival Diversification

'Survival' diversification enables a firm in a bad competitive position to survive. Because of the firm's poor financial situation, the size of the new business cannot be too large; the organization must consider the need for short-term profitability on the one hand and the growth potential on the other. These two elements are the keys to success in any survival diversification strategy. The operation is extremely delicate because it challenges the existence of the firm itself. More than in any other situation, the process of diversification must be carefully controlled. As far as possible the new business must use the bulk of existing skills within the firm. Also, a majority interest is essential because it must control the activity on which its survival depends.

Diversification and Risk

It is important, when the risk involved by diversification is to be assessed, to differentiate between the risk of the new activity itself and the risk to the firm of finding itself in a worse situation after it has diversified. From this perspective it is necessary to separate the short term from the long term according to the time horizon of the diversification. The Investment and the Branching Out Diversifica-

---

*Malcolin S. Salter and Wolf A. Weinhold, Diversification via acquisition: creating value, *Harvard Business Review*, July (1980).

tion involve relatively limited risk in the short term, but they have important implications for the future of the company. A firm which makes a bad choice of activity may damage its financial strength in the long run. On the contrary, Survival Diversification has to face only a short-term risk; in the long term the risk is minimum because in its initial situation the firm was dying.

Too often, many factors: the personality of the managers, their technical training, the corporate identity, etc. which determine the attitude of the firm towards diversification, may prevent it from making the right changes in activity at the right moment or lead it to certain types of diversification which correspond neither to its needs nor to the resources available. For example some companies in a weak position make Financial or Branching Out investments when they do not have the means to pursue such a policy in the long run.

Diversification is neither the privilege nor the prerogative of the wealthiest firms: the strategy is open to everyone. But each step of the decision process must be carefully examined in order to minimize the risks of failure. These steps are given below:

The Diversification Decision Process

Step 1.	Thorough understanding of the business and expertise of the firm: distinctive skills and key factors for success;
Step 2.	Growth rate and potential for the activity;
Step 3.	Definition of the main elements of the competitive environment: understanding of the relevant market and study of the competitive position of the firm;
Step 4.	Study of the strategic consequences of this diagnosis, especially in terms of financial results;
Step 5.	Definition of the key strategic orientations: the choice between specialization and diversification.

It is a Long Way to a Successful Diversification

Once the strategic choice of diversification has been made, it has to be implemented very carefully, because throughout the decision-making process, many difficulties arise. Indeed, it is during the implementation that the chances of failure are the highest. The decision process followed by companies clearly indicates that certain steps are compulsory, the logical sequence of which enables the firm to have the best chance of avoiding future difficulties. The analysis of case studies reveals that very often inadequacies exist. They usually concern the neglect of strategic variables or more generally,

psychological and organizational factors which relate to the identity of the firm and are not taken into account. These omissions may cause important setbacks although the solutions may seem obvious to the managers.

Five Rules for Success

Rule 1. Make the Management Aware of the Importance of the Diversification Decision

The project receives its first outline and must overcome the barriers to acceptance throughout the line of command of the firm. Two elements have to be taken into account: the external influences and the internal driving forces. At this stage of the process, some firms take a risky position under the pressure of these external influences: the 'me-too' attitude has dangerous consequences. To follow in other people's footsteps has never been a sensible strategy. The internal driving forces are of two kinds: the technical and the strategic forces. The psychological reasons are not so often mentioned. Nevertheless, they sometimes appear to be decisive especially in small firms. Many interviews have led us to the conclusion that the initial decision to diversify originates in feelings of *frustration* in relation to competitors, of *aggressiveness* towards the environment which is considered as hostile, and sometimes of *pleasure*. Thus, for example, in a sub-contracting company, with a good competitive position in a growing market, the sub-contracting activity was perceived as unrewarding by the managers as well as by all of the personnel. The decision to diversify therefore appeared as a means to achieve independent production.

Such feelings encourage managers to diversify and to proceed with diversification immediately. Obviously, the firm must build its future on its specific and distinctive skills and not on inspiration, hazard or mimicry.

During this initial phase, which is often disregarded, a lack of thorough strategic thinking is to be common. Certain firms begin a diversification process when a careful analysis of their financial and strategic requirements would lead them to employ their finances to secure growth in their original market and to protect their competitive position. Other firms diversify on a basis which has nothing to do with their traditional skills and distinctive competences.

Rule 2. Ensure that the Firm has the Skills Suited to Market Needs

A company seeks diversification projects which will enable it to capitalize on its specific skills, either technical or commercial, by maximizing the synergy effects. During this second phase, 'prototypes' will be elaborated. It is therefore necessary to have a research department within the firm as well as an organization to study the market opportunities. In general, technical assessments are made in a

Stages of Process	Key Issue	Factors for Success	Factors for Failure
1 Awareness of Need to Diversify	Separation of Internal and External Influences	Carefully Analyse Strategic Requirements	Rely on Chance or Inspiration
2 Search of a New Business	Keep Close to Present Know-how	Get the Commitment of the Operational Executives	Force the Diversification Decision Upon the People Below
3 In Depth Analysis and Tests	Understand the New Market Characteristics	Focus on the Real Size of Geographical Area	Overestimate Salesforce Potential
4 Starting Operations	Identification of the Point of No-return	Be Careful to Get the Required Competences	Eagerness to Obtain Profitable Results Too Fast
5 Ongoing Management of Operations	Face Potential Reactions of Corporate Identity	Protect and Defend the New Business	Consider that New and Old Business Should be Managed the Same Way

Figure 2. Diversification: the key factors for success

complete and detailed manner but that this is not the case for the marketing studies. This is all the more true when the manager of the firm considers its activity as the application of a particular technology. Usually, the objective is to develop technology or know-how.

In analysis of the market and competition, the major deficiencies which are traditionally found are as follows:

☆ *ignorance of the real size of the market* and the underestimation of the competitive structure, which makes the profitability calculations, and thus the choice of investments, extremely hazardous;

☆ *a poor knowledge of the consumers' needs* which leads practically always to supplementary research study costs. Very often, the necessity of having a complete product line is not really perceived;

☆ *underestimation of the costs and limits to distribution.* It is certainly the most difficult obstacle to surmount. To a large extent, it explains part of the difference between the anticipated and the effective profitability;

☆ *overestimating the savings to be obtained by the use of their commercial synergies.* Usually, when the firms diversify by offering a new product to their customers they think they can do so by using their existing sales force. Such a solution is all the more tempting as the new and original products are closely connected. Unfortunately, it is extremely difficult to foresee such phenomena.

Next, the compatibility between the objectives and the resources which the firm is able to devote to the diversification project has to be carefully examined. What is the investment required? How many people should be employed? Generally speaking what are the human and financial resources required to implement the project? This step is essential, for it is not uncommon to find an average of 60 per cent underestimation of the resources needed. As a result more than 60 per cent of the firms interviewed achieved poorer results than they had expected, in terms of sales as well as profit. The underestimation of the task of the firm is all the more important as the new project may seem easy to implement from a *technical* point of view. Because of limited human resources in smaller firms, which do not have much time to devote to a thorough study of various diversification opportunities, the choice is generally reduced to a Yes or No decision. Alternative projects are rare. Because of these reasons small firms seldom envisage a diversification via acquisition; it usually stems from the firm itself.

Rule 3. Test Before Going Broadscale
This is the point where the project will be tested. This third phase is the moment to assess the size of the market, to determine the reactions of potential customers and to examine the problems of the production process. It is the last chance for the managers to acquire the necessary skills and to test their capacity to adapt to the new project while limiting the risks. Obviously, the duration of the test phase varies, depending on the firm and on the activity. It is often the source of disillusion for the finishing touches are always the most difficult to

make. Of course, one of the conclusions that can be drawn from this third step is that the diversification project is not feasible. In this case other research studies must be carried out, but because of the failure of the first proposal, the alternative projects must be examined with particular care.

Rule 4. Identify the Point of No Return
This is the time for investment in the production, administrative and human resources. It is also the time when the most important problems will be faced, for the firm has gone beyond the turning point:

☆ *in marketing,* the choice of the distribution channels and of the sales force has to be made and the sales prices have to be fixed;

☆ *in finance* a solution has to. be found to cash flow problems as well as to the financing of the working capital;

☆ *in accounting,* cost accounting must be developed for the new product, accounts must be opened for the new customers and suppliers;

☆ *in the organization* many human problems may arise from the conflict between persons working on the original and the new products.

Rule 5. Take Account of the Human Problems and the Corporate Identity
All of the difficulties and conflicts brought on by the commencement of a new activity have to be solved at once. The analysis of successful diversifications shows clearly that these problems and conflicts had been anticipated and that a procedure to solve them had been previously thought through. In particular, the system of control for the original activity may not be adapted to evaluate the new business. Consequently, the diversification may appear to be a total loss before it has had the chance to reveal its profitability, especially since the point at which the business breaks even is not always as early as was expected. What kind of organization must be established? What system should be used to control the new activity? Is it necessary to appoint a Product Manager? What is the relevant legal form? All these practical problems will have to be dealt with during this last phase of the diversification process. The answers which are given will determine to a large extent the success or the failure of the diversification.

The start up of the new business will inevitably disturb the management, the production and the human relations system of the traditional activity. These disturbances are usually taken into account much too late in the fifth step. The integration of the new business into the existing organization, its total separation, or its affiliation are solutions which have to be examined carefully; otherwise the capacity of the organization to adapt to its new markets is likely to be questioned and the diversification may be progressively edged out. Indeed it is vital to protect the new business being cannibalized by the tradi-

tional activities. Of course total separation is often difficult, almost impossible, because the diversification is based on complementarities, on technical and commercial synergies which mean that the same factors of production, and the same sales force is being used. The lack of thinking observed in the field of organizational and managerial problems results in a situation in which the system of control considers the diversification too much as a traditional activity: in this case, the new activity faces a terrible handicap.

The Corporate Identity

Throughout the decision process, an important role is played by certain factors such as the training of the management, their conception of diversification, the personality of the managers, etc. These elements, which serve as filters, are the components of the corporate identity.

The identity of the firm is the point of convergence of three images:*

Image 1. The image that every employee has of the company. The understanding of the firm's activity, which follows the perception of its mission, will play a decisive role in the motivation of the employees in implementing the new strategy.

Image 2. The image which the staff have of their working group and of the networks of influence and power. This is related to the personality of the existing managers but also with the image of the staff who will have to work in the new activity. The changes involved in diversification have a good chance of disrupting the balance between the different groups and of generating fear and uncertainty in the face of a new distribution of power. That particular factor has to be carefully taken into account along with the decision process in order to avoid slowing down the implementation of the diversification strategy.

Image 3. The image that the members of the company have of the professional and ethical qualities required to carry out their task. The internal values of the firm are in question here.

The firm's identity is not an abstract concept, unrelated to its strategy and organization. In the case of diversification, in particular, it will find a source of regeneration in the new project. It is indeed thanks to or because of, this strategy that the firm will stay, or will not stay, or will not stay, faithful to its mission. The relationship between the strategy and the identity of the firm appears clearly when one examines diversifications which succeed and fail. The former usually benefited from a positive identity and the latter had to try to overcome a conflicting identity.

*Jean-Pierre Nioche et Bernard Ramanantsoa, Decision and corporate identity, *Strategic Management Society,* Paris (1983).

These negative attitudes arise from the perception of the traditional product or of what is called 'the style of the house'. They appear every time the new products are perceived as too different from the original production of the firm; each time, the internal values are questioned. The three images of which the identity consists are no longer in harmony with the strategy. There is loss of interest, employees point to the 'traitors', i.e. those who agree to work in the new activity. There may be a general desire to stop the diversification strategy from being implemented, although it may be necessary or even vital for the continued existence of the firm. It is mainly between step one, Awareness and two, Research and Development, that the filter of identity will play a decisive role: beyond the know-how and the ability to do something, there is a *will* to do. All the projects which do not respect the identity of the firm, take the risk of being rejected. This will indeed strengthen the original image the personnel have of what the company should or should not do. The conflicting identities are often found in firms where the fundamental values proceed from high technology or thorough specialization.

The driving identities are, on the contrary, centered on the personality of the executive manager, 'one has to follow the leader', or originate from the overall sense of superiority over the environment 'we have the power to do everything'. The risks involved in that kind of attitude are exactly the opposite of the previous one: a belief that anything can be accepted across the board without any detailed strategic financial or marketing analysis. When the firm's identity is supported by the general manager, which is often the case in smaller companies, the diversification project needs only to be desired and begun by the boss for it to be accepted by everyone without discussion. The risks are naturally those inherent to a lack of strategic analysis but also in underestimating the necessity to modify certain structures and management procedures. Similarly, in the firms where 'everything is possible provided there is the will to do it', the identity works as a distorting filter which may lead to underestimating the strength of a competitor, ignoring the effects of growth on the financial commitments, and miscalculating the research and development costs and the distribution costs.

The identity of the firm is a fundamental factor which managers have to examine carefully, especially when they wish to make an important strategic change such as diversification.

Environmental change, the strategic and competitive position, the decision processes, the organization structure and the corporate identity of the firm are important factors which managers have to take into account when they begin a diversification process. In a time of crisis, increasing uncertainty, and dramatic changes, it is one of the ways to ensure the firm's survival. But the process is difficult and complex to manage. It is, indeed, a long way to a successful diversification.

Bibliography

(1) Corporate Strategy

D. F. Abel, *Defining the Business: the Starting Point of Strategic Planning,* Prentice Hall (1980).

D. F. Abel, et J. S. Hammond, *Strategic Market Planning—Problems and Analytical Approaches,* Prentice Hali (1979).

H. I. Ansoff, *Strategie du développement de l'entreprise,* Hommes et Techniques (1971).

Boston Consulting Group, *Perspectives sur la stratégie d'entreprise,* Hommes et Techniques (1974).

Boston Consulting Group, *Les mécanismes fondamentaux de la compétitivité,* Hommes et Techniques (1980).

J. P. Detrie et B. Ramanantsoa, *Stratégie de l'entreprise et diversification,* Nathan (1983).

C. W. Hofer, *Strategy Formulation: Analytical Concepts,* West, St Paul, MN (1978).

M. Leontiades, *Management Policy, Strategy and Plans,* Little Brown (1982).

A. Martinet, *Stratégie,* Vuibert (1983).

F. Paris, *Missions stratégiques de l'équipe dirigeante,* Dunod (1980).

M. E. Porter, *Choix stratégiques et concurrence,* Economica (1982).

J. Savary, *Les multinationales françaises,* PUF (1981).

J. C. Tarondeau, *Produits et technologies: choix politiques de l'entreprise industrielle,* Paris, Dalloz (1982).

(2) Corporate Identity

J. Ardoino, *Management ou commandement,* Epi (1970).

C. Argyris, *Participation et organisation,* Dunod (1974).

G. Asplund, *An Integrated Development Strategy,* Wiley, Chichester (1982).

S. B. Bacharach and E. J. Lawler, *Power and Politics in Organizations,* Jossey-Bass (1980).

R. Beckard, *Le développement des organisations, sa pratique, ses perspectives et ses problèmes,* Dalloz (1975).

F. Bourricaud, *Esquisse d'une théorie de l'autorité,* Plon (1961).

T. E. Deal and A. A. Kennedy, *Corporate Cultures,* Addison-Wesley (1982).

M. Fourcault, *Surveiller et punir,* N.R.F. (1975).

A. Jardim, *The first Henry FORD,* MIT Press (1970).

P. Jarniou, *L'entreprise comme système politique,* PUF (1982).

R. Kaes, *L'appareil psychique groupal,* Dunod (1976).

G. Lapassade, *Groupes, Organisations, Institutions,* Gauthier Villars (1974).

J. P Larcon et R. Reitter, *Structures de pouvoir et identité de l'entreprise,* Nathan (1979).

H. Levinson, *L'art de diriger,* Publi Union (1971).

C. Levy-Strauss, *L'identité,* Grasset (1977).

W. Ollins, *Corporate Identity,* Heinemann (1979).

M. Pages et al., *L'emprise de l'organisation,* PUF (1979).

P. Selznik, *Leadership in Administration,* Harper and Row (1957).

A. Zaleznik, *Human Dilemmas of Leadership,* Harper and Row (1966).

A. Zaleznik et M. Ketz de Vries, *Power and the Corporate Mind,* Houghton Mifflin (1975).

Section Five

New Ventures and Small Business

Strategic Management: New Ventures and Small Business

Professor Arnold C. Cooper, Krannert Graduate School of Management, Indiana

This paper examines the factors influencing the formulation and implementation of strategy in new and small firms. Small businesses vary substantially in their resource positions, the goals of their founders and their potential. They also vary in stage of development: thus strategic management is examined separately in the start-up stage, the early-growth stage, and the later-growth stage. Intracorporate entrepreneurship in established firms is also considered. Despite this diversity, small firms create an environment for strategic management in which both the opportunities and constraints are different from those in large organizations.

New and small firms provide a distinctive environment for the formulation and implementation of strategy. This paper, based upon a review of the literature, examines the processes by which strategy is developed in such firms and the nature of the resulting strategies. Because new ventures within established firms have many of the characteristics of new and small businesses, strategic management within this context will also be considered.

Most firms in the United States, the United Kingdom, and other Western countries are small. For instance, about 95 per cent of all U.S. firms have fewer than 20 employees.[1] However, the diversity among these small firms is enormous, so that statements which are descriptive of some do not apply to others. They differ in types of founders, in management sophistication, in stage of development, and in performance. Vesper has suggested that small firms might be classified as 'mom and pop' companies, stable high-payoff companies, and growth-oriented companies.[2]

By far the majority of small businesses would be classified as mom and pop firms, particularly in retailing and service industries. Many have no hired employees and rely only on the proprietor or members of the family. Their founders often lack formal managerial training, but may have technical skills, such as being able to sell real estate, cut hair, or do automobile repairs. Capital barriers to entry are usually low, management methods intuitive, and profits moderate or low. Start-ups and discontinuances are frequent and the founders often move from blue-collar or clerical jobs to entrepreneurship and back again. Some such places of business need revolving doors, not for the few customers, but for the entrepreneurs who come and go.

Some small retail and service firms and a higher percentage of small manufacturing firms might be classified as stable, high-payoff companies. Their founders often have more formal education and higher expectations than the mom and pop founders. Often they enjoy strong competitive positions deriving from specialized know-how, patents, or a virtual monopoly in a particular local market. Management methods, although informal by large company standards, may be very effective. Without the pressures of growth, the founder may be able to engage in civic activities or achieving a lower golf handicap, while maintaining a high standard of living.

Growth-oriented small firms offer the possibility of high payoff through selling out, through floating public issues of stock, or through controlling a large enterprise. They are started more often by groups, with the founders usually having had managerial experience. Their strategies usually position them in growing markets or involve innovative methods or products which give them clear competitive advantages. However, their growth may impose heavy demands on the founders, in personal commitments and the need to take risks. Capital requirements may bring outside investors and loss of control. Management methods may change to such a degree that the original founders must be replaced.

Arnold C. Cooper is a professor at the Krannert Graduate School of Management, Purdue University, West Lafayette, Indiana 47907, U.S.A.

...fluid and it is certainly
...ve from one category to
...ral, these types of firms
...rces, follow different
...ve different internal
...ation and implemen-

...hich strategy is managed also
...stage of development of the small
...this paper, we shall think of three stages:

(1) *the start-up stage*, including the strategic decisions to found a firm and to position it within a particular industry with a particular competitive strategy;

(2) *the early-growth stage*, when the initial product-market strategy is being tested and when the president maintains direct contact with all major activities (many firms stabilize at this stage);

(3) *the later-growth stage*, often characterized by multiple sites for retail and service businesses and by some diversification for manufacturing firms; organizationally the firm usually has one or more levels of middle-management and some delegation of decision-making.

All of the types of firms just considered pass through the start-up stage and, if they are successful, move on to an early-growth stage. However, only the growth-oriented firms are likely to be found in the later-growth stage.

As a firm grows, at what point is it no longer small? Any answer to this question is somewhat arbitrary, but the focus here, even for firms in the later-growth stage, is upon organizations with less than 500 employees.

Strategic Management in the Start-up Stage

The decision to found a new firm is, in every sense, a strategic decision by the entrepreneur. It involves non-routine decisions to commit major resources to create a particular new business at a particular time and place. The new business then has a strategy (which may or may not have been carefully considered); it provides selected goods or services to particular markets and it emphasizes (whether wisely or not) particular policies to provide a way of competing.

The decision to found a new firm seems to be influenced by three broad factors.[3] They are:

(1) the entrepreneur, including the many aspects of his background which affect his motivations, his perceptions, and his skills and knowledge;

(2) the organization for which the entrepreneur had previously been working, whose charac-

teristics influence the location and the nature of new firms, as well as the likelihood of spin-offs; and

(3) various environmental factors external to the individual and his organization, which make the climate more or less favorable to the starting of a new firm.

Of these factors, the characteristics of the entrepreneur have been most extensively examined. Psychological research suggests that entrepreneurs have a high need for achievement and a belief that they can control their own fate.[4] One group of manufacturing entrepreneurs was characterized as having had poor relations with their fathers, their teachers and their employers. They seemed to be driven to entrepreneurship by their need to avoid being in a subordinate relationship to others.[5] A number of studies have shown that entrepreneurs often come from families where the father or a close relative was in business for himself.[6,7] Some sub-groups of societies have higher rates of entrepreneurship than others; young members of such sub-groups (such as the Chinese in South-East Asia or the Indians in East Africa) are surrounded by 'role-models' of entrepreneurship. They may also choose this career path because other career paths are closed to them in the larger society.[8] The thrust of these findings is that some people, by virtue of their family background and early childhood influences, are much more likely to start businesses. However, entrepreneurial inclinations, like musical talent, may or may not be capitalized upon. A number of other factors, discussed below, interact to create a climate more or less favorable to starting a new business.

The typical entrepreneur with technical or managerial training starts his business when he is in his thirties.[9,10] It is then that he has the track record, experience, and savings to make founding feasible, while still having the energy level and willingness to take risks which are necessary. Thus, the conditions which exist when potential technical entrepreneurs are in their thirties, including the organizations they then work for and the environmental climate then extant, determine whether they will be likely to found new businesses. However, evidence on the founders of mom and pop firms suggest a wider range of ages at the time of founding.[11]

A second major factor influencing whether a potential entrepreneur will start a new business is the nature of the organization for which he works. This organization, which might be termed an incubator, seems to play a particularly important role in the founding of high technology firms. It locates the potential founder in a particular geographic area which may or may not have a favorable entrepreneurial climate. (A number of studies have shown that most entrepreneurs start their businesses where they are already living and working; it is the rare founder who moves at the time he is starting a new business.)[12]

The incubator organization also provides the entrepreneur with the experience which leads to particular managerial skills and industry knowledge. Since industries vary widely in the extent to which they offer opportunities for new ventures, this means that the strategy of the incubator organization determines to a great extent whether its employees will ever be in a position to spin off and start their own businesses. Thus an established organization in a mature industry with little growth and heavy capital requirements is unlikely to have many spin-offs. Its employees, no matter how motivated, are not acquiring the technical and market knowledge which can easily be translated into the strategic decision to start a new business.

The policies of potential incubator organizations also appear to determine, to a marked degree, the motivations of the entrepreneur. In brief surveys such as questionnaires, founders tend to report the socially acceptable reasons as to why they became entrepreneurs; these include such factors as the desire for independence and financial gain. However, depth interviews often disclose that the founder was 'pushed' from the parent organization by frustration.[3] Studies of spin-off rates from established organizations show that internal factors influence spin-off rates, with internal problems being associated with high rates of spin-off and placid times being associated with low rates.[9] Thus, the extent to which the strategic and operating decisions of the established firm satisfy or frustrate its employees influences whether spin-offs occur.

A complex of factors external to the individual and to the parent organization also appears to influence entrepreneurship. Much of the research in this area is only suggestive, but it seems that climates can change over time and that past entrepreneurship makes future entrepreneurship more likely. The credibility of the act of starting a company appears to depend, in part, upon whether the founder knows of others who have taken this step.[7] Venture capital availability and particularly the existence of well-developed communication channels vary across geographic regions and help to determine the feasibility of entrepreneurship. The presence of experienced entrepreneurs also influences future entrepreneurship; they serve as sources of advice and venture capital and they sometimes do what they know best—start additional new businesses.[3,13] Their companies become excellent incubators for other spin-offs and also offer consulting opportunities for fledgling founders who are seeking income while trying to get started. It seems clear that past entrepreneurship influences the climate for future entrepreneurship. What is not so clear and what deserves additional research is how an area begins to become enterpreneurially active or how an area which has been active becomes less so.

The three broad factors just discussed influence the entrepreneurial decision as summarized in Figure 1.

The Competitive Strategy of the New Firm
The decision to start a new firm is clearly a strategic decision. However, also of interest here is the cluster of decisions which determine the nature of the new business, including the products of services to be offered, the markets to be served, and the policies to be emphasized. What has been learned about the influences upon these decisions in the new firm and about the relationship between particular strategies and performance?

Since the new business draws primarily upon the knowledge and skills of the entrepreneur, one might expect that the product/market choice would be closely tied to the experience gained in the incubator organization. For the most part this is true, although it varies by industry. New companies are closely related to the nature of the business of the parent firms for about 80–85 per cent of high technology firms; for nontechnical manufacturing and service firms, the corresponding percentages are 50–55 per cent.[9,11,14] For new franchises, the percentage is probably very low,

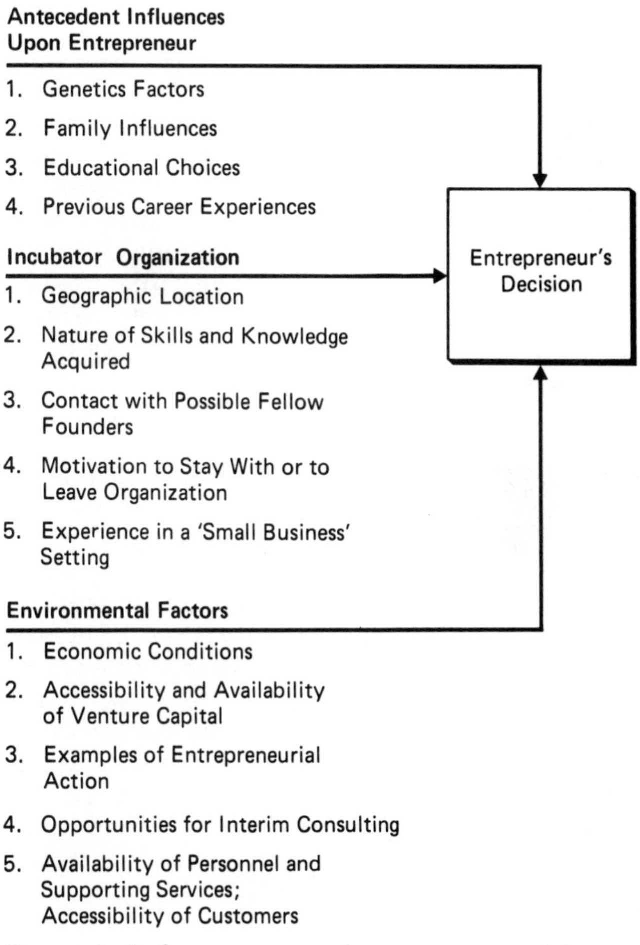

Antecedent Influences Upon Entrepreneur

1. Genetics Factors
2. Family Influences
3. Educational Choices
4. Previous Career Experiences

Incubator Organization

1. Geographic Location
2. Nature of Skills and Knowledge Acquired
3. Contact with Possible Fellow Founders
4. Motivation to Stay With or to Leave Organization
5. Experience in a 'Small Business' Setting

Environmental Factors

1. Economic Conditions
2. Accessibility and Availability of Venture Capital
3. Examples of Entrepreneurial Action
4. Opportunities for Interim Consulting
5. Availability of Personnel and Supporting Services; Accessibility of Customers

Entrepreneur's Decision

Figure 1. Influences upon the entrepreneurial decision

since the franchisor supplies the expertise rather than the founder.

Although there has not been much explicit research on how the founder decides upon a business strategy, we can draw some inferences from general descriptions of the process and from case studies. For larger, more professionally-based ventures, and particularly for those seeking venture capital, there typically is a new business plan. Such a plan describes the way in which the proposed firm is to compete and often reflects considerable thought. For that much larger group of new ventures which start without the discipline of seeking outside capital from professional sources, the process of deciding upon a basis of competition seems to be informal and intuitive. It may be based upon an excellent, first-hand 'feel' for the market. However, many new service businesses of the mom and pop type seem to be started opportunistically, with the availability of particular facilities or sites being important determinants.[11]

We don't know very much about the relationships between characteristics of founders, the strategies of their firms, and subsequent performance. There has been some research on high technology firms, though, which suggests that successful new firms are more likely to be started by multiple founders, have more initial capital, transfer more technology from the parent organization, are more likely to have a marketing function, show greater concern for personnel matters, and are more likely to have spun-off from large organizations than from small ones.[15,16] With regard to strategy, those new high technology firms whose strategies were related to the parent firms, in markets served and technology utilized, were more likely to be successful. In addition, longitudinal study of 95 new manufacturing firms indicated that those judged to be successful were more likely to have been started by two or more founders and more likely to have founders with both relevant experience and post high school education.[14]

Strategic Management in the Early Growth Stage

As the new firm becomes established, the founder typically continues to be in direct contact with all activities and decisions. Many businesses of modest potential stabilize at this point, often with no hired employees. Other firms continue to grow, adding employees and sometimes additional management. At this time the founder or founders may delegate operating decisions, but not strategic decisions. Management methods continue to be informal, with few policies and with control exercised primarily through direct contact.

As the new business gets started, it immediately begins to receive 'feedback' from the market.

Sometimes, the assumptions underlying the new firm's strategy prove to be faulty, and the firm seems likely to run out of cash before reaching the break-even point. It appears that founders often change their strategies at this point. Thus, an electronics component manufacturer switches to sub-contract work or an ice-cream shop becomes a steak-house. The entrepreneur has the opportunity to change quickly at this point; there is no organization to convince and there is little commitment to the status quo. However, much will depend upon how the entrepreneur perceives the environment, whether he perceives it as it really is or as he would like to see it.[17] Founders are sometimes stubborn people with a dream and not really amenable to dispassionate analysis of their plans.

As the new firm becomes established, the extent to which management confronts strategic decisions varies with the kind of firm and the characteristics of its industry. For the mom and pop business in a stable environment, the focus is usually upon operating decisions. Whether the strategy is re-examined and whether opportunities are then pursued appears to depend on the characteristics of management. In experiments conducted in India, owner-managers who had received achievement-motivation training frequently investigated or undertook changes in strategy.[18]

For those businesses which grow to become what we have classified as stable, high payoff firms or growth-oriented firms, there are decisions associated with evolving successful strategies. However, we lack systematic research to indicate whether these firms have high-potential strategies from the time of founding or whether these strategies evolve from the feedback of the market place. One study of 270 manufacturing firms indicated that companies which achieved annual sales of $100,000 or more in sales did so in their first 10 years; old small companies usually didn't grow.[19] The firms in this sample also showed great stability in their strategies, with only one in twelve making substantial product changes in a 9 year period.

There is substantial 'wisdom-based' literature analyzing the characteristics of small firms and suggesting the most suitable strategies. Small firms, particularly in the early stages, have limited financial and human resources. They have almost no reputation and little in the way of economies of scale or benefits from experience curves. There is a concentration of risk in one or a few products, markets, and people; there is usually no cushion to absorb the results of bad luck or bad decisions. The capabilities of the new firm are often uneven, reflecting the unbalanced experience of the entrepreneur.

Against these disadvantages, the new firm has no

ties to the past; it can innovate, without worrying about the effect on existing sales. This, coupled with the talents and drive of the founding group, is undoubtedly one reason why new and small firms have been such remarkably fertile sources of technical innovation, accounting for major new innovations all out of proportion to their R & D expenditures.[20] (Of course, most small firms are not particularly innovative; it is the growth-oriented small firms which are most likely to have this characteristic.) New firms also have the ability to move quickly; the chain of command is short and decision methods are informal and, if not carefully documented, at least timely. Management often has a first-hand 'feel' for the realities of customers and operations, based not upon the abstractions of reports, but upon day-to-day contact. Small firms also can avoid the departmentalization and co-ordination problems which characterize large, complex organizations. There may be a lack of staff specialists and formalized analysis, but there is the opportunity to focus the attention of the organization upon opportunities. The small organization, with its shared sense of the need to survive, can create a cost consciousness and dedication which are difficult to achieve in large, profitable firms where each individual knows that his contributions are only a small part of the whole. Of course, in all instances these are potential advantages which may or may not be realized, depending upon the competence and commitment of management.

To summarize the advice of most writers, it would be that the small firm should choose a 'niche' and avoid direct competition with larger companies. Some would modify this advice to say that direct competition is possible, but that the small firm should concentrate on where it has a competitive advantage or where the large firm is complacent or doing a poor job.[21-23] Thus, large firms tend to concentrate on mass markets, so small firms should concentrate on specialized markets. Large firms tend to be slow to react, so small firms should concentrate on opportunities arising from rapid market change. Large firms tend to be organized to produce in large production runs and to offer standardized service. Small firms can concentrate on short production runs, quick delivery and extra service. Large firms must be concerned about whether raw material supplies, work forces, and manufacturing and personnel policies are suitable for large volume operations. Small companies can use scarce materials, locate in areas with small labor forces, and utilize unique approaches, unconcerned about the implications if these were applied throughout a large corporation. Large firms must be concerned about government regulatory attitudes and their visibility to communities and unions. Small firms have a low profile and can move more quickly and be less concerned about the reactions of such groups. The evidence supporting these recommendations is anecdotal and based upon general observation. Much of it appears to be sound, but there is no systematic research examining the strategies of large number of firms and their performance over time.

The process of strategic planning in small firms has received attention in several articles.[24-27] The small firm environment makes heavy demands upon management for day-to-day operations and there are usually no staff specialists to provide support. Explicit efforts to set aside blocks of time for planning and to shield management from day-to-day pressures may be necessary. Structured approaches to the process of planning have been recommended by several authors. Unlike large organizations the emphasis is not upon deciding how to allocate resources among businesses or upon formal planning as a communication mechanism. The primary focus is upon mechanisms for identifying problems and for 'stepping-back' to look at the implications of current strategy. Recognizing the flexibility of small firms, particular emphasis should be placed on short-term planning.[28]

Strategic Management in the Later Growth Stage

Many small businesses stabilize and maintain an environment in which the president is in direct contact with the key activities, possibly with a small management team, each member of which is responsible for a key function. However, growth-oriented small businesses may continue to grow, adding additional levels of management.

The internal environment for management then begins to change, as the sheer volume of activities compels the founder to turn some duties over to others. Typically, the role of the founder changes, with 'doing' activities largely delegated and with the job becoming more managerial in character. Many operating decisions may be delegated, although the president continues to be deeply involved in strategic decisions. One of the distinguishing characteristics of the very small firm, the president's direct contact with employees, with products, and customers, begins to change. More formal ways must be developed to keep management informed and to control operations. Policies must be developed and increased formality occurs. Top managment must try to develop new skills in managing through others and in developing an organization. Some entrepreneurs are not suited for this kind of managerial task and their shortcomings may prevent the firm from growing successfully or may lead to the entrepreneur's departure.

These changes in the internal environment both aid and hamper effective strategic management. The growth in the organization may give the president more time for planning. The growing firm may have more resources to pursue particular activities and to withstand competitors' challenges. However, growth may cause management to 'lose touch'; control of operations may suffer and management's feel for markets, competitors, and organizational capabilities may diminish. Implementation of strategy, which is typically one area where a small firm has a real advantage, becomes more of a problem as the organization grows.

Many growth-oriented small firms seem to be positioned in newly-developing industries. As such, management faces the challenges of adapting strategy to the changing demands of an evolving industry. The strategic implications of industry life cycles become particularly important for these firms.[29] It is widely believed that new industries are characterized by a high rate of new company formation and a high rate of entry by established firms, both small and large. Later, there is often a 'shake-out' as the stronger competitors enlarge their market shares. The extent to which small firms survive and prosper as an industry matures appears to vary widely, but the reasons for these differences have not been examined systematically.

Growth-oriented small firms sometimes owe their success to innovative strategies. A number of authors have commented on how the small firm environment is conducive to innovation, with its informal decision processes in which relatively few executives must be convinced, its lack of commitment to the status quo, its low sales requirements to be successful, and its low costs of development.[20,30] However, the small firm may sometimes pioneer and then be faced with severe competition. It is surprising that there has been very little research on the most appropriate strategies for small firms which have been successful in innovation, but then face severe competition in a growing market.

Strategic Management in Intracorporate Ventures

A number of writers have suggested that large firms seem to be better at developing existing businesses than at growing new ones.[31-33] The large firm can bring great resources to bear upon new opportunities and can absorb failures. However, performance measurement systems often penalize those divisions and executives who assume risks. New ventures can disrupt existing manufacturing and marketing activities. New ventures often require different kinds of people and facilities and an orientation toward working closely with customers, short production runs, and continually changing technology.[34]

An increasing number of corporations have developed new venture departments to facilitate intracorporate entrepreneurship. Two surveys, both published in 1973, indicated that the number of new venture departments was increasing.[35,36] As might be expected, large firms have adopted formal intracorporate entrepreneurship programs to a greater degree than smaller firms. However, more recent research suggests that many new venture departments are short-lived.[34]

New venture department organizations may range from *ad hoc* task forces with no formal training, to departments with established budgets, to separate legal entities. Typically, these intracorporate entrepreneurial groups study proposed ventures and sometimes proceed to start new businesses— developing, producing, and marketing new products. They usually can call upon the resources of the larger organization, although this sometimes presents problems because of lack of authority over other departments. The performance measurement system may be modified to place less emphasis on short-run profits. If the product is promising or becomes firmly established, it may be transferred to an existing department or become the basis for a new department.

Practices vary in the extent to which new ventures are separate, the timing of when products are transferred to the regular organization, and how venture managers are rewarded. An extreme form of venture management might be termed 'sponsored spin-offs' in which, with the parent firm's blessing, a separate new enterprise is created, possibly with the parent company holding some of the equity.[37]

Some of the issues associated with organizing venture management departments include determining how managers are to be rewarded and how their careers are affected if they return to the main organization. Other issues relate to the extent to which they can call upon resources from the main organization and the degree of delegation—the extent to which they can act as if they were managing their own firms.

Research by Fast indicates that new venture departments usually evolve, becoming operating divisions, staff departments, or new venture departments which differ in size, objectives, and corporate impact from their earlier versions.[34] Sometimes the departments are disbanded. The two major influences upon the evolution of a new venture department appear to be the changing nature of the firm's strategy and its political support within the organization.

In general, these approaches have demonstrated some success, but many companies are experimenting with different ways of creating an environment for intracorporate entrepreneurship.

Conclusion

Small businesses differ greatly in their resource positions, the goals of their founders, their stages of development and their potential. Yet, within this diversity, we can note certain common characteristics. These result in an environment for strategic management which creates both constraints and opportunities different from those in large organizations.

Acknowledgements—This paper is adapted from a chapter in D. Schendel and C. Hofer (Eds.), *Strategic Management: A New View of Business Policy*, Little, Brown & Co., 1979.

References

(1) 1967 *Enterprise Statistics, Part 1*. U.S. Government Printing Office, Washington, DC (1972).

(2) LaRue Hosmer, Arnold Cooper and Karl Vesper, *The Entrepreneurial Function*. Prentice-Hall, Inc., Englewood Cliffs (1977).

(3) Arnold Cooper, *The Founding of Technologically-Based Firms*, The Center for Venture Management, Milwaukee (1971).

(4) David McClelland, *The Achieving Society*, C. Van Nostrand, Princeton (1961).

(5) Orvis Collins and David Moore, *The Organization Makers*, Appleton-Century-Crofts, New York (1970).

(6) Edward Roberts and H. Wainer, Some characteristics of new technical enterprises, *IEEE Transactions on Engineering Management*, EM-18 (3) (1971).

(7) Albert Shapero, Entrepreneurship and economic development, *Entrepreneurship and Enterprise Development: A Worldwide Perspective*, Proceedings of Project ISEED, Project ISEED, Ltd. and The Center for Venture Management, Milwaukee (1975).

(8) Everett Hagen, The Transition in Columbia, in *Entrepreneurship and Economic Development*, P. Kilby (Ed.), The Free Press, New York (1971).

(9) Arnold Cooper, Technical entrepreneurship: what do we know? *R & D Management*, 3 (2), February (1973).

(10) Patrick Liles, *New Business Ventures and the Entrepreneur*, Richard D. Irwin, Inc., Homewood (1974).

(11) Kurt Mayer and Sidney Goldstein, *The First Two Years: Problems of Small Firm Growth and Survival*, U.S. Government Printing Office, Washington, D.C. (1961).

(12) Jeffrey Susbauer, The technical entrepreneurship process in Austin, Texas, in *Technical Entrepreneurship: A Symposium*, A. Cooper and J. Komives (Eds.), The Center for Venture Management, Milwaukee (1972).

(13) Lawrence Lamont, What entrepreneurs learn from experience, *Journal of Small Business Management*, July (1972).

(14) William Hoad and Peter Rosko, *Management Factors Contributing to the Success or Failure of New Small Manufacturers*, University of Michigan, Ann Arbor (1964).

(15) Arnold Cooper and Albert Bruno, Success among high-technology firms, *Business Horizons*, 20 (2), April (1977).

(16) Edward Roberts, Influences upon performance of new technical enterprises, in *Technical Entrepreneurship: A Symposium*, A. Cooper and J. Komives (Eds.), The Center for Venture Management, Milwaukee (1972).

(17) Harry Schrage, R & D entrepreneur: profile of success, *Harvard Business Review*, 43 (6), November–December (1965).

(18) David McClelland, Achievement motivation can be developed, *Harvard Business Review*, 43 (6), November–December (1965).

(19) Joseph McGuire, *Factors in the Growth of Manufacturing Firms*, Bureau of Business Research, University of Washington, Seattle (1963).

(20) Robert Charpie and others, *Technological Innovation: Its Environment and Management*, U.S. Government Printing Office, Washington, D.C. (1967).

(21) Alfred Gross, Meeting the competition of giants, *Harvard Business Review*, 45 (3), May–June (1967).

(22) W. Arnold Hosmer, Small manufacturing enterprises, *Harvard Business Review*, 35(6), November–December (1957).

(23) Robert Katz, *Management of the Total Enterprise*, Prentice-Hall, Englewood Cliffs (1970).

(24) Frank Gilmore, Formulating strategy in smaller companies, *Harvard Business Review*, 49 (3), May–June (1971).

(25) Preston LeBreton, *A Guide for Proper Management Planning for Small Business*, Division of Research, College of Business Administration, Louisiana State University, Baton Rouge (1963).

(26) George Steiner, Approaches to long-range planning for small business, *California Management Review*, X (1), Fall (1967).

(27) S. C. Wheelwright, Strategic planning in the small business, *Business Horizons*, XIV (4), August (1971).

(28) Theodore Cohn and Roy Lindberg, *Survival and Growth: Management Strategies for the Small Firm*, Amacom, New York (1974).

(29) Charles Hofer, Toward a contingency theory of business strategy, *Academy of Management Journal*, 18 (4), December (1975).

(30) Arnold Cooper, Small companies can pioneer new products, *Harvard Business Review*, 44 (5), September–October (1966).

(31) Mark Hanan, Venturing corporations—think small to stay strong, *Harvard Business Review*, 54 (3), May–June (1976).

(32) Richard Hill and James Hlavacek, The venture team: a new concept in marketing organization, *Journal of Marketing*, 36 (3), July (1972).

(33) Russell W. Peterson, New venture management in a large company, *Harvard Business Review*, 45 (3), May–June (1967).

(34) Norman Fast, The evolution of corporate new venture divisions, unpublished D.B.A. dissertation, Harvard Graduate School of Business Administration, Boston (1977).

(35) Jeffrey Susbauer, U.S. industrial intracorporate entrepreneurship practices, *R & D Management*, 3 (3), June (1973).

(36) Karl Vesper and Thomas Holmdahl, How venture management fares in innovation companies, *Research Management*, XVI (3), May (1973).

(37) Arnold Cooper and Arthur Riggs, Jr., Non-traditional approaches to technology utilization, *Journal of the Society of Research Administrators*, VI (3), Winter (1975).

The External Corporate Venture Capital Fund—A Valuable Vehicle for Growth

Knut Bleicher and Herbert Paul

Corporate venture capital is becoming an important tool for business development. In addition to attractive financial returns corporate venture capital provides strategic benefits which result from establishing strategic alliances between small entrepreneurial companies and large mature corporations. There are several approaches to corporate venture capital. Each approach requires a different level of commitment with respect to corporate resources and yields specific strategic benefits. At present there appears to be a trend for establishing focused corporate venture capital programmes in co-operation with an external venture capital organization. The successful introduction and management of such a programme require that a few important guidelines are observed.

Venture capital, which is a seminal force for jobs, economic growth and entrepreneurism, is what corporate America supposedly is all about these days. Also, if the investor has the patience and the staying power, no other investment medium in the last 20 years has come close to the returns on venture capital. However, it is not only the financial returns which make venture capital attractive. Its strategic value in forming alliances between small high-tech companies and large mature corporations is becoming ever more important. Some of the largest U.S. corporations are among the participants in various venture capital programmes: Xerox, Monsanto, AT & T, Eastman Kodak, INCO, Standard Oil of Indiana, IBM and General Electric. Since the United States is the world leader in the development and commercialization of technology, foreign corporations are also forging strong links with U.S. venture capital firms. The list of multinational corporations having established such links includes

Siemens, British Petroleum, Rhone-Poulenc, Olivetti, N.V. Philips, BMW and Mitsubishi.

While the importance of innovation is accepted by all corporations, countless dollars and hours spent in attempting to foster innovation internally have often yielded frustratingly poor results.[1] All too frequently large corporations lack the flexibility to respond easily and quickly to transform a new idea into a successful product that provides a corporation with new growth and financial returns. Studies of the National Science Foundation have shown that large established corporations spend their R & D dollars four times less efficiently than do small ones and that between 1953 and 1976 the majority of innovations in the United States have come from small companies with less than 1000 employees.[2]

In view of these findings for many of the large well-established corporations, the perplexing question is: Why is most of the action on the outside with these new upstarts and how can we participate in it ourselves? Clearly, a corporation has several alternatives to participate in new ventures. Besides traditional approaches, such as taking a minority position in one or more of the start-up companies or an outright acquisition, the focus has shifted to various venture capital funds.

Venture Economics, a major consulting organization to the venture capital industry, keeps track of corporate venture capital investing.[3] It reported a decrease for passive venture capital partnership investments from 131 in 1984 to 88 in 1985 (Figure 1).

Many corporations which made passive partnership investments in prior years began establishing strategically oriented corporate venture funds. This trend results from a growing attitude that to remain competitive, large corporations must have a means

Dr Knut Bleicher is Professor of Management at the Graduate School of Business, St. Gall University, Switzerland. Dr Herbert Paul is responsible for the Corporate Venture Capital Programme of F. Hoffmann-La Roche & Co. AG in Basel, Switzerland.

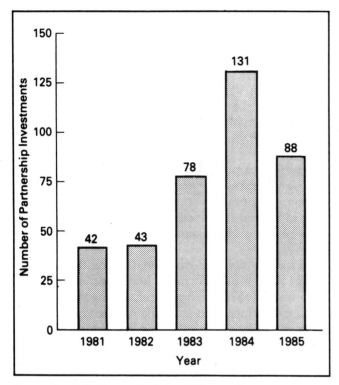

Source: *Trends in Venture Capital,* p. 7, Venture Economics, Wellesley, Massachusetts (1986).

Figure 1. Corporate venture capital—passive partnership investments

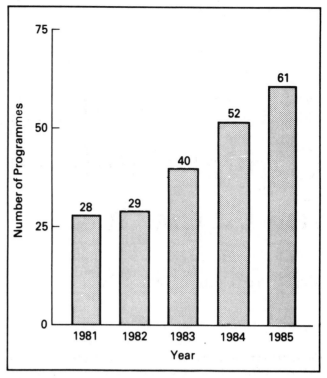

Source: *Trends in Venture Capital,* p. 8, Venture Economics, Wellesley, Massachusetts (1986).

Figure 2. Corporate venture capital—focused corporate programmes

to access the stream of advanced products and new market opportunities developed by small, entrepreneurial companies. At the end of 1985 there were 61 corporate industrial venture capital programmes (Figure 2).

These programmes cover a broad range of industries: computers and electronics, chemicals, medical and pharmaceuticals, telecommunication, oil and gas, defence, automotive, metals, public utilities, construction and industrial products. Of the 61 corporate programmes currently active in the United States, 15 programmes have non-U.S. parents.

Venture Capital Management as a Tool for Corporate Development

When looking at venture capital as a business development tool one can distinguish different approaches. Each alternative requires a certain level of corporate resources and has the potential for yielding specific strategic returns.

Major Corporate Venture Capital Options

There are basically four alternative approaches to corporate venture capital: traditional venture capital partnerships, specialty venture capital funds, internal venture groups and external focused venture programmes.

Traditional venture capital partnerships. The tradi-

tional venture funds focus primarily on financial returns. TA Associates, Kleiner, Perkins, Caufield and Byers as well as Hambrecht & Quist are some of the larger well-known traditional venture capital firms. Corporations, amongst other investors, invest as limited partners in the venture partnership which is managed by experienced venture capitalists. This approach requires a limited financial commitment with the possibility of significant capital appreciation if the fund is well-managed. Even though the investing corporation gets a limited exposure to the technologies of the dozen or more growth companies a venture fund will typically hold in its portfolio, most of these start-ups are of no or little strategic relevance to the corporation. Also the investing corporation has hardly any control over the investment strategy carried out by the fund's management.

Specialty venture capital funds. These funds attempt to attract a clientele that seeks a more tailor-made or special venture capital service. Of the venture capital funds that raised capital from institutional investors in 1983, for example, roughly one half advertised a specialty of which the management team had certain unique delivery skills.[4]

These funds can be set up to provide two benefits to the investing corporations:

(1) The fund invests in a broad spectrum of industries and generates a window on technology to the investors by providing regular reports about the development of the portfolio

companies. Two good examples for this approach are Oxford Partners and Vista Ventures.

(2) The fund can be set up with a very narrow focus on a specific industry such as the Hambrecht & Quist Health and Medical Fund or the Rothchild Life Sciences Fund. These funds are managed by individuals with experience in the industries in which they intend to make investments. The purpose of the fund is to exploit a specific industry trend.

In both cases there are many—sometimes competing—corporate investors which makes it very difficult to realize technology transfer objectives. In addition, services provided to the investing corporation are usually very limited.

Internal corporate venture funds. Towards the end of the 1960s many major U.S. corporations created new venture divisions as a means to stimulate external investments and internal entrepreneurship that would catapult them into new exciting growth areas. But the results have not lived up to such expectations. Most of the new venture divisions sank without a trace before they had a chance to prove their worth.

The biggest problem in using internal venture funds as a diversification tool may lie in reconciling the strategic goals of the large corporation and the independent-minded interests of the small ones. The differences between the informal flexible and entrepreneurially oriented culture of the start-up company and the formal, bureaucratic culture prevalent in most of the large mature corporations certainly contribute to the problems of internal venture divisions. More specifically, there are four major reasons for the failure of internal venture divisions:[5]

(1) Inability to adequately compensate the fund's management, i.e. to enable the venture division's managers to earn equity interests in the portfolio companies. The compensation problem is a major reason why many corporations with an internal venture division were unable to hire qualified venture capital personnel and keep them on the payroll.

(2) Unwillingness to fund the venture division in advance. Corporations generally require that the fund managers obtain funding on a deal-by-deal basis subject to the approval of a corporate executive committee. Without advanced funding, the programme becomes extremely vulnerable to major alternative corporate capital needs or corporate operating problems which generate cash constraints.

(3) Lack of flexibility to find co-investors and work with them in an investment syndicate. This is again a result of working with the often cumbersome and slow-moving corporate decision process.

(4) Major policy changes related to flipping back and forth between different priorities, i.e. realizing various strategic benefits vs financial returns. In addition, frequent reshuffling of senior management has contributed to this problem.

A visible example of the pitfalls in diversification through venture capital was the painful effort by Exxon Corporation to gain a foothold in specific new industries (advanced materials, energy conversion, information systems).

As Exxon's venture division (Exxon Enterprises) grew and required new levels of investment, corporate involvement expanded. Exxon's management procedures and strategic objectives conflicted with the independent start-up environment of the ventures and pushed them toward a more structured, control-oriented mode of operation. After a short period of time, the managements of the ventures were so much driven by controlling and accounting that the environment stimulating development of the non-conventional solutions was lost. Consequently, profitability and growth of the ventures were seriously hampered. About 10 years later Exxon dissolved Exxon Enterprises.[6]

A study by Hardymon, DeNino and Salter concluded that internal venture divisions do not live up to the original goals.[7] The authors recommended that corporations should replicate the conditions of the 'stand alone' venture capital firms as much as possible. By co-operating with these venture capital firms, corporations could realize specific strategic benefits without getting directly involved in the management of the portfolio companies.

To sum up, almost all internal venture funds were financially successful, but most internal funds had major difficulties on the strategic side.[8] However, there are a few exceptions. The programmes of Xerox and Lubrizol are widely considered strategically successful even though both programmes had a relatively long start-up time to resolve the aforementioned problems.

External focused corporate venture funds. Despite the inherent problems of internal venture funds, the idea of using small start-up companies (i.e. their technological and entrepreneurial know-how) to revive mature corporations remains intriguing. Based on the negative experiences of realizing strategic objectives with internal venture funds there appears to be a trend towards more external focused corporate venture funds.[9]

External corporate venture investing generally takes the form of setting-up a limited partnership. The general partner (i.e. the venture capitalist) will manage the partnership's investment portfolio. The investing corporation as the sole limited partner provides the funding and defines the investment charter. Since a typical investment has a time horizon of 5–7 years, most partnerships set 8–10 years as their lifetime. A typical partnership formed today is funded with $15–30m. The general partner is paid an annual management fee of 2·5–3·5 per cent of committed capital and, in addition, receives an incentive allocation of 20 per cent of the partnership's realized net gains. There are several benefits associated with such a fund:

(1) Above-average financial returns.

There has been much written about the financial returns of venture capital. If history is any guide to future performance, the pre-tax internal rate of return on investment for a professionally backed venture capital fund should reach between 20 and 25 per cent.[10]

(2) Identification and initial entry into related and new areas of business.

Strategic benefits refer to the opening of a window on technology which provides continuing intelligence on emerging technologies, possibly causing the corporation to redirect its internal R & D efforts. Equally important, the corporate venture fund can assist the corporation in getting access to new technology and products via licences, joint R & D projects, joint ventures and eventually, acquisitions.

(3) Assistance in spin-outs and divestitures.

The venture fund can also provide an outlet for business opportunities which are created by internal programmes but do not fit in the current or future business strategy of the parent corporation.

(4) Exposure to entrepreneurial practices.

Finally, the corporation may derive benefits from cross-fertilizing skills by interfacing entrepreneurs with corporate managers during the process of evaluating investment opportunities.

An excellent example of a successful external focused venture programme is that of Monsanto, a company in transition from a traditional chemicals producer to a company balanced between chemical sciences, life sciences and engineered materials. Monsanto has by far the largest international venture capital involvement of any corporation in the world, having committed a total of over $100m, with over $10m in Europe alone.[11] Since 1981, Monsanto has become an investor in the network of Advent funds in both Europe and South East Asia. Monsanto used the venture fund successfully to get a window on technology in the bio-technology field. After having monitored this industry for a few years, Monsanto decided to actively support and expand its bio-tech ventures. Today bio-technology is one of Monsanto's most promising growth areas.

Corporate Commitment and Strategic Returns
As the above discussion indicates there is a close relationship between the level of corporate resources (i.e. human resources and capital committed) to a venture capital fund and the potential strategic benefits related to a specific venture capital option. The potential for strategic returns increases as more resources are invested into a fund. Strategic returns and corporate resources are relatively low for a traditional venture capital partnership. An external focused venture programme yields the highest strategic returns but generally does not require as much commitment of corporate resources as the internal venture groups. This relationship is depicted in Figure 3.

Five Guidelines for Setting up an External Focused Corporate Venture Fund

The following guidelines have been used successfully in starting an external focused venture capital fund in a major multinational corporation. They may be adaptable to other established corporations which intend to set up a focused venture programme in co-operation with a venture capital firm.

Guideline 1: Assuring Top Management Commitment
The first and most important point about a focused corporate venture fund is that the Chief Executive Officer as well as the top divisional executives recognize the potential contributions of such a programme to long-term growth and profitability of the corporation as well as the risks, time frame and costs associated with the venture process.[12] The CEO's commitment in this regard must be widely communicated and understood by all of those directly or indirectly involved in the venture programme.

Guideline 2: Establishing Clear Understanding of Objectives and Time Frame
Focused corporate venture funds typically have the dual objectives of gaining access to innovations in preferred industries, coupled with attractive returns on investment. This duality, however, may lead to confusion within the corporate organization about which objective has priority. There are basically two reasons for giving the financial return objective first priority:[13]

(a) The strategic value of a start-up company to the investing corporation is improved if the small company is profitable and if its technology and products are accepted in the market-place.

(b) Attractive financial returns will help ensure that management supports the venture fund over an extended period of time.

It should also be clearly understood that the benefits of a focused venture fund are long-term in nature

E–H

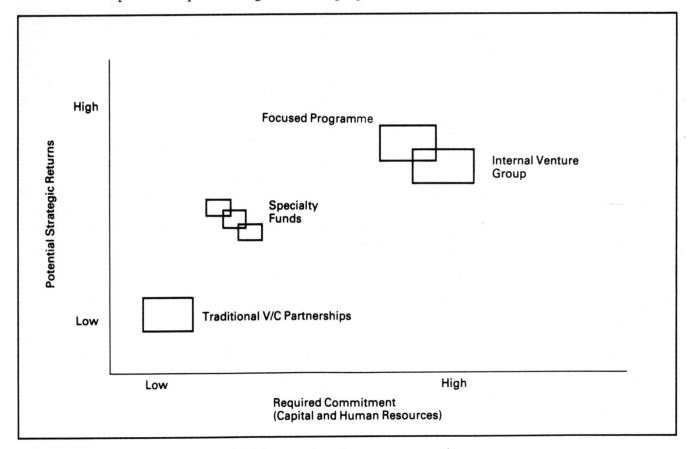

Figure 3. Corporate venture capital options—commitment vs strategic returns

and require a continued commitment of management over time. A venture portfolio usually experiences its losses and problems early, while the successes often take more time to develop than anticipated. Experience indicates that a time frame of 7–10 years is appropriate.

Guideline 3: Selecting of Venture Capital Firm

It is obvious that one should compare the performance and services of several venture capitalists before entering a contractual agreement. There are five important criteria for evaluating venture capital firms:

(1) Past performance with respect to financial returns.

(2) Services being offered to realize strategic benefits.

(3) Size of venture capital firm which is related to deal flow and expertise in specific industries.

(4) Relationships with major competitors of the investing corporation.

(5) International network affiliation of the venture capital firm, if the investing corporation pursues global strategies.

Guideline 4: Formulating an Investment Charter

The investment charter defines markets and technologies in which the investing corporation wants to be active.[14] Formulating the investment charter is an interactive process between the corporation and the venture capitalist so that the intentions of both sides are clearly understood. It must be based on the strategic plan of the corporation and should be considered as a 'living document' which changes in accordance with changes in strategies. Depending on the strategic importance of each of the corporation's businesses it may be useful to classify the various investment areas into those with primary and those with secondary priority. The charter should neither be defined too narrow nor too wide. In the first case the risks increase and make it less likely to achieve an attractive financial return. If the charter is too wide, the corporation may not get the full strategic benefits it looks for. A solution to this dilemma depends on the corporation's specific interests.

Guideline 5: Setting-up an Internal Organization Structure and Procedures

There are several interrelated organizational issues, namely structure, process and people associated with the venture programme, which must be clarified and focused before the venture programme begins to operate. In order to realize the strategic benefits of a focused venture fund almost all corporations have to overcome the 'Not Invented Here' (NIH) syndrome, i.e. a negative attitude of the corporation with respect to innovations coming from the outside. Therefore, any organizational arrangement has to specifically address this syndrome.

(a) *Internal venture organization.* Involving the operating divisions and the relevant functions at different levels of the corporate hierarchy in the venture capital programme through an appropriate organizational structure helps to reduce the NIH syndrome. Even though there may be other approaches, the following three-tier organization has been successfully used for starting a venture fund in a major multinational corporation:

At the top of this organization is an *Advisory Board* which consists of three top-level executives. Its members act as the corporation's representatives to the partnership. They oversee the fund and approve changes in the investment charter. On the second level a *Venture Committee* acts as a forum of discussion for strategic priorities of the programme and issues of technology transfer. Its members come from the operating divisions and corporate R & D. This committee meets four times a year. At the third level there is a *Venture Co-ordination Team* consisting of one representative from corporate development and one from corporate R & D. Both provide a liaison between the venture capitalist and the corporation. They also co-ordinate all venture related information flows within the corporation's organization.

(b) *Decision procedures and due diligence.* The question to what extent the corporation itself should be involved in making investment decisions may lead to some discussions within the corporation. As mentioned before, the limited decision-making authority and the slow corporate decision process have been identified as major problems for internal venture groups. Therefore, the corporation should not make the final investment decisions. However, the corporation determines the areas of investment in the investment charter. Also, investment decisions of a venture capital fund organized as a limited partnership must be made by the General Partner (i.e. the venture capitalist). Otherwise the corporation runs the risk of losing the special tax and liability treatment associated with the status of a limited partner.

An area closely related to decision-making is the due diligence process, i.e. the detailed process of evaluating an investment opportunity by the venture capitalist. Sharing due diligence with the investing corporation allows the venture capitalist to draw on the corporation's expertise in specific areas. On the other hand, participating in the due diligence process gives the corporation the opportunity to influence the investment decisions to a certain extent. In addition, the early involvement of various divisional and functional staff in evaluating a technology will arouse their interest and may pay off later if a technology transfer is considered.

(c) *First quality personnel.* The final and most important point is that the corporation must put first quality resources behind the venture fund.[15]

This is certainly not the place to send the executive who has been twice passed for a promotion and who is looking for a place to wait until retirement. The essential qualities are an open entrepreneurial mind, an excellent understanding of the corporate culture as well as high credibility within the corporate organization. Personnel selection and training plays a pivotal role in addressing the NIH syndrome. Having the corporate personnel directly involved in the venture capital process (i.e. the Venture Co-ordination Team) spend at least 3 months for training at the venture capitalist's headquarters will help to overcome the NIH syndrome whilst also building relationships with key members of the venture capital firm.

Managing Change Through Corporate Venture Capital

Today one measure of corporate excellence is management's ability to cope with a changing environment. Most industrial corporations compete in markets which are constantly being impacted by the emerging new electronics, communications, bio-technology and manufacturing technologies. A surprisingly large share of significant advances in these fields are being made by entrepreneurial, often venture capital-backed small companies. Venture capital provides corporations with a creative means to manage change by staying as current as possible on these developments and by gaining access to the small companies. At the same time venture capital generates an attractive rate of return on the capital employed.

However, in many respects, the way that venture capital firms operate is antithetical to the way that corporations operate. A corporation that thinks about it immediately realizes that the corporation cannot have a tame, in-house, captive venture capital team, as this is a contradiction in terms. An established corporation that intends to use venture capital as a systematic instrument of corporate development should thus seek the co-operation of an external venture capital firm rather than starting an internal venture division. This holds especially true if the corporation is getting involved with venture capital for the first time. Once an external venture programme has been started successfully, direct investments can be made alongside venture capitalists, and later, if properly organized, exclusive direct investments may prove rewarding.

The guidelines recommended have been designed to minimize both financial risk and the near-term organizational cost associated with setting-up an external focused venture fund. It should be noted that a venture capital fund does not replace existing corporate development activities. Venture capital can be a challenging and powerful investment to augment the other more traditional business development efforts.

Acknowledgements—In writing this article we would like to recognize the helpful comments of the staff from Advent International, Boston.

References

(1) *Trends in Venture Capital*, pp. 5–10, Venture Economics, Wellesley, Massachusetts (1986).

(2) Richard N. Foster, *Innovation: The Attacker's Advantage*, McKinsey & Co., New York (1986).

(3) National Science Board, Science indicators—1976. In *Report of the National Science Board*, pp. 92–93, National Science Foundation, Washington DC (1977).

(4) A. David Silver, *Venture Capital. The Corporate Guide for Investors*, p. 14, John Wiley, New York (1985).

(5) A. David Silver, *Venture Capital*, pp. 6–10; and John W. Wilson, *The New Ventures. Inside the High Stakes World of Venture Capital*, pp. 149–165, Addison-Wellesley, Reading, Massachusetts (1986).

(6) Hollister B. Sykes, Lessons from a new ventures program, *Harvard Business Review*, **64**, 69–74, May–June (1986).

(7) G. Felda Hardymon, Mark J. DeNino and Malcolm S. Salter, When corporate venture capital doesn't work, *Harvard Business Review*, **61**, p. 120, May–June (1983).

(8) See, for example, ref. (7), pp. 114–120; and Paul T. Bailey, *Venture Capital and the Corporation*, Presentation to the European Chemical Marketing Research Association in Berlin, West Germany, pp. 13 and 14, Baring Brothers, Hambrecht & Quist, London (1985).

(9) See, for example, G. Felda Hardymon, Mark J. DeNino and Malcolm S. Salter, When corporate venture capital doesn't work, p. 120; Paul T. Bailey, Venture capital and the corporation, p. 14; and Robert C. Perez, *Inside Venture Capital. Past, Present, and Future*, p. 70, Praeger, New York (1986).

(10) John W. Wilson, *The New Ventures*, p. 26; see also Craig A. T. Jones, *Investing in Venture Capital by Pension Funds*, Research paper published by Centennial Research & Development Company, L.P., Denver, Colorado (1985).

(11) C. E. Anagnostopoulos, Managing change: a corporate imperative (The Monsanto Experience), Presentation to the Conference on New Business Development, *Business Week* Executive Programs in New York, 28–29 January (1985).

(12) Charles L. Gautschi and Richard E. Werner, Planning and organizing for internal growth ventures, *Managerial Planning*, **32**, p. 23 (1983).

(13) John W. Wilson, *The New Ventures*, p. 156.

(14) Richard M. Hill and James D. Hlavacek, Learning from failure. Ten guidelines for venture management, *California Management Review*, p. 7, Summer (1977).

(15) Charles L. Gautschi and Richard E. Werner, Planning and organizing for internal growth ventures, p. 23.

Alliance: The New Strategic Focus*

Barrie G. James, Pharmaceutical Division, Ciba-Geigy, Basel, Switzerland

Alliance between companies has long been a major corporate strategy. However, the recession and increasing protectionism have combined to raise the costs of doing business which in turn have favoured the increasing use of business alliances. While alliances have proved to be valuable competitive manoeuvres, there are inherent risks in relying on alliances as the sole or the major strategy for a company. This article discusses the key factors behind the change in focus for alliance strategies and identifies the major alliance thrusts being adopted in response to changing conditions.

Introduction

> Alliances are held together by fear, not by love.
>
> Harold Macmillan (1959)

Alliance between companies has long been a *modus operandi* in business. Until recently, business alliances were exceptions to normal operations since they were formed on an *ad hoc* basis to deal with specific situations generally linked to product access and market control.

The significant change in the business environment due to economic conditions, high costs, the globalization of business and increasing political control has changed the focus of alliance strategies to the point where they are now becoming the rule rather than the exception.

The Elements of Change

The recession of the late 1970s and early 1980s has had a profound impact on the business environment. High growth has turned into stagnating demand for many products and services and companies are faced with increasing levels of competition in the fight to secure share in conditions of low growth or declining demand.

Survival and growth under such conditions depend on the ability of firms to take business away from competitors, to protect existing business from competitive attacks, and to deter competitors from aggressive acts. Firms under current market conditions face a combat situation with strong analogies to typical forms of military combat of which alliance strategies are a fundamental component.

The costs of doing business have increased substantially. A period of sustained inflation; the heavy expenditure required to develop and bring to market new technologies, processes and products; the growth in and complexity of regulatory compliance; the need to compete on a world-wide basis and the increased marketing costs associated with competing in a mature market have combined to increase business expenses.

Business in general has become more international in nature. While new technologies have aided large-scale international communication and transportation, companies themselves have moved internationally to seek new markets both to obtain new sources of growth outside mature home markets and to amortize the increased costs of research and development and regulatory compliance over a wider catchment area.

Political intervention in business has increased. While much early legislation was aimed at curbing business abuse, legislation in the 1970s was triggered by political concern of the effects of business activity on the environment, health and safety and corruptive practices. In the 1980s the significant trade imbalances particularly between the West and Japan began to trigger a round of protectionism designed to safeguard indigenous companies and markets in the U.S. and Western Europe. These legislative changes have not only made the operating environment of the firm more complex but also costs of regulatory compliance have risen substantially adding to the expense spiral.

Barrie G. James is Head of Marketing Development for the Pharmaceutical Division of Ciba-Geigy AG, CH-4002, Basel, Switzerland.
*This article is based on the author's book *Business Wargames*, published by Abacus Press, London (1984).

The Alliance Strategies

The basic objective of a business or military alliance is to combine the forces of actual or possible combatants either to overwhelm an opponent or opponents or to dissuade potential belligerents from conducting a future conflict. Both forms of alliance are based on a commonality of interest between the members of the alliance. In business alliances, the members generally seek to combine financial, marketing, production or technological resources in such a way as to serve the common objective of increasing market share. The most widely used alliance strategies cover licensing, marketing agreements, joint ventures, franchising, private label agreements, buyer–seller arrangements, forging common standards and consortia. Alliances, however, are dependent on the ability of members to sustain their commitment to the alliance through a mutuality of interest and alliances can be weakened by the changing interests of the members (Figure 1).

Both business and the military depend heavily on the use of alliance strategies in modern combat for essentially the same reasons. The rising cost of market and battlefield conflict, the need to match competitive resource deployment and the global nature of conflict require the increased use of effective alliance strategies for both survival and growth.

The New Alliance Focus

The increased use of alliance strategies in the 1980s and the changing focus reflect a new range of interests on the part of alliance members dictated by current economic, political and competitive considerations.

These new interests centre on an amalgam of factors

including market access, technology acquisition and control, financial support, competitive reality and political insurance.

Market Access
Local conditions and start-up costs in new markets are major barriers to successful market penetration.

Import restrictions on personal computers in South Korea have resulted in IBM negotiating with Hyundai on a co-operative venture to produce IBM's 5550 personal computer while Mexican value-added requirements led Ford to decide to establish a 400,000 unit engine plant in Mexico to serve its U.S. and Canadian operations.

In Japan the complexities of import regulations, tariffs, product standards and the distribution system have made direct market penetration a difficult and costly undertaking. Western companies largely take the view that a partnership with a local company is the most successful way of establishing a viable operation in Japan. Volkswagen, for example, gambled that its co-operative Santana car in Japan with 70 per cent local parts sourcing would provide the leverage in cost and marketing to make a strong penetration of the medium-size car market—which no other foreign car manufacturer has yet attained. By mid-1984, 10,000 Santana's had been sold in Japan compared to 17,000 in the whole of Europe in 1983 illustrating the value of such alliances. Similarly, Japanese companies are faced with high start-up costs and a lack of knowledge of the radically different business environment in the West and have frequently sought local partners to obtain operating experience. Takeda's joint venture with Abbott in the U.S.A. and with Roussel in Europe to market Takeda's drug products are examples of efforts to cope with both the complexities of health care regulatory agencies and the distribution and

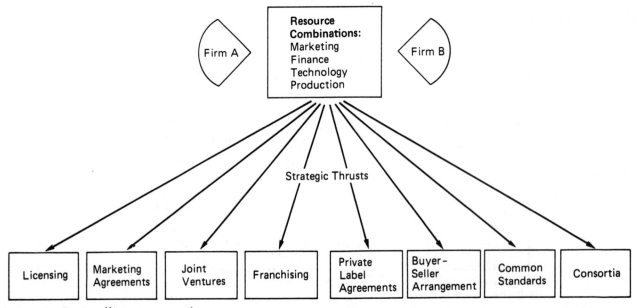

Figure 1. Basic alliance strategies

marketing systems which are markedly different from those in Japan (Figure 2).

By using alliance strategies, companies can offset, to some extent, some of the high cost/high risk syndrome associated with penetrating new markets—an essential business development manoeuvre in the global market for products and services.

Technology Acquisition and Control

The exploitation of new technology has become the driving force in many industries; however, indigenous access through internal R & D to new products is time-consuming, costly and high risk.

To cover gaps in the product line and to supplement internal innovation, companies in many industires are increasing their search for new technology developed by other firms. Product licensing has become a key strategic manoeuvre in the chemical, drug and electronics industries. Production cost escalation has been such that companies have also moved into alliances to obtain access to low-cost

manufacturing technology. Bendix, for example, transfers its machine tool technology to Murata in Japan and Murata ships the finished product to Bendix for sale in the U.S. at some 30 per cent lower than U.S. manufacturing costs. By astute licensing-out of technology, licensers can also gain a measure of control over the use to which the technology is put, the markets where it is sold and the price to avoid the spectre of the firm competing with itself. RCA's failure to provide its colour television technology to the Japanese in the 1950s with such safeguards enabled the Japanese electronics manufacturers to decimate the U.S. colour TV market in the late 1960s and 1970s (Figure 3).

Licensing-out also provides the licenser with the ability to deflect the licensee from developing a competitive product. Pilkington's wide licensing-out of its float-glass technology to the 16 major world plate-glass manufacturers in the early 1960s forestalled much larger companies from developing competitive technology to rival Pilkington's process and enabled the company through signifi-

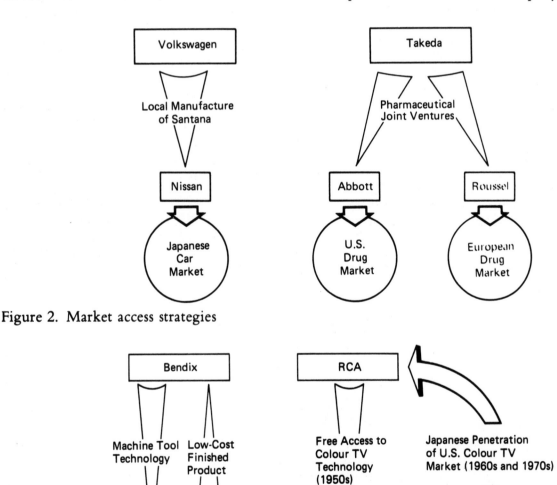

Figure 2. Market access strategies

Figure 3. Technology access and control strategies

cant licensing fees to become a major force in its own right.

Financial Support

Alliance strategies are being widely used for funding major new product programmes where high levels of sustained expenditure and long-term payback are major deterrents to one company development.

BL's agreement to manufacture and market Honda's Acclaim car; the BWR consortium of General Electric (U.S.A.), Asea (Sweden) and Hitachi and Toshiba (Japan) to develop atomic reactors and the Rolls-Royce, IHI–Kawasaki–Mitsubishi (Japan) together with Pratt & Whitney and MTU (Germany) and Fiat (Italy) to develop the new V2500 jet engine at an estimated cost of $3bn to power a new generation 150 seat airliner are typical examples of underwriting major project costs through alliance strategies.

Similarly IBM's progressive acquisition of ROLM, a leader in the development of private branch exchanges, will provide ROLM with the finance to support its development of pbx's, which are critical to IBM to develop its computers to fit voice and data communications networks. Even companies of the size of IBM can no longer afford to pursue developments in all facets of their markets and alliances with small, innovative firms can provide strategic leverage, particularly with emergent technologies (Figure 4).

Competitive Reality

In many industries, competition has reached a point where, apart from surrender, only two options are open to companies if they wish to survive—either join the competition or form an alliance with other contenders to fight the competition on more favourable terms.

By joining the competition, the emphasis is on gaining by drawing on each partner's relative strengths. Western companies have, for example, linked their product innovation with low-cost Japanese process and production technology. Searle's artificial sweetener, Aspartame, uses low-cost production expertise from the world's largest producer of amino acids, Ajinomoto, plus large-volume production capacity to keep the price competitive with other artificial sweeteners and to meet volume demand. Airbus Industries' strategy falls into the second category. The world market for medium-sized wide-bodied jet airliners was the exclusive preserve of Boeing, McDonnell-Douglas and Lockheed. Airbus recognized that a number of factors were required, besides an excellent product, to gain a viable market share. By forming a consortium of Aerospatiale (France), AerItalia (Italy), British Aerospace, CASA (Spain), Fokker (The Netherlands), SABCA (Belgium) and VFW (Germany), Airbus could compete on more favourable terms. Government and private company finance was available for development and customer credit incentives, multi-company involvement provided access to the necessary skills and multi-country participation ensured launch orders from most of the major European government owned airlines (Figure 5).

Political Insurance

Political conditions have also favoured the greater use of alliances as a means both to enter and stay in the market.

Joint ventures are becoming the rule to deal with both demands for local content and materials in new production units in Brazil, India and Saudi Arabia, and with local majority equity stakes in foreign companies in Indonesia, Malaysia and Nigeria.

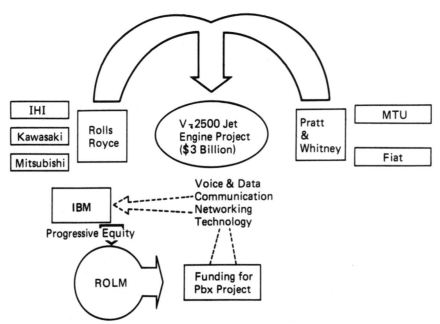

Figure 4. Financial alliance strategies

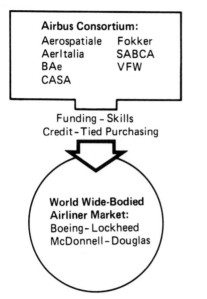

Figure 5. Strategies reflecting commercial reality

Political interests are such that military products sold in volume to the U.S. armed forces push a foreign manufacturer into alliances to build the product under licence or to build a U.S. production plant. British Aerospace joined with McDonnell-Douglas to develop and produce an advanced Harrier Vtol jet (AV–8B) for the U.S. Marine Corps. Similarly, the large offset manufacturing arrangements offered by General Dynamics to aerospace companies in Belgium, Denmark, The Netherlands and Norway were an instrumental political factor in selling the F16 fighter to the air forces of these countries.

The large trade imbalances with Japan have spurred a number of Japanese companies to seek a political umbrella through alliances with local companies. Toyota plan to build a small car in a joint venture with General Motors in a $300m refitted GM plant in California and Fujitsu's supply of computer products and technology to Amdahl (U.S.), ICL

(U.K.) and Siemens (Germany) for joint marketing are clear attempts to avoid political censure but still enter or remain in markets (Figure 6).

The award of choice oil exploration contracts in the South China and Yellow Seas to a consortium dominated by state-owned oil companies—BP, Petrobas (Brazil) and Petro Canada—is a form of political insurance since the Chinese government felt more secure in dealing with a consortium that could be viewed virtually as an intergovernmental deal.

Summary

Alliances are now becoming a *sine qua non* for business strategy and are emerging as the norm across a wide range of markets, technologies and countries. Economic and competitive conditions are now such that joint arrangements for technology development, funding and sharing, financing, manufacturing, marketing and distribution are necessary to avoid fratricidal wars of attrition in the market place. In addition, political circumstances which are frequently rooted in protectionism are strong motivators for alliances with local companies.

While alliance strategies are highly relevant to current economic, competitive and political conditions there are drawbacks to their use and limits to their value. There are great difficulties in tracking experience; accountability is weak; communications are often slack; and joint decision-making takes too long and is frequently tackled in an *ad hoc* manner—all of which cause severe operating problems in alliances. The Tornado multi-role combat aircraft produced by the British Aerospace–MBB (Germany)–AerItalia (Italy) alliance was well over budget; the collaborative development of the System X telecommunications project by British Telecom, GEC and Plessey in the

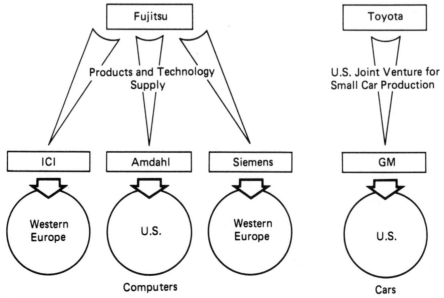

Figure 6. Political insurance strategies

U.K. suffered considerable technical delays and the BMW–Steyr–Daimler–Puch project to manufacture diesel engines in Austria was eventually abandoned. Temporary alliances to protect long-term independence may weaken rather than strengthen a company's activities since it can lose the ability and capacity to produce a fully integrated product. British Aerospace's collaboration to build the wings for Airbus Industrie has probably placed BAe in a position where it has lost the staff, experience and finance to build an Airbus-sized jet airliner on its own in the future. Critical proprietary information can easily flow to alliance partners and a partner may become too dependent on another company for essential components, making them subordinate and vulnerable to those who possess a broad base of volume components.

Alliances hold up only as long as the conditions which favoured their formation remain in force and the interests of the partners are homogeneous. A joint venture between Ampex and Toshiba in Japan to produce magnetic tape and videotape recorders collapsed due to a major difference of opinion between the partners on how to restructure the deficit-ridden operation. A change in world economic conditions to sustained growth could bring greater regulatory pressures to bear on alliances which are deemed as lessening competition and the specific internal conditions within partners of an alliance can change rapidly—both undermining the aims and operations of alliances. When McDonalds' relationship with a French franchisee, Dyan, collapsed over a standards and quality dispute, McDonalds was faced with a major competitive challenge from its former ally. Dyan coverted its 14 well-located McDonalds restaurants in Paris overnight to the O'Kitch hamburger chain, forcing McDonalds to start from scratch in a market where the fast-food hamburger was approaching saturation. With no independent strategic approach, McDonalds was completely vulnerable to Dyan's shift from an ally to an enemy.

While alliance strategies under the right conditions can be valuable competitive manoeuvres they are a means to an end and not an end in themselves. The use of alliance strategies in business to the exclusion of other strategic moves robs a company of the flexibility to manoeuvre in the market place. Alliance strategies, while playing a useful role, must be considered a part but not the core of the central strategic theme for most companies.

Section Six

New Venture Management

Venture Management—Success or Failure?

B. C. Burrows, Milton Keynes Development Corporation

The considerable amount of published literature on venture management is reviewed in an attempt to see how successful this technique is in promoting new products. It was found that earlier articles were optimistic but later articles were more realistic with several describing failed projects.

An attempt is made to relate this with the published literature on the failure of traditional Research and Development but little published evidence is available. The role of New Towns in innovation is briefly mentioned. Finally the reasons for failure are identified and guidelines are established as a means of making venture groups more successful.

Venture management has been described as a corporate strategy for creating new products via new businesses. It is a team approach to internal growth. The term venture capital is also in use but in venture management the company organizing the venture approach to innovation has 100 per cent ownership of or a controlling interest of the project.

It developed as an answer to the failure of Research and Development. Here in most cases a group of scientists were expected to produce new products. Certainly they produced new knowledge but there was no system to exploit this knowledge. Also the new knowledge was not necessarily marketable.

In order to develop a new product a multidiscipline team is needed. This should consist of:

- a research scientist;
- a market researcher;
- a design engineer;
- a production engineer;
- an information scientist.

Without this team a systems approach is not possible. There are several methods of venture management. These are:

The Task Force Approach

This is the most informal of the methods used. In this one person acts as a leader of a temporary team which is set up to develop a product.

The Venture Management Department

Here a formal structure is used in that there is a full time commitment of staff with an established budget. The approach is broader, in that ideas are evaluated from other departments or from outside the organization.

The Venture Management Company

Here a separate company is set up which is a wholly owned subsidiary. With this there is a total commitment by the staff to succeed. If not the company is wound up.

The venture approach is divided into several stages:

(1) The search for ideas. This in many cases is an information search and is the role of the information scientist.

(2) Idea screening. This is a selection process of the ideas, a team effort with particular reference to market research.

(3) Idea investigation. This is the role of the research scientist, who decides if the idea is scientifically sound.

(4) Venture development. This is the role of the design and production engineers.

(5) Commercial exploitation. This is, of course, a marketing exercise.

In theory this concept appears to be a way of limiting the considerable risk of failure in the development of new products. There have been a number of articles on this subject describing the

B. C. Burrows is Marketing Intelligence Officer, Milton Keynes Development Corporation, Wavenden Tower, Wavendon, Milton Keynes MK17 8LX, U.K.

technique in detail. But how successful is this technique? In reviewing the literature it should be possible to find out what success there has been. It will be necessary to read between the lines in the more recent articles as there is a pattern for describing all new ideas. The first article describes things in glowing terms. This is followed by a more realistic assessment. But if there is no success to report there is a complete silence or just passing references to failure. This is a great pity because we can often learn more from studying failure than success. There may be an unknown factor in success but with failure we can examine the complete environment and find out what went wrong. Several articles mainly by academics were found on failed venture groups but the companies were not named.

In a literature search many articles were identified and these will be reviewed in chronological order, starting with the earliest.

In 1961 Don C. Wheaton uses the term 'Venture Projects' and discusses the financing of these. He regards all new projects as venture projects, including the raising of finance and venture money. He deals with the problems of raising finance from outside sources, so in the strict sense this is not venture management.

In 1963 Donald A. Schon published a very influential paper in which he linked the theory of innovation with the project champion. Later Schon was to coin the useful phrase 'dynamic conservatism' in which large organizations are very active in attempting not to change. There is the logical desire for change and the emotive desire to stay the same. From this paper the idea of small groups with some autonomy in large organizations was developed. There were also signs that R & D organizations divorced from the reality of business were not producing new products only new ideas, which were not being examined in a commercial environment.

In 1965 Harry Schrage discussed the R & D entrepreneur. He collected evidence on how the R & D man operates and applied this data to 22 R & D companies selected at random as regards:

(1) sales volume;
(2) annual profit.

From this he was able to identify the psychology of the successful entrepreneur namely:

(1) honesty with self;
(2) total awareness.

The interesting conclusion is that the successful person was high in achievement motivation, low in power motivation, and high in the awareness of self, the market and his employees.

The thinking behind venture management is the problem of large organizations stifling innovation and small firms lacking the resources even if they have the motivation.

In 1967 James Hillier gave a talk 'Venture Activities in the Large Corporation' to the IEEE which was published in 1968. In this he was concerned with all research and development which was separate from central research. He described groups set up to promote and develop products by first residing in the central research department and then transferring the new technology for development. He visualized permanent and temporary groups. The temporary group he describes as a task force. Examples are quoted of the success of these techniques within the electronics industry. The concept of venture management is beginning to emerge.

Also in the same year a description of a Sibany Manufacturing Corporation appeared in *Business Week*. This company was set up for the sole purpose of venture management. In 1974 William H. Shames wrote a book on this which will be reviewed later.

A paper by Russell W. Peterson in the *Harvard Business Review* described this approach to new product development by the Du Pont Company. This was an attempt to combine the advantage of size of the large organization with the entrepreneur spirit found in small companies. The relationship of this venture team with the Central Research Department is discussed and the structure of the venture group is described. This is the same multidiscipline team found in other venture groups. Reference is made to the approach of the Minnesota Mining and Manufacturing Company who have also used this approach. In conclusion it is claimed that Du Pont are in favour of this approach but it is also stated that it is still under review.

A key paper by M. Hanan published early in 1969 was called 'Corporate growth through venture management'. The author, a management consultant, states 'Venturing is an attempt to make innovation more predictable and less random. It represents a corporate effort to manage its new business development as a continuing commitment rather than as a sporadic or periodic crash programme.' He is concerned with the poor return of R & D and says 'many manufacturers have more or less abandoned their laboratories . . . in search of greener pastures in the form of acquisitions'. He sees venture management as a means of continuing the internal development of new products with a greater success ratio and with less expense. The venture approach is seen as venture selection, information gathering and evaluation followed by recommendation. He quotes companies using this technique but there is no information on what results are obtained. He claims that with this approach emphasis is placed on market needs. Venture management seemed to become a reality in 1969 and a number of papers were published on this subject.

There were three papers in Research Management by Robert M. Adams, General Manager, New Business Ventures Division 3Ms Company, Robert C. Springborn, Vice President of the Technical Group, General Manager New Ventures Division W. R. Grace and Company, and Robert T. Wallace, Vice President New Product Planning and Development Owens-Illinois Incorporated.

Robert M. Adams emphasizes that the environment must be right. The venture group should be housed with the marketing function. To develop the entrepreneur spirit the group should have a great deal of independence. He concludes,

To summarize, then, internally generated new business ventures have the best chance to succeed when the corporate climate is favourable; when a development concept is adopted that gives freedom of action, individual responsibility, a chance to become wholly involved, and adequate rewards; and when the project is placed in the hands of an entrepreneur who is excited by the potential business and dedicated to making it go, go, go ...

Robert C. Springborn reports that the New Ventures Division of W. R. Grace and Company is 1 year old with an initial 5 year plan. The organization of this project is described and the methods used in its management. The techniques adopted are similar to other venture groups.

Robert T. Wallace also describes the structure of Owens-Illinois and how the venture management section will operate. All projects are too recent for any firm data on results.

A paper by Herbert A. Wainer and Irwin M. Rubin studied the motivation of entrepreneurs in an R & D environment. Fifty-one technical entrepreneurs were studied, focusing upon the relationship between their motivation and company performance. The results confirm the findings of an earlier paper by Schrage that the motivation is a high need for achievement and less need for power. The need for power appears to derive from leadership patterns. Although this paper and the one by Schrage are not directly concerned with venture management they are essential reading in relation to the motivation of venture teams. It is encouraging that the team with the right people will identify with the project more than with power.

A. B. Cohen gave a paper 'Venture Management' at the University of Bradford which was published in 1969. In this he described the Riston Venture which involved penetrating an unfamiliar industrial market with a radically different product. He is

Manager, New Product Development Photo Products Department, E. I. du Pont de Nemours, and he published a further paper in 1970 'New Venture Development at Du Pont'. A new venture group was started in October 1966 and successfully concluded in August 1969. It was then set up as a separate profit centre within the Photo Products Department. The organizational structure of this and the new venture development phases are described and in conclusion the future of these types of activity are viewed with favour.

A key paper by the consultant Frederic Cook gives examples of venture management as a means of growth. It is a report of a survey of the hundred largest industrial corporations in the U.S.A. and a large number of them are using this technique as a means of growth. The methods used are described but the companies are not identified although some are named at the beginning of the article. These include Standard Oil, Scott Paper Company and Leasco. Quotations are also included from people working for GTE, Boise-Cascade and St. Regis Paper Company.

Possibly the most important paper in 1971 was written by Arnold C. Cooper for the recently founded Center For Venture Management, Milwaukee, Wisconsin, U.S.A. This is an empirical research study which examines the history and performance of innovative individuals who seek to become entrepreneurs. The nature of the new technologically based firms is analysed, based on data collected in 1969 with the support of Dr. John Komives of the Centre for Venture Management. The study was undertaken in the San Francisco Peninsula which includes the inventive centre of Palo Alto. In his examination of the entrepreneur in this area the author found him to be a person in his thirties with a masters degree who had achieved considerable success in a prior situation. This is followed by an interesting chapter entitled Incubator Organizations. These technologically based firms recruit, train, bring together and motivate entrepreneurs. This enables the inventive person to set up on his own and establish spin off enterprises. These spin off rates were calculated for each year and related to regional employment and the death of firms. Thus a relationship between the birth and death of firms was established. It was found that once established the technologically based firms had a low failure rate.

Douglas Foster wrote a paper from the marketing point of view in which he pointed out that the main barrier to innovation is the traditional authoritarian structure of the company. Techniques such as brainstorming are described which lead on to the concept of venture management. The author sees a venture as being related to the parent company in three ways. The management team may be intra-corporate, inter-corporate or supra-corporate.

The relationship between the entrepreneur and the venture management team was explored by Donald I. Orenbuch. He feels that present day society is a 'temporary society' and that new products are vital to the survival of an organization and concludes that the venture management team is the answer for innovation. Reference is made to the venture management team of M. and T. Chemicals Incorporated, a subsidiary of the American Can Company. This New Venture Division is responsible for the first three phases of a product: exploration, screening and business analysis. the author says 'This is a key role for as the Booz, Allen and Hamilton study indicated of every 58 ideas only six or seven get through the screening stages, and only one winds up as a successful product'. The author concludes with six points he feels necessary for a venture project to succeed.

(1) It has to be dedicated to change.

(2) The team must be multidisciplined.

(3) The team must be single minded.

(4) Venture management is wide ranging. It has no sympathy with 'not invented here'.

(5) Easy communication is essential.

(6) The team is entrepreneural, its goal is to make significant breakthroughs.

A paper given to the American Society of Mechanical Engineers by A. W. Blackman deals with the role of technical forecasting in the analysis and planning of new ventures. This provides a structure for the application of logical, mathematical and scientific procedures to decision problems which involve a significant portion of an organization's resources, have a long term effect on a firm's future success and are characterized by uncertainty in many of the factors important to the decision. The system is based on a synthesis of analytical techniques, decision analysis and system dynamics for determining the resource allocation level for new venture portfolios designed to achieve long term growth objectives. The role played by technological forecasting in new venture planning in the selection of engineering projects is also discussed.

In dealing with the problems of organizing new venture teams David Wileman and Howard Freese face the relationship between the theory of the venture teams and the practical problems of making them operate successfully. The problems the venture teams face are outlined. One is that they act as a buffer between the marketing man and the research scientist. The person in marketing wishes to sell the new product as soon as possible and the research scientist wishes to hang on in order to improve it. Unless the venture team breaks the deadlock it will not succeed. The authors also see conflict developing in the group because of differing backgrounds and the fact that the 'free wheeling

maverick' entrepreneur could be motivated to join the team. The role of the manager is vital here as a unifying force. The question of creativity is also discussed with the danger that venture teams will burn themselves out. The recycling of people in differing ventures teams is suggested. The article concludes as follows 'In short there is a delicate balance between too much and too little structure and freedom, and its important that this balance be struck at the outset of any new venture activity'. In fact if the group is not accepted as part of the organization by the rest of the personnel its chances of success are greatly reduced.

A paper by Richard M. Hill and James D. Hlavacek, July 1972, studies the marketing aspects of the venture team. This article consists of a full description of a venture team followed by a survey to identify the characteristics of the team. All these characteristics have been described in previous papers but the authors do make the point that venture teams are informal and often split off into sub-groups or task forces. The article concludes that the new venture team possesses considerable advantages over other forms of organization such as committees or the product manager system for achieving market growth.

In 'New Venture Analysis' David W. Brown describes a procedure for reducing failure in new venture activities. The first approach is to assess a new venture in relation to the overall objectives of the organization. A warning is given about being carried away by the glamour of a new product and the necessity of assessing the profitability by the use of marketing and financial analysis. The article concludes with a study of financial means of reducing the risk of a new venture.

David L. Wileman collaborated with Kenneth A. Jones in November 1972 to examine the 'Emerging Patterns in New Venture Management'. This reported the results of a recent study that investigated the following areas:

(1) the nature of venture teams;

(2) characteristics of venture managers;

(3) organizational importance assigned to venturing;

(4) management of venture teams;

(5) intraorganizational contributions of other company operating units;

(6) organizational acceptance and opposition to the venture management concept.

The study was conducted during 1970 and involved 24 large consumer and industrial goods companies, all of which were among Fortune magazines 500 largest industrial companies. It was discovered that 25 per cent of the firms listed among these 500 companies had venture teams in operation.

(1) The nature of venture teams. These are seen as about 9 or 10 full time members, with part time members ranging from 0–50 persons.

(2) Venture managers. These were found to be in their early forties with about 24 per cent holding a technical degree, 32 per cent had a background of R & D, 16 per cent engineering and 24 per cent corporate planning.

(3) Organizational importance. It was found in most cases that the venture manager had the authority to make decisions.

(4) Management of venture teams. The source of new ideas was examined and it was found that 30 per cent came from external sources, 24 per cent from R & D, 14 per cent from marketing, 10 per cent from the chairman and board of directors, 7 per cent from line staff, 5 per cent from the venture team, 4 per cent from literature searches, 3 per cent from customers, 1 per cent from competitors and 1 per cent from Corporate Planning Department. I find the 5 per cent figure for the venture team and 4 per cent for literature searches surprisingly low.

(5) Intraorganizational contributions from other company operating units. These are listed as marketing, manufacturing, legal, finance, engineering and research and development.

(6) Organizational acceptance and opposition to the venture management concept. This is not dealt with in detail and there is only a short section on co-operation and conflict. Despite this failing this is a most useful contribution to the study of venture management and contains a great deal of useful information based on firm data.

The first article traced in 1973 was by J. B. Gardner describing a new venture concept at BOC. The author describes the doubts that industrial firms have from the results of conventional R & D particularly from central research establishments. This article describes how the British Oxygen Company Limited have changed the central R & D function to a pilot venture structure.

Details are given of the structure of this project but no conclusions are given as to its success because of the early stages of this operation. A short paper by Karl H. Vesper and Thomas G. Holmdahl describes the results of a survey on firms in the innovation business. The results were that about 65 per cent of these firms were using venture management. Details are given of what happens to venture teams. In fact 82 per cent became integrated into the parent company. Of the venture managers 37 per cent stayed with the project, 28 per cent went on to new projects and 26 per cent returned to other parts of the organization and 9 per cent left.

David L. Wileman and Gary R. Gemmill report on a survey they conducted on venture managers and their problems. The role of the venture is described and his need for support from the corporation. The following table is of interest.

Sources of information on corporate objectives for venture management literature, independent research on venture management	%
research on venture management	24
Chairman of the board	12
Executive committee	12
President	12
Vice president	8
Immediate superior	16
No reponse	8
Other	8
Total	100

The conditions in which a venture manager would accept another similar position is described and the stress problems which he faces are analysed. A table is given of the types of risk which the venture faces. The highest is in failure to produce tangible results. This was 40 per cent.

A paper by James D. Hlavacek and Victor A. Thompson examined the relationship between bureaucracy and innovation. The well known problem of bureaucracy being a barrier to change is stated as well as the fact that the larger the organization the greater the bureaucracy with less chance of the development of new products. The authors point out that in order to survive large organizations must innovate. The venture team is seen as the answer to this. Personal interviews of 14 firms in the petroleum, automative, electronics and chemical industries were undertaken. This was followed by an in depth study of three of the largest U.S. chemical firms. It was found that 'what appears to be taking place is a structuring of new product management in a non bureaucratic direction'.

The methods used to do this were the setting up of a product manager and the setting up of a venture team. The product manager had no organization or staff. This is a direct translation of Donald Schon's concept of the product champion. In the other method, the setting up of the venture team, emphasis was made that this team is both interdisciplinary and temporary. A detailed study was made of the type of people who make up a venture team, their professional and educational background and the number of published periodical articles. No mention is made of any new successful products, presumably due to the fact that these venture teams had not been in existence long enough to be judged.

In December 1973 Fortune published an article by Sharon Sabin. This is on the concept of the 'severed venture'. After a firm has set up a venture team they may decide not to develop the product which the venture team have developed. This system gives the venture team the chance to do so. At General Electric U.S.A. David J. Ben Daniel developed a method of spinning off GE's unwanted products. In this case a separate business is set up. In most cases GE retains about a third of the capital assets of this venture. The article describes the setting up of this venture team. This is a method which could be more widely used for reducing failure in innovation. Many new projects change in their development and do not fit into the long term plans of the organization. In this case the team responsible should be given the chance of 'going it alone'.

Martin Christopher gave a paper on venture analysis at the University of Bradford. This paper describes a framework for the sequential evaluation of new products. No mention is made of venture management but the technique outlined is of use to any venture team.

A major contribution in 1974 was a book by William H. Shames entitled *Venture Management*. The author established the Sibany Manufacturing Corporation and went into the venture management business in 1967. The aim was to invent new products and set up new companies either by venture capital or by licencing. In 1968 and 1969 five companies were started, two of which were operating successfully in 1974. The author also describes the setting up of new venture management groups in large companies. These include General Electric, Alcoa, Boise Casade, Coca Cola, General Mills, U.S. Steel, International Paper, Singer, Mobil Oil, Travelers Insurance, Dow Chemicals, 3M and Exxon. Most companies would not comment on the success of these ventures. A G.E. executive is quoted as saying that 1975 will be the year for assessing success or failure as the time span of activity is seen as being from 5 to 7 years. William H. Shames feels that most products in large organizations fail and will continue to fail without venture management. He claims that the research scientist in the laboratory falls in love with his project and forgets the market. Details of contracts with other companies are given. It can only be concluded that this is a most useful contribution to the understanding of the innovation process with a most practical approach.

In the same year Patrick Liles wrote a book on *New Business Ventures and the Entrepreneur*. This work is designed as a means of providing basic material for individuals who wish to start up or purchase a business. This is done by a study of entrepreneurs and a description of the methods of setting up of a business in the U.S.A. Case studies are given in many cases. An article by A. Vernon describes a new business venture at the Pharmaceutical Division of ICI Limited. This new venture was in the area of medical aids and was started in 1971. The new venture concept is defined and the resulting

experience is described. The conclusion is that so far results are encouraging.

Donald M. Collier, Vice President, Borg Warner Corporation in a paper in R & D management, argues that innovation is applied invention. He gives examples of how small firms are innovative and large firms are not. He concludes that a research based venture should be set up by a large organization under the protective umbrella of the R & D department and, when ready, transferred to the operating company. He does not describe the structure of the venture group.

A paper by James D. Hlavacek made a major contribution to the study of venture management as the reasons why projects fail were analysed. In all 21 innovation failures were studied and the results of the interviews are given below.

Table 1 presents the reasons for venture failures given by top management at the corporate and divisional levels. These responses and further interviews with these executives revealed that top management's concern in venture failures focused on costs and profits.

Table 1. Top management responses, causes of venture failures

Causes	Frequency reported*
Sunk costs became too great	8
Market was too small	8
Did not fit distribution system	8
Technical problems	6
Wrong venture manager	6
Drain on corporate-divisional profits	5
Low return on investment	5
Conflicts with divisions	5
Termination of federal funds	2
Weak lobbying effort	1

*The frequency totals more than 21 because multiple causes were given for many failures.

Table 2 shows the causes of failure as reported by venture managers. In contrast to the top management causes in Table 1, the venture managers

Table 2. Venture manager responses, causes of venture failures

Causes	Frequency reported*
Market was too small	7
Distribution problems	6
Conflicts with divisional managers	6
Impatient top management	4
Resistance from existing sales force	4
Marketing research inaccurate	4
Budget too small	5
Inexperienced venture team	2
Termination of federal funds	2
Decline in corporate profits	1
Venture team too small	1

*The frequency totals more than 21 because multiple causes were given for many failures.

reported more operational problems as causes of failure.

Four venture stages were studied (see below).

Stage I
One of the main causes of failure most frequently reported by top management was that sunk costs became too large.

Stage II
The problems of business planning and integration of teams are described and the main problem was the threat of new products to traditional business.

Stage III
In most cases technical obstacles caused the project to be abandoned.

Stage IV
Failure due to decrease in a corporations profits is the main cause here. The severed venture technique is described. The author concludes with the following points:

(1) Develop a venture charter from top management that specifically defines the function, operational procedures, and boundaries of all venture management activity.

(2) Make top management and division managers aware of the long-term corporate growth benefit of venture management by stressing minimum ROIs and yearly growth rates.

(3) Adopt a uniform format for composing and reviewing business plans within the proposed time frames.

(4) Maintain multiple sources of internal sponsorship for ventures.

(5) Maintain a limited number of ventures with independent budgets at varying stages of development or maturity.

(6) Maintain top management involvement and quarterly reviews of ventures in light of the venture alternatives of forming a new division, transferring to an existing division, entering a joint venture, selling, severing, or liquidating at each of the four venture stages.

(7) Select product-champion-type venture managers and high-calibre key team members.

This very useful article does not deal with any percentage of venture management failures so that we still do not know what improvements there are on conventional R & D methods.

Little and Cooper studied the relationship between market research and new technologies ventures. They see the role of market research as the key to success and give examples of failure when this is not done.

In *From Invention to New Business Venture* Roy Rothwell describes the types of venture groups and product teams followed by a step by step description of the innovation process and the structure of venture groups. This is a most useful guide to the range of activities in the venture approach but no examples of the application of this approach are given.

In Chemtech, D. W. Collier discusses the link between the market and technology which he considers vital for success. A brief mention of venture management concludes this article.

A book with the interesting title of *Entrepreneurship and Venture Management* was published in 1975. This consists of a selection of previously published articles. The papers of interest have already been referred to but the others are of background interest.

In the same year a collection of papers was made and edited by J. Mancuso. Again all the papers on venture management have been described, but again the other papers are of background interest.

Table 3. Venture stages

Stage I	Stage II	Stage III	Stage IV
R & D or markets surveyed for new products or ideas	Venture teams compose and submit total business plan to divisional or corporate review committees for acceptance or rejection	Team's plan accepted in Stage II, receives independent budget to begin advanced product and market development	A. Form new division
Determine market need— value analysis			B. Move to an existing division
Build working model			C. Joint venture
Obtain early qualitative market response			D. Sell or license
Conduct primary financial-profitability analysis			E. Severed approach
			F. Liquidation or abandonment

C–F may also occur in stages I, II, or III

An interesting paper by D. S. Hopkins was based on a study to find out what experts consider to be the relative merits of differing ways of organizing new product activities including venture groups. The advantages and disadvantages of these groups is discussed. The article also shows that many top executives have mixed feelings about the setting up of a group outside of the conventional organizational structure.

M. Hanan deals with the setting up of venture groups by large corporations and finds out that most of these have failed. The reason was that the methods of the large organization were applied to the small organization with the result that the venture team was not given enough freedom to operate.

As a result of this most corporations are now aware that new business ventures must be treated as small start up businesses, and not a large business in miniature. The author goes on to stress the need for an entrepreneurial manager. One interesting point he makes is that many businesses have originated in garages.

A short paper in *Business Europe* describes BOC's special outlet for new products. This is a New Venture Secretariat which is an autonomous unit with a general manager who reports to the company's executive committee. This has been successful and reference is made to new successful products which have been developed.

The relationship between small and large companies in operating joint venture is described in a paper by J. D. Hlavacek and others. It was found that 74 per cent of technical innovations originate in small companies and the authors describe in detail the relationship between the two types of company. It is concluded that 'The joint venture can be an excellent marriage of small company, technology, and large company, marketing and manufacturing. . . . '.

Edward B. Roberts describes methods of generating effective corporate innovation within a company. The structure is the entrepreneur, the project manager, the sponsor and the gatekeeper (the information gatherer). Reference is made to the research of Professor Allen on gatekeepers. The author only deals with venture management in relation to venture strategies.

Richard M. Hill and James D. Hlavacek undertook a post mortem on 21 venture group failures at 12 large multidivision firms. The stages of development in the setting up and running of these groups were identified as well as seeing how the groups progressed.

Stage 1
This was the setting up of the venture team in order to conduct early technical and commercial evaluation and concludes with a working model embodying the venture craft.

Stage 2
This consisted of detailed planning by the venture team.

Stage 3
Major product and market development activities were undertaken at this stage by the venture groups which served stage 2.

Stage 4
This was the commercialization stage. Only six venture teams reached this stage. However all these new divisions were disbanded after a period because the project's long term growth and profits were not considered to be sufficient by the parent company.

In conclusion 10 guidelines were established for setting up and running a venture team. These are:

Guideline 1
Formulate a venture charter (a model charter is given in an appendix).

Guideline 2
Indoctrinate top management concerning the contribution to long term corporate growth.

Guideline 3
Adapt a standard format to be followed in developing venture plans.

Guideline 4
Maintain a limited number of ventures at different stages of development.

Guideline 5
Assign each venture which reaches stage 3 its own budget.

Guideline 6
Formalize the relationship between top management and venture management.

Guideline 7
Install as head of each venture team a person who has demonstrated both competence as a manager and championship of the product assigned to the venture.

Guideline 8
Ventures earmarked for transfer to operating divisions should not be moved until earnings are far enough above the breakeven point to satisfy the divisional managers concerned.

Guideline 9
Allow division managers at least five options in disposing of their new development projects.

(a) Continue them and attempt to raise their revenue beyond the breakeven point.

(b) Liquidate them and recover as much cost as possible.

(c) Sell them.

(d) Transfer them to another division.

(e) Release them to venturing.

Guideline 10
Include the venture team manager in the revue process at the end of stage 2.

Dan T. Dunn studied 10 venture groups in 10 different companies. All of these failed and have in many cases been replaced by more traditional methods for developing new products. The question to be asked is why did they fail and the author identifies some of the reasons for failure.

The venture groups were questioned on the reasons for their establishment and the philosophy behind this. It was clear that one venture team had too wide a brief on the basis that they did not want to turn anything down. The question of what sort of business are we in or what sort of business do we wish to be in was not asked. Other teams were given privileged treatment with no time limit in which to develop new products. Others developed organizational methods which were unnecessarily expensive.

Of the 10 venture groups studied, six had to be disbanded and four were curtailed. This was partly due to an unfavourable economic outlook.

The author found that the firms who closed down their venture groups still needed new products and that 'most venture-type development effort must be limited to those few projects that have a reasonable chance of early payoff'.

The lessons learnt from these failures are:

> involve senior managers in the development;
> avoid the high profile 'crown prince' syndrome;
> use a blend of people;
> recognize 'staff' and 'line' development functions.

In the last paper identified in 1977 on venture management, the success and failure of internal corporate ventures are discussed and the literature reviewed. The author, Eric Von Hippel, finds the use of venture management to be both widespread and successful. He finds that there is a strong relationship between venture success and the prior experience of the parent company and the venture success with the venture team personnel and the customers on a specific project. Another point he makes is that a venture manager should not be given the post if he has managed resources greater than

that involved in the venture. Tables are given of successful and failing ventures. Of these ventures listed, 11 were successful and 7 failures. This article gives the impression that most venture projects succeed.

During 1978 there appears to have been little published on this subject. The only reference traced was in Dun's *Review on Venture Capital*. Major U.S. corporations such as Exxon, General Electric (U.S.) and Motorola are providing both finance and management know-how to firms in the high technology areas such as electronic devices, radar games, solar energy systems and biological research. These range from just an investment with no direct control of the firm to the setting up of small subsidiaries. The president of General Electric is quoted as saying 'We are looking for things that at some point in time will open a new technology or a new business for the Company'. It is clear from this that the investment is seen as long term and it will either create a new market or be written off. General Electric has spun off nine operations in which it retains an interest from 19 to 45 per cent and has also invested in 11 outside firms.

Exxon also has a similar approach but it is interesting to note that the word processing equipment manufacturer, Vydec Corp, is under the control of Exxon. The flexible approach by large organizations is an interesting development.

A further description of the approach was published in the *Financial Times*. The differing approaches of 3M, whose policy is to promote internal ventures only, is contradictory with the more flexible approach of Exxon. The article is based on the research of Dr. Edward B. Roberts of MIT. The following techniques are described, Venture Capital, Joint Ventures, Composite Approach (Exxon) and the Internal Venture (3M). The conclusion is that 'to achieve their objective, large companies' new ventures should be in new organizational forms as well as in new business areas'.

Ralph Biggadike deals with the problems of developing new products and quotes figures to show that failure is both common and costly. For example, General Food had to write off $59·9m in 1972 on its entry into the fast food business. Guidelines are open as to how long a company should stay with a line before they know that a product is a success. The average time is 10–12 years for a return on capital. The author advocates that large scale resources should be made available if a company is to succeed in new ventures. No mention is made of the management structure for the implication of innovation but the information on the risks involved in developing new products is most useful as well as the information on the time needed to develop a new product.

The article is useful to the venture management team but it is a pity that the author does not deal with the type of organization needed to develop innovation.

The year of 1979 was the year of Norman D. Fast. His first contribution was detailed study of 'The Rise and Fall of Corporate New Venture Divisions'. This was first published late in 1978 in the U.S.A, but as far as I am aware, was first available in the U.K. early in 1979. Norman D. Fast defines a New Venture Division (or NVD) as an organizational unit whose primary functions are:

(1) the investigation of potential new business opportunities;

(2) the development of business plans for new ventures;

(3) the management of the early commercialization of these ventures.

The author found that of the NVD's established in the 1960s and 1970 a high proportion of these were short lived. He states that of the 18 NVD's studied in this thesis, seven were inoperative by 1976. The rest, in order to succeed, had to change and evolve. This process of evolution is studied in this thesis.

The result consisted of two phases:

(1) a broad exploratory survey of 18 companies engaged in NVD;

(2) a detailed study of what factors influenced the evolution of the ventures. This is followed by an in depth study of three companies.

Two types of NVD were identified, a MICRO and MACRO and there was a natural evolution from the MICRO type to the MACRO type. It was a fact that an NVD either grew from a MICRO type or declined and failed.

The author quotes evidence that over a long period, organizations that develop new products grow at least for a longer period. He also stated that it has been estimated that almost three quarters of more than $20bn annual expenditure on R & D in the U.S.A. does not yield a profitable product. Leading on from this the author traces the resources for the development of NVD.

These are:

(1) to create a centre of responsibility for new business development to ensure it receives sufficient attention;

(2) to provide the organizational climate and structure appropriate to new business developments;

(3) to insulate new business development activities from dominant values and norms of the parent company.

The ways in which NVD's develop and change is described. This is illustrated in the following figure:

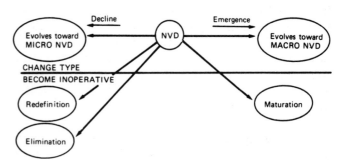

Figure 1. Emergence and decline of an NVD

This work then examines in detail a series of case studies of firms engaged in NVD. These are:

> The Standard Chemical Company;
> Du Pont;
> Ralston Purina.

This is followed by an exmination as to why these projects were not particularly successful.

With MACRO NVD's it was found that expectations were so high that the results were considered to be disappointing. With MICRO NVD's a low profile is maintained which gives this team more time to develop successful products.

Another point is that there were not sufficient mechanisms for the control of the evolution of NVD's.

These are considered to be:

(1) Varying top management support for the NVD.

(2) Changing the organizational positioning of the NVD.

(3) Selecting the staff of the NVD.

(4) Specifying criteria for the screening of ventures.

(5) Establishing integrating mechanisms for the NVD.

(6) Creating a new NVD.

(7) Assaying additional functions of the NVD.

(8) Modifying the level of expedients for the NVD.

(9) Deciding the timing of the venture spin offs from the NVD.

(10) Modifying the NVD charter.

In conclusion the author argues 'that companies should stay with those businesses which fit their existing capabilities or venture into closely related areas'. Research results are quoted proving that unrelated diversification is less successful than related diversification.

In *A Visit to the New Venture Graveyard*, Norman Fast continues his study of venture management failures. In the 1960s it achieved widespread popularity in the U.S.A. and many firms set up these ventures. The author studied the failure rate and life span of these groups. It was found that the average life span was only 4 years.

The following figures show the life span of 18 new venture groups established in 1966. By 1976 half of these had become inoperative.

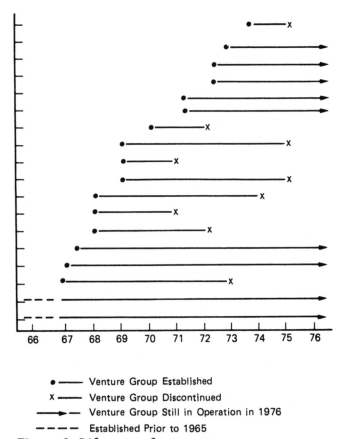

Figure 2. Life span of new venture groups

The conclusion is made from this that most venture groups are a failure and the following reasons are given for this.

Strategic Reversal

The aims of the venture group are long term but before a group can prove itself, a company will undergo several crises which will make it alter its long term strategy. When this happens the venture group is in danger.

It was found that a decline in profits resulted in a decline of venture groups and a rise in corporate profits causes an increase in venturing.

The Emergence Trap

This relates to internal political problems as a result of a successful venture group. There are four factors identified in this.

(1) Resentment by the rest of the organization and the resulting attempt to cut off resources to the venture group.

(2) Conflict by the rest of the organizations because of the favouritism shown to the venture group by management.

(3) The infringement of traditional territory in the rest of the organization. An example is when a venture group sets up its own sales group.

(4) The promotion of the head of a successful venture group can result in resentment at this short cut to bypassing the corporate hierarchy who will attempt to undermine this approach.

The author suggests the following solutions to this.

(1) The question should be asked whether the product is truly innovative. If there is any overlap with traditional products there will be conflict.

(2) When long term high risk venture groups are established it is best to have a small lean organization using a beachhead strategy.

(3) When a venture group pursues a lower risk venture, a large scale organization is needed with a frontal assault type strategy aimed at a large section of the market. The author does not say so but the implication of this approval is that a much quicker result will have to be obtained in order for this venture group to survive. Norman Fast makes this clear with the following figure.

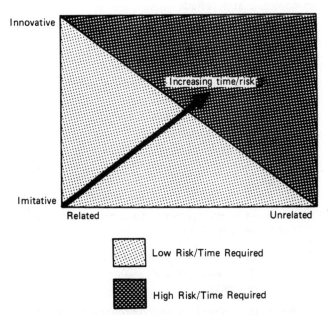

Figure 3. Relationship between type of venture and risk/time

By using this it is possible to study the interface between the two types of venture group.

The author concludes with some guidelines for success.

Pay Your Own Way

It is not possible for venture groups to generate finance until their product is successful, but it is possible to utilize under utilized corporate assets which will not be affected by a financial crisis. An example is given of a major oil company which was given the petrol pump business. This was very profitable but low growth business.

Balance Top Management Support

This is a question of top management support with a keen eye on the expenditure of the venture group. An example is given of a major chemical company drowning a venture group in money. This equates with my experience. If money is obtained too easily it is spent on status symbols such as high quality furniture, secretaries for everyone etc.

Reviewing the Venture Group Charter

A venture group should have a clearly defined charter setting out its objectives and how these are to be achieved. The conclusion that Norman Fast comes to is that all venture groups evolve and that the regular reviews of the charter is a way of monitoring these changes in structure and objectives.

The author concludes this article as follows.

> The real tragedy of the venture graveyard is not that venture groups in many companies have been killed or pared down, but in many of these companies the spirit of venturing has also been a casualty.

A further article by Norman Fast in 1979 deals with the 'Key Managerial Factors in New Venture Departments'. Much of this deals with the research covered in the previous work but it is important that it was published in an Industrial Marketing Journal. Two clusters of factors are described as the 'corporate strategic posture' and the New Venture Department 'political posture' which will determine the direction of the NVD. The relationship between the corporate strategic posture and the cycles of diversification are explored. These can be seen as a continuum, one end of which is a diversifying position and the other end is a consolidated posture. As well as his own research work and experience the author reviews a great deal of published work on this subject. When I wrote the first draft of this literature review, I was not aware

of the valuable contribution by Norman Fast but on checking his references it was found that all had been reviewed and that a consensus of agreement was evident. It is interesting that since this major contribution by Norman Fast only one publication on NVD has been identified.

This is an article by Robert Sweeting who sets out to attempt a management framework for internal venture management. This framework is being used by the author for an empirical study of venturing in U.K. companies. The elements of the framework are listed as follows:

Corporate planning and business environment.
Venture evaluation and selection.
Organizational form and personnel.
Management planning and control.
Communications.
Venture disposition.

Reference is made to the work of Fast and other authors listed above and it is concluded that any failure is due to top management not being clear in their objective to what they require from venture management. In order to overcome this the following guidelines are listed. They should be written and widely available.

The objective of venturing.
The type of environment that will be provided by the parent company.
The management control system to be incorporated in ventures.
The process of assessing and reviewing venture.
The process for funding ventures.

The question now needs to be asked as to the success or failure of venture groups and it is evident that most of them fail but it is possible to learn from these failures to make them more successful.

As well as this the further question needs to be asked. Are venture groups more successful than traditional R & D? The problem here is the lack of evidence on the failure rate in central R & D establishments. One thing is certain. Innovation is risk taking to a high degree and most new products will fail. The problem we face is that of short term thinking, which is why we take the risk. I am reminded of this attitude by a story of Bob Hope to some students leaving college. The advice was 'don't go'. Everyone knows we live in a competitive world and that although we can innovate new ideas in the U.K., other countries exploit them. We are prisoners of our past history in being the first industrial country. Therefore it is essential to examine all aspects of innovation to make this country competitive again.

The only survey of failed R & D projects known to me is 'On the Shelf', but there is no attempt to equate these abandoned projects with those which were a success.

Until then there was a complete silence on these projects. Failure is not liked and is forgotten as quickly as possible, but we can learn more from studying failure than success, because we have more facts. With success there can be an unidentified factor which can play a major role without it being realized.

Another survey on failed R & D was by Ieuan Maddoch. He gives some interesting figures relating expenditure to results which contrast unfavourably in the U.K. to other countries. His conclusions are in line with the development of the venture team. Another factor to take note of is that a number of centralized R & D laboratories have been closed down within the last 10 years.

Although we have a great deal of evidence on the failure of venture groups we do not know the names of the companies or the type of product they attempted to develop. Thus we are unable to make any conclusions on what type of product is suitable for NVD or if in fact the failure was due to the method used in development. A number of firms were mentioned in the setting up stage of this process but it is not possible to identify which firms abandoned these techniques. The problem is that there is a stigma to failure and nobody likes to admit they have failed. Also there is the scapegoat syndrome in which the total blame is shifted to a person or group of people even though they may not be fully responsible. Therefore most organizations will only allow their failed projects to be studied if they cannot be identified. At the same time success is measured by greater profits and market penetration. Successful techniques which achieve this are kept confidential as long as possible. No firm is interested in helping a competitor.

The only two firms which have used this technique where progress can be followed are General Electric (U.S.A.) and Exxon. General Electric used this technique for developing new products but missed out on the micro-electronic revolution. They are at present buying their way back into this and the information technology business by taking over much smaller firms.

Exxon have been much more successful. They in fact developed a computer firm Zilog and the following firms in the office automation business; Delphi, Vydex, Quip and Qyx by using venture management techniques. The sales side of this is now being grouped together under Exxon Office Equipment. They were exhibiting under this name at the recent Info 81 exhibition. Their aim is to challenge IBM and Xerox in this market.

Because of the converging of information technology equipment this was the correct thing to do but it has created problems with staff differences and even some leaving. It appears that from an assessment in the *Financial Times*, not enough thought was given to overall strategy and the establishment of common norms and objectives. Therefore it is not yet clear if Exxon have succeeded with NVD.

It does illustrate a new problem facing NVD teams which due to convergent technology could happen again. It would be interesting to learn how or if Exxon solve this problem. One point is vital and that is that in any merger there must be objectives set by the teams in co-operation with each other and not the values of the parent body.

These objectives are set by both the type of product and the market it is intended for.

This leaves one to make conclusions on the basis of one's past experience and emotive reactions. My experience of 15 years in R & D as an information scientist is that in most cases projects fail in the final stages. Improvements of traditional products can be achieved within the operating company. Therefore, we need new forms of organization to promote innovation. One of the reasons for the failure of centralized R & D was the complete lack of communication between the market researcher and the scientist. In venture management things are brought together. This should result in a better success rate.

It seems likely that despite the high failure rate of NVD, the success rate is higher than in centralized R & D. Therefore, I feel that the work of Norman Fast should be widely read and studied in the U.K. in order to make our industry more innovative. The reasons for failure should be implemented in all new venture groups and their progress closely monitored. However, we should continue to look for any other new forms of organization.

Innovation and New Towns

New ventures can be actively promoted and assisted in different ways by various agencies. New Town Development Corporations, for example, are able to encourage new ventures in a number of different ways. In Milton Keynes these take the following forms:

First, concentration is directed toward certain key industries for which the opportunities offered by the new city are particularly appropriate, and which show a high incidence of innovation. One such industry is electronic components, where availability of small premises on a flexible basis, good access to other similar companies and availability of skilled labour is of prime importance.

Second, special centres for small businesses have been provided such as the Kiln Farm Business Centre where shared facilities and consultancy advice are available.

Third, the Corporation is prepared to act as an agent to raise venture capital, and is actively trying to promote a fuller range of advice and information services to all firms within its area of influence.

In conclusion it is possible to identify the main points of failure in the operation of a venture group. These are:

(1) The failure to conduct extensive information searches.

(2) The failure to conduct extensive marketing studies.

(3) The failure to set up a series of screening processes in selecting new projects.

(4) The failure to monitor progress in the NVD.

(5) The application of the rules of large organizations to the NVD.

(6) The failure to win acceptance by the rest of the organization.

(7) The failure to make sure that funds will be available when there is a crisis.

(8) The failure to use the severed 'venture' approach.

(9) The failure to establish a working relationship within the venture team. The boundaries of the organization are the market researcher and the scientist. Within these boundaries the production, design and systems engineer should have full say. An information scientist should also be available to monitor the external environment for the team.

(10) The failure to fit the venture management project into the overall corporate strategy of the organization. NVD is not the answer to long-range planning but is a part of it. It is an innovative technique which must be designed to be part of the corporate strategy of the enterprise.

(11) The failure of resources to see a project through to the break even point. It is of interest that Exxon (who own Esso) is a very large oil company with considerable resources and that they should be interested in venture management. With oil reserves limited the oil companies have to move into new ventures. Will it be venture management in its present or modified form or some new technique?

Finally there is an unexplored area relating innovation to its surrounding environment. We know that like innovation attracts like innovation, i.e. route 128 and Silicon Valley. This is due to a pool of skilled labour being available. However, what happens when a new town is built which attempts to attract high technology? Milton Keynes has and is being successful in doing this but so far no study has been made of the differing market techniques within new and expanded towns, local authorities and traditional areas. This would be a fruitful area of research within the next few years.

We have the classic work by Aguilar on scanning the business environment. A recent article in *Long Range Planning* shows there has been little progress. The question still needs to be asked about the impact of the external environment on the business. When a business relocates it enters a new environment and often becomes very different in operation. We like to think that in a new town environment it will be easier to encourage the new thinking which this country needs.

Another aspect not mentioned is raised by F. M. Smith. He makes the point that a new venture stands more chance of success if it is launched just as a recession is ending than if one is just starting. He also refers to the Kondratieff cycle. This is now being recognized as a very far sighted piece of forecasting.

This cycle can be seen as

Industrial manufacturing.
Railways.
Electricity and chemicals.
Information technology.
Space technology and the environment.

All these developments result in a period of prosperity.

With information technology we may be able to end the present world recession. This means we need to study and use new innovative methods in the United Kingdom to a much greater degree than in the past. The next market in my view is the use of space technology to monitor the environment.

Acknowledgements—This study started out as a project for Dr. R. C. Parker at Ashridge Management College and I would like to acknowledge the assistance of both Dr. Parker and the Planning Department of Milton Keynes Development Corporation in the final draft. However, the views expressed are my own.

References

D. C. Wheaton, Financing of venture projects, *Research Management*, 4 (4), 301–306, Winter (1961).

Donald A. Schon, Champions for radical new inventions, *Harvard Business Review*, pp. 77–86, March–April (1963).

Harry Schrage, The R & D entrepreneur: profile of success, *Harvard Business Review*, 43 (6), 56–69, November/December (1965).

Arnold C. Cooper, Small companies can pioneer new products, *Harvard Business Review*, pp. 162–179, September/October (1966).

Inventions for hire, but not for sale, *Business Week*, 25 March (1967).

Russell W. Peterson, New venture management in a large company, *Harvard Business Review*, **45**, 68–76, May/June (1967).

James Hiller, Venture activities in the large corporation, *IEEE Transactions on Engineering Management*, **EM-15** (2), 65–70, June (1968).

M. Hanan, Corporate growth through venture management, *Harvard Business Review*, **47** (1), 43–52, January/February (1969).

R. M. Adams, An approach to new business ventures, *Research Management*, **12** (4), 255–270, July (1969).

R. C. Springborn, New ventures of W R Grace and Company, *Research Management*, **12** (4), 271–278, July (1969).

Robert T. Wallace, New venture management at Owens—Illinois, *Research Management*, **12** (4), 261 (1969).

H. A. Wainer and I. M. Rubin, Motivation of R & D entrepreneur: determinants of company success, *Journal of Applied Psychology*, **53**, 178–184, June (1969).

A. B. Cohen, Venture management, in *Proceedings of the Management of the Technological Innovation Conference*, University of Bradford, pp. 101–104 (1969).

A. B. Cohen, New venture development at Du Pont, *Long Range Planning*, **2** (4), 7–10 June (1970).

Frederick Cook, Venture management as a new way to grow, *Innovation*, **25**, 28–37, October (1971).

Arnold C. Cooper, The founding of technologically based firms, *The Center for Venture Management*, p. 63 (1971). (Reprinted in *Entrepreneurs Handbook*, Vol. 2, Edited by Joseph Mancuso, Artech House, U.S.A. 1975 pp. 175–233 (1974)).

Douglas Foster, Venture management: a new approach to major problems, *Industrial Advertising and Marketing*, pp. 2–7, June (1971).

D. I. Orenbuch, The new entrepreneur, or venture management in practice, *Chemtech*, **1** (10), 584–587, October (1971).

A. W. Blackman, The role of technological forecasting in analysis and planning of new ventures, *American Society of Mechanical Engineers*, Design Engineering Conference Paper No. 72; p. 20, 26 December (1972). (Reprinted in *Technological Forecasting and Social Change*, **5**, 25–49 (1973)).

D. L. Wilemon and Howard Freese, Problems new venture teams face, *Innovation*, No. 28, pp. 40–47, Feburary (1972).

D. W. Brown, New venture analysis—playing to win, *Innovation*, No. 30, pp. 30–37, April (1972).

Richard M. Hill and James D. Hlavacek, The venture team—a new concept in marketing organization, *Journal of Marketing*, pp. 40–50, July (1972).

K. A. Jones and D. L. Wilemon, Emerging patterns in new venture management, *Research Management*, **15** (6), 14–27, November (1972).

J. B. Gardner, Innovation through new ventures. New venture concept at BOC, *R and D Management*, **3** (2), 85–90, February (1973).

K. H. Vesper and T. G. Holmdahl, How venture management fares in innovative companies, *Research Management*, **16** (3), 30–32 (1973).

D. L. Wilemon and G. R. Gemmill, The venture manager as a corporate innovator, *California Management Review*, **16** (1), 49–56 (1973).

James D. Hlavacek and Victor A. Thompson, Bureaucracy and new product innovation, *Academy of Management Journal*, **16** (3), 361–372, September (1973).

Sharon Sabin, At Nuclepore they don't work for GE anymore, *Fortune*, pp. 143–153, December (1973).

Martin Christopher, Venture analysis—Paper in *Creating and Marketing New Products*, Edited by Gordon Wills, etc., Crosby Lockwood Staples, pp. 193–211 (1973).

William H. Shames, Venture management—the business of the inventor, entrepreneur, venture capitalist and established company, Free Press, p. 289 (1974).

Patrick R. Liles, New business ventures and the entrepreneur, Richard D. Irwin Inc., U.S.A., p. 517 (1974).

A. Vernon, A new business venture, *R and D Management*, **4** (2), 85–88 (1974).

Donald M. Collier, Research based venture companies and the link between market and technology, *Research Management*, pp. 16–20, May (1974).

J. D. Hlavacek, Towards more successful venture management, *Journal of Marketing*, **38** (4), 56–60, October (1974).

Blair Little and R. G. Cooper, The marketing research decision in new technology ventures, *The Business Quarterly*, **39** (4), 58–64, Winter (1974).

Roy Rothwell, From invention to new business via the new venture approach, *Management Decision*, **13** (1), 10–21 (1975).

D. W. Collier, The creative link between market and technology, *Chemtech*, **2**, 90–93, February (1975).

C. Baumbeck and J. Mancuso, Editors, *Entrepreneurship and Venture Management*, Prentice-Hall, p. 355 (1975).

Joseph Mancuso, Editor, *The Entrepreneurs Handbook*, 2 Vols., Artech House, U.S.A. (1975).

David S. Hopkins, The roles of project teams and venture groups in new product development, *Research Management*, **18** (1), 7–12, January (1975).

Mark Hanan, Venturing corporation—think small to stay strong, *Harvard Business Review*, **54** (3), 139–148, May/June (1976).

BOC Limited, Developing new products. BOC's special outlet for innovation, *Business Europe*, pp. 191–192, 11 June (1976).

James D. Hlavacek, Brian H. Dovey and John J. Biondo, The small business technology to marketing power, *Harvard Business Review*, **55** (1), 106–116, January/February (1977).

Edward B. Roberts, Generating effective corporate innovation, *Technology Review*, **80** (1), 27–33, October/November (1977).

E. von Hippel, Successful and failing co-operative ventures—an empirical analysis, *Industrial Marketing Management*, **6**, 163–174 (1977).

Richard M. Hill and James D. Hlavacek, Learning from failure. Ten guidelines for venture management, *California Management Review*, **19** (4), 5–16 (1977).

Dan T. Dunn, The rise and fall of ten venture groups, *Business Horizons*, No. 5, pp. 32–41, October (1977).

Lynn Adkins, Venture capital: the latest corporate game, *Dun's Review*, **112** (4), 82–84, October (1978).

Christopher Lorenz, Venture management—3M and Exxon show the way, *Financial Times*, p. 19, 20 February (1979).

Ralph Biggadike, The risky business of diversification, *Harvard Business Review*, pp. 103–111, May–June (1979).

Norman D. Fast, The rise and fall of corporate new venture divisions, *UMI Research Press* (Published 1978 in U.S.A).

Norman D. Fast, A visit to the new venture graveyard, *Research Management*, **2**, 18–22, March (1979).

Normal D. Fast, Key managerial factors in new venture developments, *Industrial Marketing Management*, **8**, 221–235, June (1979).

Robert Sweeting, Internal venture management: analytical aspects, *Journal of General Management*, **7** (1), 34–45, Autumn (1981).

Other References

Centre for the Study of Industrial Innovation, *On The Shelf*, A survey of individual R & D projects abandoned for non-technical reasons (1971).

Ieuan Maddock, End of the glamorous adventure, *New Scientist*, pp. 375–378, 13 February (1975).

Exxon's Next Prey: IBM at Xerox, *Business Week*, pp. 92, 95–97, 28 April (1980).

Financial Times, Management Page edited by C. Lorenz—Will Exxon close the office door? 8 February (1982).

F. J. Aguilar, *Scanning the Business Environment*, Collier-MacMillan (1967).

Liam Fahey, William R. King and Vadake K. Narayanan, Environmental scanning and forecasting in strategic planning—the state of the art, *Long Range Planning* 14 (1), 32–39, February (1981).

F. M. Smith, Innovation: the way out of the recession? *Long Range Planning*, 15 (1), 19–33 (1982).

The Delusion of Intrapreneurship

C. Wesley Morse

The purpose of this article is to provide some insight into the limitations in the concept of intrapreneurship, the definition of an 'intrapreneur' being an entrepreneur operating within a large comany rather than in his own business. The author believes that intrapreneurship is not a formula for successful innovation in large companies as a bureaucratic system cannot provide the rewards and the personal autonomy which the true entrepreneur requires.

In the wake of Japanese management techniques and with a broad backdrop of behavioural research, which has emphasized more trusting and creative group relationships for more than 20 years, managers in large companies are being asked to consider new structural changes which are quite unique. The latest popular prescription for the revitalization of large businesses is called 'intrapreneuring'.

Aware that entrepreneurs are the darlings of the venture capital market, and mindful of such research as the U.S. National Science Foundation study[1] which reports that each dollar spent for research and development by small firms produces four times more innovation than a comparable dollar lavished by large companies, the pragmatic advocates of this newly 'coined' practice have confidently advised, 'if you can't beat 'em, join 'em'.

Gifford Pinchot, in his book *Intrapreneuring*,[2] defines the 'intrapreneur' in the same terms that most knowledgeable people use to describe entrepreneurs. In fact, an important theme of the book is to explain that an entrepreneur can operate within a large comany in much the same way that he would proceed if he were in a smaller firm; given that the right conditions exist in the company. The *intrapreneur* then, is seen as a sort of internal entrepreneur. His charge is to duplicate the energy, resourcefulness and innovation of entrepreneurs on the outside, and the corporation is admonished to give him the tools to do it with.

The author is a Professor of Management at California State University and a visiting member of faculty at Henley—The Management College. He is currently writing a book, to be published in 1987, entitled *Business Champions: Becoming an Entrepreneur.*

It has been fairly well documented that entrepreneurial practices leading to desirable growth and profitability are inherent in many small and mid-sized growth companies.[3] What I will examine in the pages that follow is the likelihood that these arrangements can be useful in large organizations as well.

I first became uneasy about the potential for entrepreneurial activity in large companies when as part of a research project I discussed the role of entrepreneurs with a number of key executives of large firms in the U.S.A. and the U.K. The feeling I received was unanimously one of guarded unease about 'that breed of cat' as one manager described them. A number of these executives remembered attempts to institute entrepreneurial practices somewhere in the firm, but there seemed to be little evidence of success. One chief executive recalled his experience as follows:

> We have had quite a lot of experience with entrepreneurs. A number of companies we have acquired over the years were headed by people you would describe as entrepreneurs, and of course most of them came to work for us as part of the deal. I must say that, in the main, they have lacked the team spirit we require of our executives. In fact, we have had so much difficulty getting these people into our way of doing things that I am sure not one of them is still with us.

None of these executives was pessimistic about the possibility of change, or increased levels of innovation in his company. They were universally familiar with the strides of recent years in organizational development and strategies for change; in fact some of them were quite enthusiastic about increasing innovation through change in their firms. They were not, however, sanguine about the organizational role of entrepreneurs. What then are the chances of success for intrapreneurs in large business organizations?

Since we are interested in voluntary work activity on the part of a limited number of individuals (surely entrepreneurial activity is not the norm in these organizations), it seems reasonable to consider the motivational aspects of entrepreneurship, and by extension, what is needed to induce such people to exercise their entrepreneurial skills in large companies. Here we have access to considerable motivational research.[4]

While an extraordinary number of motivating factors are suggested by various studies, two stand out as universal and important. These are: the expectation of wealth, and the need for personal autonomy. Without regard for the myriad other reasons then, let us examine just these two major motivations of entrepreneurs to see if they can be provided by large firms. To do so, we will need to consider three sometimes overlapping areas of policy common to most large firms. These are:

☆ the reward structure;

☆ the locus of control in the organization and

☆ the nature of the corporate culture.

Rewards

Of all the rewards that entrepreneurs expect from business, financial gain is certainly the most widely publicized. The number of entrepreneurs in innovative businesses who have amassed sizable fortunes is impressive. The importance of the statistics can hardly have escaped anyone who has a spark of inventive genius or entrepreneurial spirit. Referring to U.S. facts alone, recent statistics show close to 1 million individuals who could claim a net worth of more than $1m, while about 5300 people report incomes in excess of $1m each year. Many of these people have been publicly associated with new ventures.

Vroom,[5] in 1964, proposed the now widely accepted Preference–Expectation theory of Motivation. His conclusions have been restated in a quite clear form by Filley and House as follows:

> Whenever an individual chooses between alternatives that involve uncertain outcomes, it seems clear that his behavior is affected not only by his preferences among outcomes, but also by the degree to which he believes these outcomes to be probable.[6]

When applied to the expectation of wealth, Vroom's motivational concept simply says that an entrepreneur's performance will be conditioned by his expectation that whatever project he undertakes not only will succeed, but will make him wealthy.

Even under the best corporate incentive plans (usually involving stock options for successful performance) the *expectation* of wealth cannot often match that of the outside entrepreneur.

Large corporations clearly have a multiplicity of factors to consider when arranging compensation, factors which generally do not burden smaller growth companies. Simple fairness in personnel policy probably heads this list. Since intrapreneurs,

by definition would be only a small part of the staff of any firm, to allow them to receive the kind of wealth that they may expect from successful performance elsewhere, might seriously unbalance the compensation system involving thousands of other people—people whose contributions are also highly valued by the firm.

Can we expect, for example, that a brilliant engineer who designs a breakthrough system, ultimately producing great company profit, will be paid more than the Chief Executive of his firm? It would seem unlikely. Yet, as an entrepreneur, or a member of a team, in a smaller company, that same engineer may have the expectation of amassing just such wealth.

Consider the likely expectations of our hypothetical engineer after he has reviewed the widely disseminated financial statistics of some entrepreneurial winners. The following are a few of the chief executives of computer companies in the U.S.A. and the value of their stock on the morning after their company went public.[7]

K. Phyllip Hwang	TeleVideo Systems	$610m
Andrew Kay	Kaypro	$245m
Lorraine Mecca	Micro D	$59m
Mitch Kapor	Lotus	$56m
Hal Lashlee	Ashton-Tate	$49m

Can we not then expect, on the basis of Vroom's theory as well as common sense, that entrepreneurs will prefer to associate with firms from which they can have a high expectation of wealth?

Or, in the words of Robert Welch, President of Zitel, a small computer memory company then on the verge of public financing, 'I can smell the Ferrari now.'[8]

Clearly, large firms are not in a position to match the wealth expectations of individuals who see themselves as entrepreneurs, able to master both the innovative and management challenges of new ventures.

The Locus of Control

The studies of organizational design reported by Joan Woodward[9] have become the benchmark research of the 'contingency' school of management thought, and serve to describe the important link between the complexity of technology and successful organization structure.

While Woodward's findings are detailed, one can safely summarize at least one dimension of her work by observing that classical, bureaucratic organizations with narrow spans of control are the most successful forms of structure in businesses that utilize simple and stable technologies.

Such businesses are characterized by highly centralized control over factors such as budgets and critical decision making.

A review of the structural arrangements in companies in the *Fortune* 500 group reveals a consistent bias for Product Division and Functional Division organization. These bureaucratic arrangements seem reasonable, particularly in companies which rely on older technologies for survival.

Such bureaucratic forms of organization however are inconsistent with the second entrepreneurial motivation I have mentioned—personal autonomy. Among the benefits of these classical structures are the stability and control which they bring to industries where growth is slow and priorities are aligned with profit maximization from relatively stable technology. This very stability and control, as we shall see in the examples that follow is a constant threat to the autonomy needed by entrepreneurs.

Corporate Culture

If it is difficult to motivate entrepreneurs in large companies, why do firms such as 3M and Hewlett-Packard seem to be successful at it? The answer lies in the deliberate establishment of a corporate culture which will support the needs of entrepreneurial people.

At 3M for example, employees across the board are allowed to use up to 15 per cent of their time to work on a pet project. Researcher Arthur Fry used this 'bootleg slack' time to develop 3M's most successful new product to date—Post-its.

While 3M's policies to encourage innovation are legend, as are those at HP and other large research-based companies, the significant issue is that the encouragement of innovation is deliberate in these firms. The culture of the entire firm has been purposely designed to promote it.

In contrast, the bureaucratic firm encourages stability, specialization and control. These factors inhibit innovation because they stifle the autonomy required by entrepreneurial people. But the bureaucratic firm cannot modify its structure to facilitate innovation as long as it is dependent on the stable technology which needs bureaucratic control.

A few years ago I attended a meeting of the Academy of Management in Phoenix Arizona. At the plenary session we were addressed by an Executive Vice President of Atlantic Richfield Corporation, the large U.S. energy company. This gentleman's topic was the encouragement of innovation within ARCO. Three hundred professorial heads nodded assent as he described the policies the firm had instituted to improve the flow of information between departments and divisions, the incentives it had provided to young managers to innovate, the new, freer atmosphere of dissent which ARCO's policies had made possible.

He described an innovative marketing programme developed by a team of young managers, which was enabling the company to increase its share of the retail market for gasoline in California.

During the question period there was considerable interest in the new marketing strategy. As we moved toward the obvious end of the session, a hand was raised with a question . . . 'I am very interested in your programme to improve innovation,' said the questioner, 'Would you mind telling us; when your company adopts a proposal of one of your innovative managers, and the project fails. What happens to the career of that manager?'

There ensued a long silence. After a while, the ARCO executive said, 'That is a very good question. I must confess that we have not yet developed a way to deal with that situation. It does seem clear however, that once a managers project has failed, it will be difficult to promote him in the future.'

Risk taking is certainly one of the most important elements in the success of entrepreneurs. While new ventures are always accompanied by risk, the style of most new venture managers involves acceptance of reasonable risks in lieu of certainty, and preservations of options to try again if failure occurs.[10] The ARCO experience displays, in this writers opinion, one of the important incompatibilities of traditional organizations and entrepreneurship. Employees of such large organizations simply cannot be expected to assume the career risks often associated with innovative projects.

There is perhaps no better example of the limitations of corporate culture than events in the aftermath of design by an entrepreneurial team of the MV8000 computer at Data General Corporation. Dubbed internally the 'Eagle', the state-of-the-art machine which was to rescue Data General from an obsolescence crunch in 1980 and contribute enormously to its cash flow, was the result of $2\frac{1}{2}$ years of intense work in a basement laboratory by a team of 30 young engineers.

While the team leader, J. Thomas West is now a Data General Vice President, the three managers who reported to him on the project have left the firm. Nine of the 14 key engineers on the design team have also left and are with small entrepreneurial companies that did not exist a few years ago.

Stephen Wallach, Eagle's chief designer now heads his own firm, Convex Computer Corporation. He says he reacted bitterly when the Eagle team was broken up after the design proved successful at Data General, and he left the firm to join a competitor.

He was subsequently 'recruited' by venture capitalists Sevin Rosen Management Company, and with partner Robert Palluck set up his own shop.

Quotations from former team members reveal how they have reacted to company policies in the wake of Eagle's success. According to Carl Alsing, now heading engineering at Palantir Corporation, the entrepreneurial thrust of the project was 'very destructive' to company loyalty. As they battled other groups for scarce resources, 'we thought we were on a different team'. In the words of Wallach, 'We didnt walk away [from the Eagle] with the feeling of coming off a high . . . we were saying, "wait a second, this isn't how it's supposed to work"'. 'It was founded on a lie,' recalls Alsing when he describes how West, the Project Manager, promised to sneak budgets for the new design concept past the Data General brass. Finally, Carl Carman, formerly Data General's Vice President of engineering and not a member of the team says, 'There was just no way to meet their expectations' with rewards that would match the value of their contributions. Carman, no longer with Data General, is now a venture capitalist.

In Table 1 the entrepreneurial motivators, 'expectation of wealth' and 'personal autonomy' are displayed to summarize the effects of different organizational systems. The terms 'bureaucratic' and 'innovative' are used to represent traditional and innovative type organizations, recognizing that these terms are generalizations. Innovative organizations may be large firms or small- or medium-sized companies where entrepreneurial values are part of the culture. The values, low and high are relative and denote tendencies in the indicated direction.

Implications for Managers

It seems clear to me that in the absence of a company-wide culture specifically designed to encourage entrepreneurial activity, large firms are well advised to consider other means to stimulate innovation. *Large companies with bureaucratic systems cannot hope to provide either the expectation of reward, or the personal autonomy which will attract and hold the best entrepreneurial people.* Intrapreneurship does not hold out hope of success in these companies because the reward structure will not permit compensation in line with the expectations of entrepreneurs, the locus of control in the organization does not allow for sufficient personal autonomy, and the corporate climate in bureaucratically organized firms promotes stability which often runs counter to the needs of innovative processes.

If it is considered essential to incorporate entrepreneurs in the innovative mix of corporate investments, these firms should consider acquiring independent subsidiary firms, where the requisite entrepreneurial culture can be allowed to take hold and grow. General Motors Corporation has recently chosen this strategy with the acquisition of Hughes Aircraft Company, an electronics and communications firm. The acquisition agreements are said to include an agreement on the part of GM to allow Hughes to be managed separately from its new parent, to protect the research environment which Hughes managers feel is essential to its continued growth.

There is a strong legacy of research and development management which emphasizes the production of creative inputs, and which has been practised successfully by the best managed large firms for many years. In the main it is these models, augmented by imaginative marketing, and not the entrepreneurial role which are most likely to produce the innovative results needed by most of our largest businesses.

References

(1) National Science Foundation, *Science Indicators*, Washington D.C. (1979).

(2) Gifford Pinchot, III, *Intrapreneuring*, Harper & Rowe, New York, pp. 32–64 (1985).

(3) See for example, Richard Cavanaugh and Donald Clifford, Jr., Lessons from America's Mid-sized Growth Companies, *McKinsey Quarterly*, Autumn (1983).

(4) Examples of this literature include: Calvin Kent, *The Environment for Entrepreneurship*, Heath, Lexington, MA (1984) and William Baumol, Toward operational models of entrepreneurship, in *Entrepreneurship*, edited by Joshua Ronen, Lexington Books (1983).

(5) V. H. Vroom, *Work and Motivation*, Wiley, New York (1964).

(6) Alan Filley and Robert House, *Managerial Process and Organizational Behavior*, Scott Foresman, Glenview, Illinois, p. 361 (1969).

(7) Robert Levering *et al.*, *The Computer Entrepreneurs*, New American Library, New York, p. 11 (1984).

(8) *Time*, 23 January, p. 49 (1984).

(9) Joan Woodward, *Industrial Organization: Theory and Practice*, Oxford University Press, London (1965).

(10) See David Gumpert and Howard Stevenson, The heart of entrepreneurship, *Harvard Business Review*, March–April, pp. 85–93 (1985).

(11) The Eagle project is described in *The Wall Street Journal*, 30 September, p. 1 (1985).

Table 1.

	Reward system		Locus of control		Company culture	
	Bureaucratic	Innovative	Bureaucratic	Innovative	Bureaucratic	Innovative
Expectation of wealth	Low	High			Low	High
Personal autonomy			Low	High	Low	High

Corporate Development— Preferred Strategies in U.K. Companies

D. A. Littler and R. C. Sweeting

In this paper policies available for corporate development are examined and the suggestion is made that new business development remains an option that must be considered. The time span of the growth, the 'quality' of any growth and the extent of managerial commitment to 'growth business' are identified as important factors that should influence decisions on corporate development. Results of two surveys made by the authors of U.K. corporate experience with different NBD entry strategies for new business development are also discussed in the paper.

It would appear uncontentious to argue that the majority of companies should aim at long-term corporate development which involves sustainable growth of some measure of return on resources employed. Given changes that can occur in a company's environment over time, corporate development implies the periodic review of, and where necessary adjustments to and elimination of existing businesses, and the development of new businesses. Short-term pressures stemming allegedly in particular from the furnishers of capital can obstruct if not endanger this process since the focus becomes the next interim or annual results, rather than the longer-term durable development of the total company and its constituent businesses.

In recent years the environmental pressures on many traditional businesses have intensified. Not only have many seen a maturing of their markets; they have also experienced increasing competition from

developing countries which have significant comparative advantages. In the United Kingdom from the late 1970s there has been survival cost–cutting with capacity being severely curtailed and some businesses (often those viewed as peripheral) being sold. Many of these companies have been seen to have improved financial health. They are 'leaner and fitter' and have, so it might be argued, a solid platform from which to develop further. The question arises as to the strategic direction of such companies: will many 'stick to the knitting'[1] and remain with and develop their existing core business; or will they launch new businesses organically, by acquisition or by some other route?

This paper examines the policies available for corporate development, suggests that new business development (NBD) remains an option that must be considered, and considers the available policies for developing innovative business areas for corporate development.

Corporate Growth and Development Strategic Decisions

There are various issues that should influence decisions on corporate growth and hence development:[2]

(a) The time span of the growth; short-term increases in profit may easily be obtained by, for example, restraining investment in new technology and product development, or by selling off easily marketable parts of the company; but such measures may result in the sacrifice of the company in the longer term.[3]

(b) The 'quality' of any growth: is the longer-term future of the 'growing' business going to be adversely affected by environmental factors?

Dale Littler is Senior Lecturer in the Department of Management Sciences, University of Manchester, specializing in the marketing of innovations, competitive policies and new business development. R. C. Sweeting is Lecturer in Finance and Accounting at UMIST, specializing in management accounting related to innovations and new business development.

These factors might include new legislation and threats from developing countries which may possess cost advantages.

(c) The extent of the managerial commitment to the 'growth business': is the commitment of management, especially top management, going to decline because it is not 'comfortable' and 'at ease' with the new growth business? Is management determined to 'make growth happen'?

Possible Directions for Corporate Development

The different types of options which companies may adopt in embarking on a policy of growth business development can be analysed as to the degree of new technology and new market content which they involve. We have modified an initial analysis by Ansoff[4] to create a 'directional matrix' (see Table 1) of different corporate options aimed at corporate development.[2]

Table 1. Corporate directional policy matrix

Market	Technology		
	Existing	Incremental	Radical
Existing	Market penetration	Product development	New product development
Incremental	Market extension	Product and market extension	Related business development
Radical	Market development	Related business development	New business development

Source: 'Directional matrix' after Ansoff,[4] but extended to include intermediate states of development.

The corporate options contained within the matrix can be summarized as:

Market penetration:
Securing a higher share of existing markets with existing products. This policy will usually entail intensifying marketing efforts.

Product development:
The aim here is to adapt existing products to give them a marked competitive advantage.

New product development:
This option requires introducing technologically innovative products to existing customers. This should result in high growth and profits but with inevitably high risk of new products failing.

Market extension:
Existing products are used to enter markets that are closely related to existing ones in which the company presently operates.

Product and market extension:
This option involves aiming at specialized market segments with products that are extensions of existing products.

Related business developments:
This is concerned with entry into new markets with new technologies but with either markets or technologies akin to that with which the company is familiar. These options, because of their remoteness in terms of market or technology with what the company is familiar are inevitably risky.

Market development:
This option involves the company aiming at significantly different markets. The difference may be, for example, in terms of geography or the buying behaviour of the new customers.

New business developments:
This is the most radical option which the company may consider in developing new growth business. It involves entering the completely unknown, so far as the company is concerned, in terms of markets and technology. It therefore presents managements with considerable uncertainties and problems.

Another important consideration to be taken into account when planning which approaches to adopt for corporate development are new sources of any new inputs that might be required, and this factor may often be omitted when considering whether or not to enter a new business. If, for example, new services are necessary then the already high risks and uncertainties of the NBD option will be intensified.

In general, in order that risk may be spread, it is advisable that a portfolio of approaches be adopted.[5] The criteria of a balanced portfolio of strategic opportunities would include: the stage of development of the new venture; the resources demanded; and the risk of commercial failure. Obviously the portfolio will have to be reviewed periodically to take account of changed circumstances and experience gained. NBDs are particularly vulnerable in such reviews because research has indicated[6] that new ventures may take 10–12 years before they produce comparable returns on investment to those of mature businesses. It is essential not only that top management is committed to NBD at the outset, but that this is sustained throughout the gestation period so that embryonic new businesses are given a reasonable chance to succeed. It is the NBD option that we will be focusing on in the remaining part of this paper.

The NBD Option

The NBD option may be one adopted by a company which is seeking to become less dependent on the core business activities that may exhibit a number of features such as inter alia a decline, stabilization or fall in the rate of increase in demand; overcapacity; intense competition, often from rivals with significant cost advantages; and declining margins. The prospects of attaining future growth are not promising.[5,7] The option includes a number of possible entry strategies and these include: acquisitions of small, entrepreneurial, usually high technology firms, licensing and venture management. Venture management is a generic term and and in turn involves a range of approaches which are summarized in Table 2.

Intra and Extra Corporate Environment

Demand for a company's products enters a phase of low or no growth when a high level of market penetration is attained. In order to ensure efficient use of productive capacity the competition will be intense to keep sales volumes high. Prices in the market may well be depressed. In addition rival producers from developing countries that possess cost advantages may be increasing their market presence often with large capacity, greater than their domestic demand, in order to take advantage of economies of scale. With stable technologies and access to cheaper factors of production, these overseas producers are formidable if not unbeatable rivals. With this background, retrenchment for those companies particularly in developed countries becomes almost inevitable.

Companies will generally be compelled to consider some form of business development if they wish to satisfy goals such as high growth and ability to secure a proprietary position in the market place. However, there are forces present such as organizational inertia which will mean incremental changes will be more willingly accepted than those where major innovation is involved with its consequent disruption. It is not argued that such incremental changes are to be rejected. Significant benefits may accrue from following extension policies, for example using developments of their technologies to aim

Table 2. Definition of the venture management approaches

Venture capital:	the investment in other companies, usually for a share of the equity.
Venture nurturing:	the provision of venture capital and management assistance from the investing company. This 'hands on' management approach is usually assured by having representative(s) of the investing company on the Board.
Venture spin-off:	the formation of a separate company to exploit an idea that is not compatible with the mainstream business of the parent company.
Special joint ventures:	a venture that involves cooperation between the Parent Company, which usually supplies capital and management services etc., and a smaller company that possesses the often advanced technology as well as perhaps that intangible ingredient 'entrepreneurial drive'.
Internal venture:	the developing of new businesses in-house, using generally internally generated ideas.

Source: After Roberts.[8]

at existing markets. However, many of the options outlined in the 'directional matrix' in Table 1 may only offer short-term amelioration of the underlying corporate problem of operating in mature markets, particularly where investment in technological innovation is not involved.

Companies which do not consider some form of business development may have decided to return funds to stakeholders and contract the scale of the company; or their managements may be so short sighted that they fail to see the significance of the opportunities offered to them by business development. It may also be that the company is able to take a pioneering position in the higher added value section of the markets in which it operates. However, the latter strategy may involve what we have termed related business development, and over time its 'proprietary' position may be eroded by the understandable imitation of its competitors.
Within the company there are possibly several impediments to the successful outcome for new business development. One of the more severe stems from the fact that parent organizations are probably highly bureaucratic and do not consequently possess the flexibility necessary for such rapidly changing new businesses.[9,10]

Senior managers in the parent organization have frequently achieved their position because they are good administrators of what were stable businesses and are therefore 'uncomfortable' with 'free wheeling' new businesses. This would suggest the need to separate new businesses organizationally from the traditional business areas in order to insulate them form a potentially stifling bureaucracy.[7,11]

A second major threat originates from the managers of the existing businesses that are generating cash. They may resent the diversion of resources to areas which seem risky and which will generally have negative cash flow. The commitment of top management is necessary to protect the new businesses and ensure they continue to receive the resources they can effectively justify over a period sufficient to gauge the potential commercial robustness of the new venture. The negative cash flow during the early years will often lead to premature termination.[7]

It is important, also, that over enthusiastic supporters for innovative NBD do not 'oversell it' to top management as an option for corporate development. Failure rates can be high.[11,12] Top management should clearly understand that there is a significant risk of failure, and appreciate the possibly long (10–12 years is not uncommon[6]) periods before reasonable financial returns flow from the *successful* ventures. During these long time spans it will be necessary for the new business to have adequate resources necessary for them to succeed.

Quinn[13] found that, 'few, if any, major innovations result from highly structured planning systems'. It could therefore be argued that an incremental approach to decision making in innovative new business areas should be adopted. The major problem is that business plans established at the outset rapidly become redundant as uncertainties clarify and new uncertainties surface. Detailed long-term plans under such circumstances are irrelevant and perhaps managements should be only looking to outline the future of NBDs.

Corporate managements, when considering the possible options for development described in the 'directional matrix' will therefore favour incremental options and NBD will only be attempted when:

☆ external pressures are so severe that the company is compelled to consider such a radical option;

☆ other preferred alternatives have failed to satisfy desired objectives even though these objectives may be unrealistic;

☆ the company feels that it is failing to capitalize on NBD opportunities that are being exploited by others, in particular its competitors; the firm's management wants to project a dynamic and progressive image;

☆ the firm is rich in cash and there is a dearth of suitable investment opportunities in existing business areas.

U.K. Corporate Involvement with NBD

As we have described above acquisition, licensing or some form of Venture Management may be adopted as entry strategies for NBD. Table 3 indicates the relative popularity of these entry strategies for NBD from a survey we performed in 1983 in which 88 U.K. companies responded to questions of how they developed new business. These companies in *The Times* Top 1000 Companies of 1981 covered an extensive range of industries.[14]

The results in Table 3 may be compared with those in Table 4 which details how 19 U.K. companies surveyed in 1985, involved in a range of industrial and commercial sectors, adopted different entry strategies for NBD. The 19 companies were a subset of 23 U.K. companies who responded to a range of questions related to their NBDs.

Acquisitions

Acquisitions in the context of strategic corporate development offer apparently easy and low-risk routes to tangential or related business areas. In our definition of NBD we indicated that the 'new'

Table 3. New business entry strategies ($n = 82$) (1983)

	Number	% of respondent
Acquisition	65	(79)
Licensing	43	(52)
Venture management:		
Venture capital/nurturing	36	(44)
Venture spin-off	7	(8)
'Special' joint venture	31	(38)
Internal venture development	33	(40)

Table 4. New business entry strategies ($n = 19$) (1985)

	Number	% of respondents
Acquisition	13	(68)
Licensing	9	(47)
Venture management:		
Venture capital/nurturing	6	(32)
Venture spin-off	2	(11)
'Special' joint venture	10	(53)
Internal venture development	12	(63)
Other:		
Distributorship	1	(5)
Product development	1	(5)

technologies and markets were new to the parent organization—they need not be 'new' in absolute terms. Therefore, it is possible in the case of an NBD acquisition that the acquired business may have some 'track record'. However, this is not necessarily so. The acquired business may be a small technologically innovative enterprise that is relatively young. The features of the acquired business will be that it has the potenial to make a significant positive effect on the company's earnings stream.

The acquired company can be an important building block, and can provide access to new technical expertise (to the purchasing firm), new markets and new personnel. But these potential benefits may not be realized: potential markets can be left undeveloped and key personnel can leave. The result can be, as one manager told us, that the acquiring company is 'left with a bag of nails'—creating more problems than solutions.

Between 1983 and 1985 acquisition has maintained its lead as the most frequently used entry strategy for NBD. In the 1985 survey, we referred to above, seven respondents viewed acquisition as the most effective of entry strategies to develop new businesses and acquisition was generally perceived as being a lower-risk route to NBD. If the company wishes to enter an innovative business area there will of course be a limited, if non-existent track record.

Licensing

Where a company does not wish to expend resources researching and developing technology

then it may be able to negotiate to license technology for the payment of some royalty or a fee. One of our survey respondents commented however, that licensing is not necessarily an easy or inexpensive process. Moreover, it may be rather limiting. It is possible that the company may be restricted from employing the licensed technology in other of its product areas or from marketing in certain geographical regions. It is, however, a relatively low-risk means of gaining access to technologies which can be employed to complement a firm's existing technologies and which may be used as a foundation for future technological development. The constraints which are entailed may be substantially offset by the benefits to be gained by being able to trade in profitable markets.[2]

The results from both the 1983 and 1985 surveys indicate that licensing is a widely used entry strategy for NBD. In the 1985 survey, however, licensing, surprisingly, was mentioned by only three companies as being the 'most effective' entry strategy in their view. The one company which considered licensing the 'least effective' option complained that completion of a licensing deal was time consuming and that there was a high cash outflow.

Internal Venture Development

In the spectrum of venture management approaches to NBD, internal corporate venturing is the entry strategy which offers the parent organization greatest control but which also has the greatest risk.[8] The parent organization has absolute control over management decisions related to internal corporate ventures. Associated with this, it has total responsibility for sustaining the ventures and is exposed to all the downside risk without any partners to share it.

In our 1985 survey, internal corporate venturing was mentioned by five companies as being the 'most effective' entry strategy for NBD, mainly because it offered much greater control. One company stated that internal ventures could be undertaken in a way that was less visible to others (particularly in traditional business areas) in the organization. However, this comment contrasts with those made by one of the two firms who regarded it as the 'least effective' entry strategy. This company argued that, in their organization, internal corporate ventures were difficult to control and 'motivate' (*sic*), were 'too visible' and were 'high risk'.

A fundamental problem which we found with internal corporate ventures is that they are frequently technology rather than market driven. The ventures often originate from a research and development project that apparently cannot be commercialized in any other way. Often little regard is given to marketing considerations with often unprofitable results for the new business.[7] Other problems that we have frequently found that limit the potential for successful outcomes of internal corporate ventures include: lack of clear objectives for the venture activity and pressure for short-term returns. It may be premature to dismiss internal corporate venturing as an ineffective means of developing new businesses because of its lack of success to date; the problems may lie more with the implementation rather than the concept.

Venture Capital

Investment in the equity of start-up businesses, but not at a level to let that business be classed as a subsidiary, has been a significant factor in the development of innovative businesses in the United States for many years. The general use of venture capital in recent years has been reported to be expanding in the United Kingdom. Chancellor of the Exchequer Lawson stated that between 1979 and 1984 risk investment by U.K. venture capitalists grew from £10m to £248m.[15] In our more limited studies the use of *corporate* venture capital (CVC) was quite widely used as a route to NBD. In the 1983 survey 44 per cent of respondents employed CVC as an entry strategy, while 32 per cent of the 1985 sample claimed to be involved with it. In the 1985 survey venture capital was only seen as the 'most effective' entry strategy by two companies; one company stated that it was 'high risk, high return'. Four companies were against the venture capital approach because they felt it entailed a loss of control. The distinction between venture capital and venture nurturing needs to be drawn; the latter was mentioned favourably by a further two companies.

Careful definition of 'venture capital' is required. Where money is provided on the basis of little or no evidence of a viable business at a key early stage in the life of the new venture then this is termed 'venture capital' whereas 'development capital' is where funds are provided when the business has existed for some time and there is some evidence of a 'track record' having been achieved. It is often the case, in the United Kingdom, according to practitioners in the venture capital market whom we have interviewed in our research, that 'development capital' is more frequently available than 'venture capital'. Indeed they find it difficult to give cases where true venture capital has been provided on a significant scale.

Corporate venture capital (CVC) is a means, maybe, of providing a 'window' on alternative technologies; if successful, the investor may increase his investment, and so develop a significant interest in a growing business area. Unfortunately, research in the U.S. by Hardymon, Denino and Salter[16] has shown that the CVC approach to corporate development may involve some difficulties. They believe that to make CVC a success the parent organization should not 'interfere' with the company's venture capital operation. They found that conflicts often arose between the objectives of the company and those responsible for managing its venture capital fund.

Concluding Comments

In considering corporate development a firm has a range of options, each of which involves differing degrees of risk, durability and potential return. There is a tendency to focus on low-risk, short-term alternatives. However, failure to develop new businesses will make the firm a 'hostage to fortune'. In fact, effective corporate development would involve investment in a portfolio of new business developments.

NBD itself—which under external pressures a company will inevitably be forced to consider—can be pursued along a number of different although not necessarily mutually exclusive routes. It is generally considered that explorations in territories akin in some way to those in which companies already operate are *more likely* to lead to profitable outcomes than entering the completely unknown.

For a variety of reasons, acquisitions and internal venture development remain preferred means of entry. There is no doubt that licensing offers considerable attractions, particularly when used to augment other methods. Corporate venture capital seems to remain on the periphery, and it is doubtful that many companies contain the requisite expertise not only to perform it effectively but also to capitalize on any opportunities that it may yield.

References

(1) J. J. Peters and R. H. Waterman, *In Search of Excellence*, Harper & Row, New York (1982).

(2) D. A. Littler and R. C. Sweeting, Policies for new business development, in *Current Research in Management*, Ed. V. Hammond, Frances Pinter (1985).

(3) R. S. Kaplan, The evolution of management accounting, *The Accounting Review*, LIX (3), 390–418 (1984).

(4) H. I. Ansoff, *Corporate Strategy*, McGraw-Hill, New York (1965).

(5) D. A. Littler and R. C. Sweeting, *Positive Approaches to New Business Development*, University of Manchester Institute of Science and Technology (1982).

(6) R. Biggadike, The risky business of diversification, *Harvard Business Review*, **57**, 103–111 (1979).

(7) D. A. Littler and R. C. Sweeting, Business innovation in the U.K., *R & D Management*, **14** (1), 1–9 (1984).

(8) E. B. Roberts, New ventures for corporate growth, *Harvard Business Review*, 134–142, July–August (1980).

(9) J. D. Hlavacek and V. A. Thompson, Bureaucracy and new product innovation, *Academy of Management Journal*, **16** (3), 361–372 (1973).

(10) R. W. Peterson, New venture management in a large company, *Harvard Business Review*, 68–76, May–June, (1967).

(11) M. Hanan, Venturing corporations—think small to stay strong, *Harvard Business Review*, 139–148, May–June (1976).

(12) N. Fast, A visit to the new venture graveyard, *Research Management*, 18–22, March (1979).

(13) J. B. Quinn, Managing innovation: controlled chaos, *Harvard Business Review*, 73–84, May–June (1985).

(14) D. A. Littler and R. C. Sweeting, *New Business Development in the U.K.—A Survey*, Department of Management Sciences, University of Manchester Institute of Science and Technology (1983).

(15) R. Pauley, *Financial Times*, 27 September (1985).

(16) G. F. Hardymon, M. J. Denino and M. S. Salter, When corporate venture capital doesn't work, *Harvard Business Review*, 114–120, May–June (1983).

Piggybacking for Business and Nonprofits: A Strategy for Hard Times

Richard P. Nielsen, Associate Professor, School of Management, Boston College

This article explains the conceptual foundations for the piggybacking strategy from the general strategic management, adoption of innovation, product life cycle, specialization and diversified portfolio strategy literatures. The strategic piggybacking strategy is compared and contrasted with the diversified portfolio and specialization strategies. Intention, dynamic investment flow, short vs long term, and mission similarities and differences are addressed. A case is made for considering strategic piggybacking as a synthesis of the specialization and diversified portfolio strategies. The conditions appropriate for adoption of a piggybacking strategy are also discussed.

Different strategies can be more or less consistent with institutional mission vs market opportunities. More specifically (and the focus of this article), the short (for both business and nonprofit institutions) or long run (for nonprofit institutions) market opportunities might favor a diversified portfolio strategy more than a specialization strategy, but the specialization strategy might be more consistent with the institution's mission than the diversified portfolio strategy. Thus, how to resolve such a conflict among mission, market opportunities and alternative strategies becomes somewhat of a dilemma. A strategy that is different from and a synthesis of diversified portfolio and specialization strategies that can help address and resolve this dilemma is 'piggybacking'. Piggybacking is investing in and/or developing a new for the institution business that is relatively unrelated to the institution's primary mission, but that is sufficiently compatible with current market opportunities so that it can generate revenues to help support in the short term (for both business and nonprofit institutions) or long term (for nonprofit institutions) the primary mission activities that are less compatible with current market

Richard P. Nielsen is Associate Professor at the School of Management, Boston College, 301 Fulton Hall, Chestnut Hill, MA 02167, U.S.A.

opportunities. A case is made for considering piggybacking as a synthesis of diversified portfolio and specialization strategies.

This article explains the conceptual foundations for the piggybacking strategy and illustrates what the strategy is, it discusses how the piggybacking strategy is a synthesis of the specialization and diversified portfolio strategies, and also considers the reasons and conditions under which a decision to adopt the strategy might reasonably be made by business and nonprofit institutions. Throughout this article, references are made to five cases: two corporations and two nonprofit institutions; and one corporation where an acquisition could be used as either a diversified portfolio or strategic piggybacking strategy.

The Five Case Studies

Case 1 is the Boston Symphony Orchestra. Its primary mission concerns the performance of classical symphonic music. Ninety years ago, ten years after its own founding, the BSO established the Boston Pops which plays established popular music before a large audience that eats and drinks liquor and wine in something of a cabaret atmosphere. The surpluses generated from the food, wine, liquor and ticket sales help support the primary mission concerning the performance of classical symphonic music.[1]

Case 2 is the Alta Bates Hospital. Its primary mission concerns primary community hospital health care. It established several sports medicine clinics in affluent neighborhoods. These clinics generate surpluses that are used to help subsidize the primary community hospital health care mission.[2]

Case 3 is the American Natural Resources corporation. Its primary mission concerns natural gas distribution. It bought five regional trucking (non-gas) companies. These highly profitable trucking companies were bought in order to provide the revenues required to develop the natural gas pipeline and distribution primary mission activities needed during a period of relatively low profitability in the natural gas areas.[3]

Case 4 is Eaton-Timberjack. Before Eaton acquired Timberjack, Timberjack defined its primary mission as concerning the development and application of mechanical equipment for woodlands use. It invested in the development of construction and mining equipment in order to generate the revenues it needed to pursue its primary mission in the woodlands equipment area. When Eaton acquired Timberjack, it modified this strategy to be more of a diversified portfolio strategy for generating profits in construction and mining for their own sakes.[4]

Case 5 is United States Steel Corporation. It acquired Marathon Oil Corporation. It could use the profits from the oil area to help finance the extensive modernization of its steel manufacturing plants if it considers steel still to be its primary mission, or it could use its oil revenues to help finance further portfolio diversification if it defines its primary mission as more in the nature of a diversified conglomerate than as a specialist in the steel area. It is not yet clear whether the acquisition of Marathon Oil was more of a diversified portfolio or a strategic piggybacking strategy.[5]

Conceptual Foundations for Strategic Piggybacking

In Alfred D. Chandler's 1962 book *Strategy and Structure: Chapters in the History of the American Industrial Enterprise*, it is revealed that there have been generalized expansion strategies successfully adopted in different circumstances, primarily in response to external market conditions. The generalized strategies are geographic expansion, verticle integration (i.e. a move into a new activity for the institution function such as extraction, processing, marketing, etc.), horizontal combination, specialization and diversification.[6]

In Chandler's 1977 Pulitzer and Bancroft prize winning book *The Visible Hand: The Managerial Revolution in American Business*, it is also revealed that another factor, the professional manager's definition of institutional mission, had a large and important role in defining and deciding strategies for realizing the mission. External market conditions and management definition of the mission interact in influencing selection and decision among alternative strategies.[7]

Definitions of strategic management have come to recognize the important interaction between market opportunities and definition of institutional mission in selecting among alternative strategies.

Uyterhoeven, Ackerman and Rosenblum explain that:

> Strategy can best be defined by looking at the purpose it serves: to provide both direction and cohesion to the enterprise . . . to give the company a sense of purpose and mission in responses to external opportunities and threats.[8]

For Newman and Logan:

> Strategies are forward-looking plans that anticipate change and initiate action to take advantage of opportunities that are integrated into the concepts or mission of the company.[9]

And similarly for Steiner and Miner:

> Strategy is the forging of company mission, setting objectives for the organization in the light of external and internal forces, formulating specific . . . strategies . . . and ensuring their proper implementation so that the basic purposes . . . of the organization will be achieved.[10]

As the above authors suggest, strategy is a function of, among other things, market opportunities and institutional mission as defined by management.

Also as suggested above, there can be a conflict among institutional mission, market opportunities, and strategies. Ideas and case experiences from the general strategic management, adoption of innovation, product life cycle, specialization and diversified portfolio strategy analysis areas help provide the conceptual foundations for a solution to the dilemma of a situation where strategies most directly consistent with institutional mission are less favored by market opportunities relative to strategies that are less consistent with institutional mission.

The French sociologist Gabriel Tarde in 1903 was one of the first to suggest that the adoption of a new idea follows a normal S-shaped distribution over time. That is, first a few people adopt the innovation, then there is a rapid increase in the rate of adoption, then a slower rate as the few remaining people in the system adopt, and then a decline as the once innovative idea is replaced by a more innovative idea.[11]

The first and also largest empirical research tradition concerning the adoption of innovation S-curve is in rural sociology which was begun during the 1920s and 1930s in the midwestern United States. This research tradition also introduced the idea of the adoption of innovation S-curve into a management and product life cycle context. For example, in the 1920s and 1930s the Iowa Extension Service and commercial seed companies cooperated in using the adoption of innovation S-curve concept to introduce hybrid seed corn. The product life cycle, in this case the hybrid seed corn life cycle, had essentially the same shape as the adoption of innovation curve. That is, first a few farmers adopted the new hybrid corn, then there was a rapid increase in the rate of adoption, then a slower rate as the few remaining farmers adopted the hybrid corn, and then a decline as the once innovative hybrid corn seed was replaced by newer and better hybrid seed products.[12]

Despite these early origins, the concept of product life cycle management was not explicitly introduced into the management literature until Theodore Levitt's 1965 *Harvard Business Review* article 'Exploit the Product Life Cycle'.[13]

Since that time Bruce D. Henderson and the Boston Consulting Group extended and integrated the concepts of adoption of the innovation curve and product life cycle with the classical diversification strategy (related or unrelated diversification) into their 'Portfolio Matrix' approach to diversified strategic planning.[14]

Uyterhoeven, Ackerman and Rosenblum explain the classical diversification alternative as follows.

> Of all the strategic alternatives, diversification is undoubtedly the most glamorous. Admittedly this glamour has paled somewhat as several well-known conglomerates have come upon hard times... Diversification is an alternative way of committing one's resources. The strategist may decide that his existing business does not hold sufficient potential. He may wish to cut back or even liquidate it and commit his resources elsewhere. Alternatively, he may keep his existing activities at current levels or exploit their growth to their full potential but seek additional growth elsewhere. Thus growth through diversification may not always be a better spreading of business risks or at achieving a growth rate which cannot be accomplished within a company's original given field of endeavor.[15]

These authors contrast the diversification strategy with the strategy of specialization. They explain as follows.

> During the boom years of the conglomerate it was not fashionable to stress the merits of a specialist strategy. Yet many companies owe their success to specialization... Indeed, the power of a single purpose can be substantial, particularly where competitors spread their energies and resources over a variety of activities. Thus, specialization may provide a competitive edge. If one asks managers of the operating divisions of diversified companies who their most dangerous and difficult competitors are, they rarely cite other conglomerates. Indeed, they usually mention much smaller specialized companies, which excel in a single product or service and which are able to react quickly and decisively. In addition to providing a competitive edge, specialization also permits companies with limited resources to use them most effectively... A strategy of specialization permits a company to exploit particular market segments, sometimes resulting in spectacular performances even where the general industry conditions are stagnant... Specialization also entails major risks. A company's fortunes are tied to a particular industry. If the industry declines, the company may be trapped. Changing market needs or major technological innovation may even put it out of business.[16]

There are of course different levels of specialization and diversification. An institution could diversify into related and unrelated areas.[17] For example, Coca Cola could diversify into an unrelated area such as the acquisition of a film company such as Columbia, or it could diversify into a related area such as the acquisition of a fruit juice company. Similarly, a classical symphony orchestra company might develop a classical chamber orchestra that is very much related to classical symphonic music or it could organize rock concerts.

Both related and unrelated diversification strategies are addressed with the diversified portfolio strategy. In the generalized diversified portfolio strategy, a product is considered a 'question mark' in the sense that it has recently been introduced and it is not clear whether it will move into the next product life cycle stage of rapid growth. Successful products that move into the second product life cycle stage of rapid growth are called 'stars'. As the 'star' product's growth slows and then begins to decline it is considered a 'cash cow'. It is considered a 'cash cow' because while it has low, no, or declining growth, it has already achieved a relatively high market share and generates high cash flow. High cash flow is generated because much of the investment required to achieve its relatively high market share was made in the past and relatively little new investment is required to maintain the cash flow. As a product continues to decline further down the product life cycle curve to the area where it has low growth potential, low market share, and poor profitability it is considered a 'dog'.[18]

The generalized diversified portfolio strategy recommended by Henderson and the Boston Consulting Group is for an institution to have a balance of businesses such that there is a dynamic where an investment is made to enter a product/market segment in its introductory (question mark) stage, then gain market share and profitability in its growth (star) stage, then generate high cash flow in its maturity (cash cow) stage to be used for financing new potential 'stars', and then gradually lose market share and profitability in its decline (dog) stage.[19]

Diversified Portfolio vs Piggybacking

While the piggybacking strategy is related to the diversified portfolio strategy, it is also different in two important ways, the intention of the strategy and the dynamic of the investment flow.

(1) Intention Differences

The intention of the piggybacking strategy is to help subsidize an historical primary mission that in the short run (for both business and nonprofit institutions) and/or the long run (for nonprofit institutions) is not very compatible with market opportunities. The intention of a diversified portfolio strategy is to spread financial risks and to help finance the development of new potential 'stars'.[20]

The Boston Symphony Orchestra established the Boston Pops in order to help subsidize its primary mission concerning the performance of classical symphonic music which it did and does not expect to be able to support itself. For 90 years since its establishment, the Boston Pops through food, wine, liquor, and ticket sales has produced surpluses which have helped subsidize the deficits the BSO has incurred in every one of its 100 years. Instead, if, for example, the intention had been to establish new, likely profitable classical or popular music businesses for their own sakes, then the strategy could be considered more in the generalized diversified portfolio than strategic piggybacking mode.

The Alta Bates Hospital established its sports medicine clinics in relatively affluent neighborhoods in order to help subsidize its primary mission concerning the operation of a primary care community hospital. The sports medicine clinics do produce surpluses which help offset the hospital deficits. Instead, if, for example, the intention had not been to help subsidize the hospital, but rather to enter new markets for their own sake, then the strategy might have been considered more diversified portfolio than piggybacking.

American Natural Resources bought its five regional trucking businesses with the intention of generating profits to improve its natural gas operations with the expectation that in the long run its primary mission concerning natural gas would be very profitable. Instead, if, for example, the intention had been to establish a profitable trucking business to be a 'star' rather than a vehicle for subsidizing its primary mission, then the strategy might be considered more diversified portfolio than piggybacking.

Before Eaton acquired Timberjack, Timberjack defined its primary mission as concerning development and application of mechanical equipment for woodlands use. Timberjack invested in the development of construction and mining equipment with the intention of generating profits it needed to pursue its primary mission in the woodlands equipment area. Instead, if, for example, the intention had been to phase out the woodlands equipment area or to develop the construction and mining areas for their own sakes, then the strategy could be considered more diversified portfolio than piggybacking. When Eaton acquired Timberjack, it modified the strategy from piggybacking to more diversified portfolio. Eaton decided to develop the construction and mining areas for their own sakes.

In the U.S. Steel acquisition of Marathon Oil case, it is not yet clear what U.S. Steel's intention was. If U.S. Steel based its investment decision in acquiring Marathon Oil on the intention of moving away from the depressed steel industry or of generating profits for a new 'star' industry, then the strategy could be considered diversified portfolio. However, if U.S. Steel purchased Marathon Oil more with the intention of using oil profits to modernize its steel business, then the strategy could be considered more one of piggybacking.

(2) Dynamic Investment Flow Differences

In the piggybacking strategy, the institution invests in new activity for the institution and relatively safe cash flow surplus producing, moderate or low growth, advanced life cycle 'cash cow' activities in order to support its subsidization needing primary mission. In contrast, the investment flow dynamic of the generalized diversified portfolio strategy suggests that an institution should use older 'cash cow' business profits from businesses it is already in to take relatively greater financial risks in newer, earlier life cycle high growth potential activities since the institution should be interested in the development of potential new 'stars'.[21] In piggybacking, the institution invests to acquire/develop a 'cash cow' to support a primary mission. In the diversified portfolio strategy, the institution takes profits from 'cash cow' businesses it already owns in order to finance new potential 'stars'.

Ninety years later it is difficult to assess how financially risky the establishment of the Boston Pops by the BSO was then. However, 90 years of uninterrupted surpluses that have helped subsidize the BSO suggest that the Boston Pops has been a very safe 'cash cow'. The idea of performing and listening to established popular music forms while eating and drinking wine and liquor is generally accepted by the public and advanced in its life cycle. If the BSO had instead decided to establish, for example, a business for the purpose of concentrating on the performance of newly composed symphonic music or new popular music for their own sakes and which had the potential of becoming 'stars', then such a strategy could have been considered more diversified portfolio than piggybacking.

The Bates Hospital did not establish any sports medicine clinics until after there had been several financially successful clinics started and operated by other institutions in California and elsewhere. The sports clinic idea was relatively advanced in its life cycle, almost immediately financially successful, and used to help subsidize the hospital. Instead, if, for example, the hospital had decided to establish a clinical genetic engineering facility, a new and potential 'star' activity, then the strategy might have been considered more diversified portfolio than piggybacking.

When ANR purchased its regional trucking companies, such businesses were neither new nor very risky. They generated substantial amounts of cash to finance the natural gas mission and trucking was relatively advanced in its life cycle. Instead, if ANR had, for example, invested in a synthetic fuel business that had the potential of becoming a 'star', then such a strategy could be considered more in the dynamic of the diversified portfolio strategy than the piggybacking strategy.

When Timberjack entered into the construction and mining businesses, it did so with the idea of subsidizing the timber business while minimally modifying its timber equipment. It was not trying to establish new 'star' businesses. However, when Eaton acquired Timberjack, it did modify the strategy and consider these new businesses as having 'star' potential in their own rights. Piggybacking was more the strategy before Eaton acquired Timberjack, while diversified portfolio was more the strategy after Eaton acquired Timberjack.

The acquisition of Marathon Oil by U.S. Steel did not represent the acquisition of a business new in its life cycle. The oil business was well advanced. In addition, the oil reserves of Marathon were well known. Marathon is more of a 'cash cow' than a potential 'star' for U.S. Steel. Instead, if, for example, U.S. Steel had acquired a synthetic fuel company or a company with a new advanced methodology for manufacturing steel, then it could be considered more in the dynamic of the diversified portfolio strategy than a strategic piggybacking strategy.

Specialization vs Strategic Piggybacking

Strategic piggybacking is similar to a specialization strategy in that they both share a concern for a specialized mission. They are different in that strategic piggybacking invests in different businesses in order to subsidize the specialized mission while specialization would call for investment within the specialized mission.[22]

The Boston Symphony Orchestra is concerned with a specialized mission, the performance of classical symphonic music. However, instead of investing its capital in the orchestra, it invested its resources in a different business, established popular music with food, wine and liquor to help subsidize its specialized mission.

The Bates Hospital is concerned with a specialized mission, primary hospital health care. However, it invested in sports medicine primarily for the treatment of nonprimary and elective health care in order to help subsidize its specialized mission.

ANR is concerned with a specialized mission in natural gas activities. However, it invested in five regional trucking companies not related to natural gas in order to help finance its specialized mission.

Timberjack was concerned with a specialized mission concerning timber equipment. It invested in mining and construction businesses in order to help finance its specialized mission. Also, Eaton modified its mission after acquisition to less specialization and more interest in these other areas for their own sakes.

It is not yet clear how U.S. Steel is defining its mission. Perhaps it has a specialized mission concerning steel and is using Marathon Oil as a piggybacking mechanism to further modernization of steel production and its specialized mission in steel. Or, perhaps U.S. Steel has changed its mission more in the direction of a diversified conglomerate and away from a specialization strategy.

Piggybacking as a Synthesis of Diversified Portfolio and Specialization Strategies

Piggybacking combines the specialized mission emphasis of the specialization strategy with the diversified investment activity of the diversified portfolio strategy. While combining elements from both strategies, it is also different from both specialization and diversified portfolio strategies. It is different from specialization in that it invests resources in relatively unrelated areas. It is different from the diversified portfolio strategy in that its intention is to subsidize a specialized primary mission while diversified portfolio strategies intend more to develop other businesses on their own merits. It is also different from the diversified portfolio strategy in that its investment flow dynamic is to seek new activities for the institution, safe, relatively advanced life cycle 'cash cow' businesses rather than using 'cash cow' businesses it already owns to help finance relatively more risky high growth potential 'star' businesses.

For example, The Boston Symphony Orchestra is concerned with a specialized mission concerning classical symphonic music, but it invests in relatively unrelated advanced 'cash cow' established popular music, food, wine, liquor activities to help subsidize its specialized primary mission.

ANR is concerned with a specialized mission concerning natural gas, but it invests in relatively unrelated advanced life cycle 'cash cow' businesses in trucking to help subsidize its specialized natural gas mission activities.

Timberjack is concerned with a specialized mission concerning timber equipment, but it invests in relatively unrelated advanced life cycle 'cash cow' mining and construction businesses to help subsidize its specialized timber equipment mission. When Eaton acquired Timberjack, it treated the construction and mining businesses more as potential 'stars'.

U.S. Steel may have either a specialized mission concerning steel production or a diversified portfolio mission. Its acquisition of Marathon could be a piggybacking strategy for helping modernize its steel operations or it could be used to help finance portfolio diversification. Time may tell.

Conditions Appropriate for a Piggybacking Strategy

For a business institution, piggybacking is an appropriate strategy when the primary mission is temporarily not being favored by the market and/or resources are needed to make the specialized mission more compatible with market opportunities. For example, in the ANR situation, it was correctly judged that the 1970s would not be boom years for natural gas activities relative to the potential of the 1980s. In the meantime, the trucking activities helped subsidize and develop the specialized natural gas mission capabilities for very good potential benefits in the 1980s. Similarly, in the Timberjack–Eaton case, while the timber markets were depressed there was relatively little demand for timber equipment, but the mining and construction equipment businesses permitted Timberjack to maintain its specialized mission capability while markets improved. It has both weathered temporary bad markets and improved its specialized technology during difficult markets. U.S. Steel is in a position with the acquisition of Marathon to either improve its specialized mission in steel through financing modernization or to adopt a diversified portfolio strategy for a modified mission as was the case with Timberjack after being acquired by Eaton.

While, for the business institutions, the piggybacking strategy was adopted primarily to help support a specialized primary mission in temporarily difficult markets, for the nonprofit institution, the strategic piggybacking strategy can also be used to help offset structural long term deficits and permit the nonprofit institution to help self-subsidize specialized missions over the longer term. For 90 years the food, wine and liquor activities of the Boston Pops have helped support the continuous deficits of the BSO's specialized mission. While it is perhaps too early to tell whether hospitals are in a similar long term deficit structural situation similar to symphony orchestras, the surplus generating activities of the strategic piggybacking strategy have the potential to help subsidize the Bates Hospital's worthwhile specialized mission in both the short and long terms.

While a nonprofit institution may wish to use a strategic piggybacking strategy for long term self-subsidization, it would probably make more sense for a business institution to change its specialized mission if that mission could not be profitable in the long term rather than subsidize a long term unprofitable specialized mission.

There is also an important caution that should be considered in evaluating whether either a business or a nonprofit institution should adopt a piggybacking strategy. Does the institution have the capability of managing effectively relatively unrelated businesses? An unrelated business activity may have actual or potential high and stable 'cash cow' benefits, but if the parent institution does not have the experience required to manage such an unrelated activity, it could lose money for both the new activity for the institution 'cash cow' as well as the parent specialized mission activities and capabilities.

Conclusion

For business and nonprofit institutions with specialized missions that are not being favored by market opportunities in the short run (for both business and nonprofit institutions) and the long run (for nonprofit institutions), and who wish to retain their specialized missions, then piggybacking should be a strategy worthy of serious consideration.

References

(1) Annual Reports, Boston Symphony Orchestra (1975–1981).

(2) Annual Reports, Alta Bates Corporation and Alta Bates Hospital, 1975–1981; Michael Waldholz, Some hospitals are entering diverse businesses, often unrelated to medicine, to offset losses, *The Wall Street Journal*, p. 46, 12 August (1981).

(3) Corporate strategies: American natural resources—a pipeliner turns trucker, *Business Week*, pp. 90–91, 5 February (1979).

(4) Derek F. Abell, *Defining the Business: The Starting Point of Strategic Planning*, pp. 116–166, Prentice-Hall, Englewood Cliffs, New Jersey (1980).

(5) Is big steel abandoning steel? *Business Week*, pp. 34–35, 7 December (1981). Richard I. Kirkland, Steel's subtle grab for quotas, *Fortune*, pp. 46–48, 8 February (1982).

(6) Alfred D. Chandler, *Strategy and Structure: Chapters in the History of the American Industrial Enterprise*, pp. 19–42, 380–395, MIT Press, Cambridge (1962).

(7) Alfred D. Chandler, *The Visible Hand: The Managerial Revolution In American Business*, pp. 1–12, 484–502, Harvard University Press, Cambridge (1977).

(8) Hugo E. R. Uyterhoeven, Robert W. Ackerman and John W. Rosenblum, *Strategy and Organization*, p. 7, Richard D. Irwin, Homewood, Illinois (1977).

(9) W. H. Newman and L. P. Logan, *Strategy, Policy and Central Management*, p. 70, South-Western Publishing, Cincinnati (1971).

(10) G. A. Steiner and J. B. Miner, *Management Policy and Strategy*, p. 19, Macmillan, New York (1977).

(11) Gabriel Tarde, *The Laws of Imitation* (translated by Elsie Clews Parsons), Holt, New York (1903); Everett M. Rogers with F. Floyd Shoemaker, *Communication of Innovation: A Cross-Cultural Approach*, pp. 53–54, The Free Press, New York (1971).

(12) Meredith C. Wilson, Influence of bulletins, news stories, and circular letters upon farm practice adoption with particular reference to methods of bulletin distribution, Federal Extension Service Circular 495, 1927, Washington, DC, USDA (1927); Neal C. Gross, The diffusion of a culture trait in two Iowa townships, M.S. Thesis. Ames: Iowa State University (1942); Bruce Ryan and Neal C. Gross, The diffusions of hybrid seed corn in two Iowa communities, *Rural Sociology*, **8**, 15–24 (1943).

(13) Theodore Levitt, Exploit the product life cycle, *Harvard Business Review*, **43**(6), 81–94 November–December (1965).

(14) Bruce D. Henderson, *The Product Portfolio*, The Boston Consulting Group, Boston (1970); George S. Day, Diagnosing the product portfolio, *Journal of Marketing*, **41**(2), 29–38, April (1977); Derek F. Abell and John S. Hammond, *Portfolio analysis, Strategic Market Planning*, Ch. 4, 173–194, Prentice-Hall, Englewood Cliffs, NJ, (1979); Derek F. Abell, *Defining the Business: The Starting Point of Strategic Planning*, pp. 3–26, 220–227, Prentice-Hall, Englewood Cliffs, NJ (1980).

(15) Uyterhoeven, Ackerman and Rosenblum, op. cit., p. 55.

(16) Ibid., pp. 52–53.

(17) Chandler, op. cit., pp. 19–42, 380–395 (1962); Uyterhoeven, Ackerman and Rosenblum, op. cit., pp. 55–56.

(18) Henderson, op. cit.; Day, op. cit; Abell and Hammond, op. cit.; Abell, op. cit.

(19) Ibid.

(20) Ibid.

(21) Ibid.

(22) Uyterhoeven, Ackerman and Rosenblum, op. cit., pp. 52–53.

PART TWO

New Venture Management in Practice

Company Cases

NEW VENTURE DEVELOPMENT AT DU PONT

A. B. Cohen

Manager, New Product Development,
Photo Products Department,
E. I. du Pont de Nemours, Parlin, New Jersey.

New Products are the life blood of a growing company, but traditional methods of introducing new products are no longer adequate. Du Pont is using a new approach called Venture Management.
A New Venture Development provides an ideal environment for making and carrying out decisions involved in introducing new technological developments. It combines the advantages in mobility and communications enjoyed by a small venture-orientated company with the strong technical and financial advantages of a large company.

Parts of this article are based on a presentation given in March 1969, to the National Conference on the Management of Technological Innovation sponsored by the University of Bradford, the Ministry of Technology and Management Today.

THE VITALITY OF A LARGE RESEARCH-oriented company like Du Pont depends on a steady infusion of new products to replace outmoded ones, and to complement and expand existing business. However, because of today's rapidly changing and more sophisticated product demands, the traditional pathways for introducing new products are no longer wholly adequate.

We can learn much about alternate pathways from certain small venture-oriented companies, which have undergone astonishing growth in recent years, often on the basis of a single technological innovation. Imaginative new ideas and remarkable vision certainly account in large measure for their growth. But perhaps even more important to their commercial success was a single-mindedness of purpose and entrepreneurial spirit, which unstintingly nourished these ideas and groomed them for commercialization in time to gain a significant competitive edge.

As a step in this direction, Du Pont is using the venture management approach, in which full responsibility for commercializing major new products is assigned to separate venture development groups. These groups are set up like small independent businesses within the Company's various industrial departments. Currently there are about two dozen New Ventures, but the number varies depending on the rate at which worthy ideas are generated and existing ventures absorbed into the established business structure. This formalized approach is not yet an exact science in Du Pont, nor does it insure automatic success. But it does set up within a large company an environment that is highly conducive to generating new ideas and provides exciting possibilities for implementing them.

Most previous papers on venture management have dealt broadly with this subject. This paper attempts to provide a more detailed view of how this type of organizational structure facilitates transfer of technology by examining a case history of a recent New Venture within Du Pont's Photo Products Department from the vantage point of its former venture manager. But first let us consider how ideas and technology for future ventures are developed and evaluated in Du Pont.

RESEARCH AND DEVELOPMENT

Each of Du Pont's eleven industrial departments functions like a separate business with its own marketing, manufacturing, research and development, and financial control divisions. The management of each department defines its own general business objectives, and is responsible for all operations needed to carry out these objectives and to maintain both the current and future profitability of the department. These same business objectives also establish the framework and scope of R & D activities carried out within the department. In addition to the industrial departments, two corporate departments carry out R & D activities and New Venture Developments which do not have an obvious fit with the interests of the industrial departments.

R & D activities in Du Pont are grouped into three broad categories according to business purpose:
- Improvement of Established Business
- Exploratory Research
- New Venture Development.

Exploratory Research programmes are, in general, longer range and more speculative than those for the Improvement of Established Business. The aim of all exploratory programmes is to seek new discoveries which can be developed into profitable and proprietary new products for existing markets, related future markets, or for diversification of current business.

Special care is taken to insure that specific objectives are relevant to the department's business interests. For example, in the Photo Products Department, this interest is defined broadly as "materials and systems for the recording, retrieval or display of information". This broad functional classification has permitted this Department to actively explore business opportunities well outside its existing product lines and has contributed significantly to its diversification and growth.

NEW VENTURE SELECTION CRITERIA

Not all new products in Du Pont reach commercialization via the new venture route. For example, innovations arising out of programmes to improve established business usually can be handled expeditiously within existing organizational structures and facilities. Similarly, with many products arising from exploratory research, there may be little need or justification for the level of effort and expenditure required to set up a New Venture Organization. Or, a new idea may fit neatly into the technological and marketing sphere of an existing New Venture and thereby expand the market opportunity of that venture.

In many cases, however, promising new products or systems are visualized in R & D programmes which do not fit well into the marketing and manufacturing capabilities of the department. It is then that a New Venture Development is considered. Since there are often more good candidates than can be developed simultaneously, prospective ventures are carefully weighed by departmental management. Among the criteria used are:
- Market Opportunity
- Profitability
- Development Timing
- Development Costs
- Investment Schedule
- Proprietary Position.

In addition, availability of critical raw materials and successful operation of pilot manufacturing facilities greatly reduce risks and increase the likelihood of a decision in favour of a proposed venture.

New Venture groups exist as separate and formally structured entities within a parent department, but there is no serious attempt to standardize the form of these units within Du Pont or even within a department. The manager of the venture is charged with very specific goals, but he has wide latitude in how he chooses to structure and operate his organization. Venture management is free to pursue unorthodox pathways toward venture objectives, and can consider, where dictated by unusual circumstances, broad departures from a department's traditional policies.

RISTON®* NEW VENTURE DEVELOPMENT

This New Venture was started in October, 1966, and successfully concluded in August, 1969, when it was set up as a separate profit centre within the established business structure of the Photo Products Department. The developments leading to this event are an interesting study of how the New Venture organizational structure facilitates decision-making and helps break down traditional barriers when transferring technology from the laboratory to the market place. Such barriers are particularly formidable when attempting to penetrate unfamiliar markets or to introduce radically different product concepts, as was the case here.

*Registered trade mark.

Market Research

Our R & D Division has its own market research staff, whose members assist the technical staff in recognizing and exploiting commercial opportunities. They constantly monitor industry trends and remain closely abreast of internal technical programmes. This group made us aware of the growing use of photographic techniques in fabricating high quality electronic components. They also pointed out the shortcomings of existing materials and processes and suggested that our strong technological background in photosensitive polymers might be a good base for developing an improved photofrabication system for making high quality electronic circuits for the computer and aerospace industries.

The best photographic techniques available prior to 1966 employed light-sensitive lacquers called liquid photoresists to reproduce a chemically resistant circuit pattern on a copper/plastic laminate. The unprotected copper was then etched away to produce the finished printed circuit.

We flirted briefly with developing an improved liquid photoresist based on our photopolymer technology. This liquid product, being similar to existing materials, would have been easiest and quickest to develop and market. However, further market studies soon indicated that a more innovative approach might be better attuned to the longer term needs of the industry: tighter tolerances, greater convenience, higher productivity and easier automation.

Exploratory Research

In an attempt to meet these needs, a dry photoresist film was devised that could be laminated to copper, to produce almost instantaneously the same kind of photosensitized surface obtained by the much slower liquid process. Next, a 'black box' was designed for rapid, continuous lamination of a roll of the film resist to a substrate. This combination of a precoated product and specially designed equipment in an integrated system offered users a new degree of uniformity, flexibility and automation, particularly in the rapidly expanding field of multilayer circuit panels.

Sample reactions to this concept among large potential users was very favourable. Accordingly, we were encouraged to proceed, and subsequently developed a prototype film resist product and a pilot manufacturing operation to provide materials for internal and external evaluations. Additional market studies and economic analyses were conducted to establish a more accurate estimate of the market opportunity and expectation of profitability. As mentioned earlier, these are among the criteria to be met in starting a New Venture. Since the outlook was still very bright, a proposal to set up and finance a New Venture Development was presented and approved by General Management.

NEW VENTURE ORGANIZATION

Personnel involved in the exploratory research programmes leading to the venture were a natural nucleus for this group. They were supplemented by experienced personnel from the marketing and manufacturing divisions of the Photo Products Department and from other departments of the Du Pont Company, who were transferred into the venture group and relieved of all other responsibilities. Persons with special skills needed in the venture and not available within Du Pont were recruited from outside the Company.

Virtually overnight, a small, semi-autonomous company was created whose sole business was to commercialize a novel system for the electronics industry. This new environment had an immediate effect in fostering greater personal identification with group objectives, while more sharply focusing individual responsibility and accountability.

The venture organization was broken down into technical, manufacturing, and marketing groups, along the lines of the parent department but on a much smaller scale. Each of these groups was headed by a manager with extensive experience in his area of responsibility. The person appointed to head the venture must be thoroughly versed in all three areas, since he is expected to assume full responsibility for setting up and operating a total business enterprise.

Figure 1 shows the three phases of development of the venture covering a period of almost three years. During this time, the number of personnel increased tenfold and groups were added to assume new responsibilities as needs arose.

Although resembling a small business administratively, the New Venture Development group had a big advantage in being able to draw on the parent company for many of the service functions normally needed by an independent business, e.g., purchasing, shipping, receiving, mechanical, accounting, business analysis and legal services. However, when these services grew to the point where they occupied an individual full-time, he was often transferred into the venture group to improve coordination with other parts of the programme.

Venture Plan

As its first important task, the venture staff formulated an operational plan detailing the steps needed to transform the venture into a profitable business in the shortest possible time. This included reaching decisions on the following major items:
- Nature and scope of product line
- Market development plan
- Manufacturing process and facilities
- Commercialization strategy and timing.

The compact organizational structure facilitated close coordination of these interdependent venture activities. During the first year of the venture, the group managers and the venture manager were at the same location with immediate access to one another. The marketing and manufacturing managers participated fully in all technical decisions to insure that targets were consistent with needed product and process specifications and with manufacturing capabilities. Because of this close association, divergent viewpoints were better understood, and usually easily reconciled. The short lines of communication also permitted bottlenecks to be recognized early and programmes for breaking them to be implemented almost immediately.

Systems Development

Products often are developed before serious work is started on devices for use with these products; sometimes, the converse is true. Responsibility for developing various parts of a proposed system is often distributed among different groups, or even among different companies. By the time close intergroup lines of communication are set up, product specifications are often fairly firm and latitude in machine design severely restricted.

In the present instance, product, process, and equipment were developed concurrently within a closely coordinated New Venture group. Continuous feedback of information between the product and equipment groups was used to establish the technical path of least resistance. This arrangement avoided freezing too soon on either product or process design and enhanced the probability of our devising an optimum system.

Market Development

While technical activities were progressing, the marketing staff continued to survey industry trends, and regularly advised technical managers of changes that would have a bearing on their programmes. These surveys also provided a basis for selecting external evaluation sites which were representative of various segments of the proposed market. Field trials were started early in order to obtain customer feedback at a time when product changes could be made relatively easily in response to changing customer needs.

The first market development representatives received their product orientation in the laboratory, while assisting R & D personnel in the final phases of product development. Similarly, technical personnel often accompanied market development representatives on field visits, and together they were able to provide customers with prompt, authoritative answers to both technical and marketing questions.

This close interaction between technical and marketing personnel within the venture gave each a better understanding of the other's problems and created a pool of technical people with marketing leanings. When the need for a separate technical service group arose, these technical people were an ideal nucleus for that group.

Manufacturing

There is often considerable loss in profit opportunity because of the time lag between the availability of pilot plant and commercial quantities of a new product. In a large established organization, much of this time is consumed in reconciling the diverse viewpoints of various functional divisions on product and process specifications. The close interaction of their counterparts within the venture made it possible to cooperatively evaluate technical and economic data derived from pilot plant activities on a current basis, and thereby, to expedite decisions needed to scale up manufacturing operations. As a result, sales of the new product were able to keep pace with market demand and were never limited by lack of production capacity.

Foreign Operations

The coordinated management possible in a New Venture permitted domestic and foreign markets to be developed concurrently. Personnel from our International Department were transferred into the venture, and with the assistance of their U.S. colleagues, set up European marketing, manufacturing and technical

service organizations. These early personal contacts promoted close relationships and later facilitated long-distance communications. Sales and some manufacturing operations started in Europe only a few months after they started in the U.S.

Profit and Loss Centre

As with any small company, the New Venture is treated as a profit and loss centre. It has its own budget, which is prepared by the venture manager and approved annually. But while the component parts of the budget are forecast in detail, the venture manager is free to reallocate funds among various segments of his programme as conditions change. Because of the magnitude of the resources involved, New Venture Developments are reviewed frequently for departmental management and for Du Pont's Executive Committee to keep all informed of progress, changes in outlook and likely needs for capital. Within the venture, costs of technical, manufacturing and marketing activities are collected separately in order to clearly fix responsibility for cost control.

The accounting procedures used are like those of our established business, but results are much more volatile and must be assessed on the basis of longer term projections. One of the criteria used for appraising the value of a venture is the expected net return on investment over a period of years. Another is forecast venture worth, which, in a simplified sense, is the net cash position derived from operating the venture for a number of years and then liquidating all assets.

If at any time, these indicators show that venture goals seem unattainable or unattractive, reduction or termination of effort would be immediately considered despite the annual budget. Conversely, if attractive new opportunities are discovered at any time during the year, an immediate increase in the authorized rate of expenditure would be recommended. While the

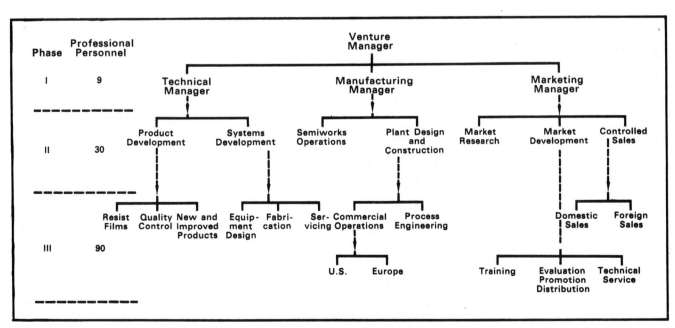

FIGURE 1. NEW VENTURE DEVELOPMENT PHASES

computer was a very useful tool in making these analyses, we found no substitute for insight or good judgment in reaching major decisions.

Dissolution of the Venture

As a successful venture matures, plans are made for integrating it into the regular business structure of an operating department. A dissolved venture may be absorbed into one of the department's existing product groups, if compatible, or set up as a separate division, as in this case.

The timing of this transition varies from case to case. One guideline is to dissolve a venture when the commercial plant comes on stream. But where this occurs relatively early in the development, as in the Riston® Venture, marketing or technical complexities may favour delaying dissolution until major problems are solved and market penetration is well under way.

The shock of the transition from venture to normal business status was minimized by setting up, well in advance, functional units that were easily spun off to form the marketing, manufacturing and technical sections of the new Riston® Products Division. Since this new profit centre retained much of the character and personnel of the venture, little momentum was lost in the changeover. It is now a healthy and growing segment of the Photo Products Department's established business.

CONCLUSIONS

An attempt has been made to relate the rapid penetration of a previously unfamiliar market to the use of the venture management approach in launching a new product. This management technique is not an end in itself, but simply a catalyst for facilitating product introduction and increasing the probability of commercial success, where the essential raw materials —marketable ideas—already exist.

Venture participation is excellent training for future management personnel. It provides an unusual opportunity for interacting with people of widely different disciplines, and for acquiring a broad range of administrative skills. Participants can observe from a privileged vantage point the dynamics of operating a total business organization and clearly see the impact of their own actions on its progress. Major decisions must be reached frequently and rapidly and prospective managers soon learn that an occasional mistake often does less harm than prolonged indecision.

Since New Ventures are treated as small profit centres, participants gain a rare glimpse of the often subtle interrelationships between costs and profits in a large company and develop greater appreciation of factors which influence profits. This is particularly important, where new technologies are being exploited, and no historical bases are available for guiding economic decisions.

In summary, a New Venture Development provides an ideal environment for making and carrying out decisions involved in introducing new technological developments. It combines the advantages in mobility and communications enjoyed by a small, venture-oriented company with the strong technical and financial advantages of a large company. ■

Regaining Your Competitive Edge

Michael E. Naylor, Corporate Strategic Planning, General Motors Corporation

The author maintains that the key to survival and growth in a world of rapid change, technological development and competitive challenge is 'Management Effectiveness'. Regaining the competitive edge in difficult conditions means developing superb management skills and translating them into effective management action. He lists and describes eight key elements of Strategic Business Management and outlines the steps in General Motors strategic planning process.

Storm warnings have been posted. Flags, flying from the flagstaffs outside most Corporate Headquarters buildings, are flapping stiffly in the strengthening winds of change. Storm clouds are gathering on many corporate horizons, or have already broken with torrential downpours that threaten to wash away many of our foundation industries with a flood of rapid changes and vigorous competitive pressures from all corners of the globe. Industry after industry is being forced to face harsh realities. The future is here, now. The old ways of doing business are inadequate to meet the competitive challenges. We are all plain out of time to take any kind of leisurely look at the situation. The waters are rising fast and many suspect that this time the dam isn't going to hold.

The simple truth; we are in the midst of a massive and swift moving transition to a new and vastly different world; a world in which all the rules are changing for all the institutions. Changes which used to take decades now happen in a matter of years, or even months. Many new products are functionally obsolete before they are out of the research and development phase. Many companies are bringing a new product to market only to find a 'next generation' product from a competitor on the same shelf before their own advertising campaign is completed.

Small wonder, then, that it has become popular to talk about re-industrialization, industrial policies, trade protectionism and a host of other catch phrases designed to fire the imagination of those who have lacked the vision to see the inevitable and who seek a quick 'solution to their problems' instead of facing the reality that we must all learn to manage new situations. What we are experiencing is a sea-change, a fundamental shift to a global economy. To deny the truth will not change it. We must seek enlightening vision, not curse the darkness.

Self-styled prophets are all around us. Most have a kernel of truth in their claims but I believe that each has offered an incomplete picture. We have heard pleas for the re-industrialization of our so-called smoke-stack industries. We have been warned that we are encountering the beginnings of the evolution to the post-industrial society, or that we are entering a period of turbulent times. Some have characterized this as a third wave of industrial evolution. Some have called it a period of industries in transition. We have been shown some of the 'megatrends' underpinning this movement that are affecting the very fabric of our society, our economy, and our own personal lives. Some are calling for an industrial renaissance or the next American revolution. Characteristically, we have no shortage of proposals to cure what ails us.

Because of their spectacular successes over the past decade, Japan, and things Japanese, hold the center stage. We can learn the art of Japanese management, the mind of Japan, and Theory-Z. Furthermore, we are exhorted to search for excellence, to look at the possibility of changing our corporate cultures, to follow the seven 'S's' to the rainbow's end. We have been offered competitive strategies, top management strategies, survival strategies—you name it.

Michael Naylor is General Director, Corporate Strategic Planning at General Motors Corporation, Manufacturing Development, B. Building (MO-47), General Motors Technical Center, Warren, MI 48090, U.S.A.

The real challenge we all face is to develop the self-discipline to hold firm in the face of the storm. To direct our efforts towards identifying those areas where we hold a comparative advantage and then institute a systematic pursuit of excellence in the basics of our businesses. There are no quick-fix solutions—no magic panaceas—no cavalry, with bugles playing and swords drawn, to come over the hill in the nick of time. We have to look after ourselves, face the realities of our competitive challenges, roll up our sleeves and get to work.

I believe the real key to success, to survival and to growth, is 'management effectiveness'. This is the common thread, the silver chain that links all the other functional elements that comprise winning performance. Perhaps a simple analogy from my own sphere of business will make this clearer. Business competition is a race, a race that never ends. In the past, most American businesses raced in a business environment that could be likened to a freeway. Even though the future (the road ahead) was unknown and unknowable it was basically surprise-free. When driving on a particular freeway for the first time you will not know the precise details of the various curves and interchanges ahead. You do know, however, that they will be well signposted and designed so that you can negotiate them without much change in speed, or even much maneuvering of your vehicle. In the past, then, in this race (or business competition) the winners were generally the people with the fastest cars, the biggest engines and the largest gas tanks. Driver skill was a secondary consideration when the roadway was broad, smoothly curved and had all the traffic going in the same direction.

Now consider what is changing or has already changed in the business environment. We are racing on what amounts to a twisting two lane mountain road. While we still need a superbly designed and manufactured vehicle, driver skill is now paramount. The highly skilled driver can compensate for some inadequacies in his vehicle and stay ahead of a mediocre driver in a highly-tuned machine. Even more significant, the highly-skilled driver actually welcomes bad driving conditions because his skill can then become an even bigger comparative advantage. Management effectiveness is directly analogous to driver skill and today's prevailing business conditions are twisty mountain roads. Regaining the competitive edge means developing superb skills as managers and translating these skills into effective management actions.

Many forget that just 15 years ago, the Japanese were not yet in the big leagues in world markets. Even 8 years ago, their products were just about the same as everyone else's. Why have they moved so far, so fast? Some people say it is 1000 years of unified cultural experience in Japan. Others cite the close cooperation between government and industry, the superior Japanese educational system, or

their preference for group accomplishment. All these things are true. But they have always been true, long before the Japanese rocked the world with their economic achievements. The only essential change is the way the Japanese decided to manage, and the result is proof in itself. We, too, can make such a change. But not an American copy of the Japanese answer. I do not think company songs and group exercise are going to do the job. We need an American response to the American problem. I believe our challenge is to convert the strategic planning concepts of yesterday into truly effective 'Strategic Business Management' for today.

There are eight key elements of strategic business management. They are:

First, STICKING-TO-IT or real commitment. This means commitment from management at all levels, and commitment from ourselves. In particular, the top management team has to accept the fundamental concepts of strategic planning and stick with them, and with their planners. Strong support from your CEO is absolutely essential if you are going to have any significant effect, or influence on your company directions. Getting real commitment from management is often difficult because of the preponderance of short-term financial measurements in our present systems, and the very natural reluctance to forego short-term gains for the sake of building long-range competitive advantage. It is necessary for both planners and managers to persist with the planning process through the start-up phase (and the re-start after the first one fails). You must learn how to live with uncertainty and not keep striving to establish certitude—for there is no such thing.

Second is THINKING THROUGH. Thinking through what your business is now, what you will become, and what you should become. Many plans end in frustration and failure because the planner or the manager did not spend the time and effort to think through the situation and the alternatives. Further, under the general category of thinking, you must give up reliance on the standard textbook methods and techniques that everyone learns in business school, and consequently, that everyone tries to use. Almost by definition, there cannot be generic strategies. If you base all your strategies on the same analytical formats as everyone else you will become dangerously predictable. You must always consider that your competitors are alert, because most of them are, and be prepared to be second-guessed because you will be much of the time. Try to think differently and more creatively, about your challenges and possible solutions. Many people believe that you are either born creative or you cannot be innovative, but that is not true. There are numerous techniques available today, like brainstorming, strategic analysis surfacing, Delphi surveys, etc. that can provide creative insights into business strategy options.

One approach is to use a sequence of structured questions that will enable you to think through your situation.

For example:

(1) What was the real key to success in this business 10, or even 20 years ago? (How many of you could answer that question, correctly, right now?)

(2) Has this key success factor changed since then, and why?

(3) What would have to happen to make it change significantly?

(4) If present trends continue, what will this business look like 10, or 20 years from now?

(5) Could this product (or service) be used, or has it ever been used, for anything else? (If the answer to this question is 'yes', you may have a potential new market and/or a potential new competitor.)

(6) Is this product still fully meeting the needs of its customers?

(7) When this business was started, what alternatives were considered and rejected?

(8) Could any of these alternatives be viable today?

(9) Who has a vested interest in seeing this business remain unchanged?

(10) Who has an interest in changing it?

(11) What relatively small changes would have a relatively large effect on the performance of this business?

(12) Are there any large changes that could be made without significant effect on this business?

(13) Is there a natural life-cycle to this business and is it changing to any great extent?

(14) What would cause this business to disappear?

(15) How does this business affect society?

(16) What complaints have been made about this business? (We should never ignore these. Our Japanese competitors consider complaints as valuable sources of information on how to improve their products and services. If you do not improve, rest assured that at least one of your competitors will.)

(17) What predictions have been made about the future of this business?

(18) What does the success of this business imply about human nature and the needs and wants of customers?

(19) What are the key features of the complete system of which this business is a part?

(20) What alternative methods could be used to satisfy the needs of this market?

This type of structured question session is a systematic way to raise the level of consciousness of your management team to the opportunities and the consequences of a wide variety of options. It is a way to stimulate thinking through your situation.

Third are the three R's of RISK, RESPONSIBILITY and REWARD. You must think through and work out the most appropriate balance between these three if you expect to see strategic behavior in your company. In particular, your incentive schemes must match the requirements of your strategic directions—and these requirements may vary widely between Strategic Business Units. The way you set up your risk, responsibility and reward system sends very strong signals to the whole organization. It is the single most effective way of reinforcing your strategic intentions. Further, if you have it out of balance, it can be the quickest and surest way to prevent or preclude strategic behavior. You cannot expect long range thinking and actions if your compensation programs reward the best bottom line each year.

Fourth is AWARENESS; awareness of your environment and, especially, awareness of your competitors. You must go out and gather data on your environment and on your competitors from a broad cross-section of sources; be receptive to feedback from as many customers as possible. What do they really want? What constitutes 'value' to each customer? How are customer tastes changing—and why? Take the time and expend the effort to understand your individual competitors thoroughly. How are they organized? Are they part of a larger corporation, and if so, what is the relationship between them and the parent organization? What are the backgrounds and the personalities of the key management people who direct each of your competitors? How are the barriers to entry and exit changing for your industry? How is technology impacting the competitive balance? Which of your competitors are developing new strengths and why? Conversely, which of them are becoming weaker, and why? Are there any new competitors entering your business environment? What is their basis for comparative advantage? These, too, are important questions. You cannot afford to guess at the answers if you hope to develop or retain any degree of competitive edge.

Fifth, you must TALK to each other. Communications, good communications, seem to elude many of us but your team is not going to score if the coach is the only one who knows the game plan. You must develop solid skills and competence in communications. It is risky to assume that your team will find out your strategic intentions by osmosis.

Sixth, is EVALUATION at each step of the implementation. It is equally important that you develop methods to evaluate the impacts of your strategies on your company 'values' as well as on finances. Return on investment is always important, but so are motivation and morale. A good approach to evaluation is to try out your Strategic Business Management process on one of the Strategic Business Units or Departments before jumping in with both feet and initiating it company-wide.

Seventh, you must accept the need and the responsibility to GROW YOUR PEOPLE. It is a continuing challenge to all managers to pick good people, but an even greater challenge to keep on training them. Perhaps the toughest challenge of all is keeping them—and this requires hard work and careful, continuous attention. Very often a major change in strategic direction will need a new mix of people and skills. It may be necessary to set up training programs for large numbers of people early on in order to have the right blend of skills and talents available to make strategies happen.

And finally, eighth, you must develop and foster YES-I-CAN attitudes. Winners have one thing in common—they have confidence in themselves. They win the competition because, deep inside, they know they can do it. Working to develop a winning attitude in your people is one of the most strategic things you can do. Somebody once said that 'Losers let it happen, but winners make it happen'. True strategic advantage comes from going out and making things happen, creating your own future, changing the rules of the game away from the areas where your competitor holds the advantage and into areas where you have the competitive edge.

The real task is to transform these elements into a workable, practical Strategic Management System that will enable your company to improve its management effectiveness and strengthen, or regain, that vital competitve edge.

At GM, we have been developing the concepts of contemporary Strategic Business Management for the past 5 years and have been in a major implementation phase for the last 3 years. Our approach has four main parts; Business Segmentation, a Negotiation Framework, a Strategic Planning Process and a supporting Corporate Culture.

In more detail Business Segmentation is the identification of each of the many different businesses that comprise General Motors. We use the typical designation of Strategic Business Unit or SBU. Each SBU is characterized by having a unique, clearly identified mission and should operate in a unique market segment. This allows the development of a clearly focused business strategy—a task that is only possible when there are clearly identified competitors. Each SBU supplies products and services that require similar skills and resources and is configured so it can assume full responsibility for its own performance and exercise significant control over its principal resources. We have found that business units offer an excellent way to establish real and direct identification with the product and lead to a strong feeling of shared ownership in the success of the business enterprise. Clearly defined objectives and sharply focused competitive strategies are produced. The business unit team recognizes that they all share in the responsibility for developing and implementing the business strategy and in the rewards for a successful effort—a real combination of the three R's (risk, responsibility, reward).

The negotiation framework (shown in Figure 1) is our structure for managing the necessary planning information flows between the SBU's and the corporation. Each SBU develops its explicit mission and objectives, the related competitive strategies and a 5 year business plan. The strategy is shown separate from the plan because it is different. The word strategy has become one of the more misunderstood and over-used words in our language. A strategy is the method to achieve and sustain competitive advantage and, as such, it must be approached in a *relative* sense. Strategies are designs to win relative to a specific competitor or group of very similar competitors. There is no such thing as a perfect strategy. What matters is the outcome relative to the other competitors. As such, strategies must be 'living things' that can change whenever necessary. Further, they should be both qualitative and quantitative. A business plan, on the other hand, is much shorter-range and more quantitative. It defines the 'what' and the 'when' of the specific actions to be taken over the next year or two and contains estimates of the needed resources that must be employed. Because it is so specific and time dependent, the business plan should be updated regularly—typically on an annual basis.

The business unit strategy and plan contain product strategies and plans for each product line and these, in turn, lead to plans for each functional area—like marketing, design, engineering, manufacturing, etc.

Negotiations take place between each of these activities, as shown by the arrows. These negotiations are key to our process of planning. They are a principal forum for talk, for communication in both directions concerning the trade-offs between business strategies and organizational capabilities and all the implications of the various plans. We have found these negotiation

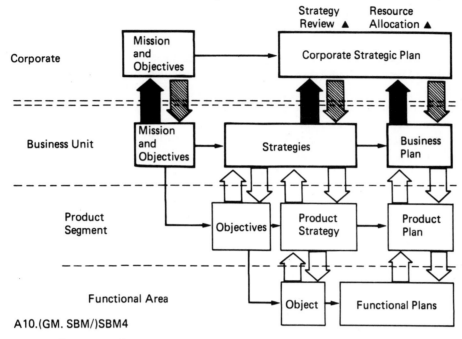

Figure 1. Management framework

sessions to be excellent ways to communicate—to get us talking to each other more frequently and about relevant things. It ensures that the impacts of the intended strategic competitive actions can be identified and evaluated by the people most directly affected—the line managers who have to implement the plans.

Over these business unit activities are the corporate level elements. The corporate mission and objectives form the overall direction for the business units. Similarly, the business unit plans also influence the corporate direction. The corporate strategic plan reflects the business unit strategies and is used to reconcile overlaps, gaps and differences between the business units during the strategy reviews. The consolidated plan also forms the basis for corporate resource allocation.

At GM, we believe strongly that planning is part of the responsibility of every line manager, rather than being entirely concentrated in a centralized corporate planning group. Planning usually fails for lack of ownership and our Strategic Business Management approach at GM is built around the concept of assigning the responsibility for planning to our line managers and making sure that they are properly trained and equipped to do this well.

The role of the planner, is to be the catalyst for change—to help make the planning happen, but not to do the planning for the operating units. The Corporate Strategic Planning Group, has the mission to 'Facilitate the continued development and implementation of Strategic Business Management throughout the Corporation'. My group sends out the planning instructions, consolidates the plans, acts as a focal point for planning expertise, acts as a planning consultant broker for multi-

divisional studies, and coordinates the training efforts for strategic business planning methods.

Our strategic planning process is straightforward. Instructions, in the form of sets of questions, are sent out each year to each division and are divided into categories that form a series of steps.

Step 1, Business Definition. This addresses where the business unit adds value and the specific definitions of market segments.

Step 2, Key Success Factors. Each business unit identifies the three or four vital factors that make the difference between success and failure.

Step 3, Situation Analysis. This is an in-depth evaluation of the relative competitive strengths and weaknesses of the business unit against each of its major competitors. This analysis seeks to pinpoint not only what a competitor could do but what is he likely to do—especially in response to possible actions we might take.

Step 4, Strategy Development. This must be somewhat unstructured. Too much dependence on a formalized or highly structured planning methodology will leave you susceptible to being second-guessed by an alert competitor—and most competitors are extremely alert today. Strategy development is done by the systematic comparison of individual strengths and weaknesses against each of the key success factors for each of the major competitors. If that sounds like a lot of work, it is! But I do not know any shortcuts that will guarantee winning strategies. Very often, the winning strategy is based on insight, but an insight augmented by the best possible information. Our planning process is a step-by-step approach to developing the essential background information.

Step 5, The Business Plan. This is the end result of the planning process. It is the careful establishment of the required capital investment, product development, marketing effort, etc., needed to implement the strategy. It is also an evaluation of the program cost, the forecasted sales and the expected return; the 'bottom line' in terms of 'is it worth it' and 'can we afford it'.

Corporate Culture
The final building block of our approach to Strategic Business Management is the establishment of a corporate culture that fosters strategic behavior. Culture is one of the buzz words that is appearing in more and more book titles nowadays but it is, and has always been, important. Back in 1921, Pierre DuPont, then Chairman of the Board of General Motors, had this to say about Alfred Sloan's reorganization plan:

> The success of any scheme of organization adopted by our company will depend on the enthusiasm and sincerity manifested by the respective heads of the departments in carrying out the plan.

Sloan, himself, had this to say about business management:

> It is not easy to say why one management is successful and another is not. The causes of success or failure are deep and complex, and chance plays a part. Experience has convinced me, however, that for those who are responsible for a business, two important factors are *motivation and opportunity*. The former is supplied in good part by incentive compensation, the latter by *decentralization*.

> From decentralization we get *initiative, responsibility, development of personnel, decisions close to the facts, flexibility*—in short, all the qualities necessary for an organization to adapt to new conditions. From coordination we get efficiencies and economies.

It must be apparent that coordinated decentralization is not an easy concept to apply. There is no hard and fast rule for sorting out the various responsibilities and the best way to assign them. The balance which is struck between corporate and divisional responsibility varies according to what is being decided, *the circumstances of the time*, past experience, and the temperaments and skills of the executive involved.

In conclusion, regaining the competitive edge will need different actions by each individual business enterprise, but the development of an effective Strategic Business Management system is an essential ingredient. Again, the precise structure of Strategic Business Management for each company will have to be thought through by its management.

However, your chances for successful implementation will be greatly improved it you remember the key word STRATEGY.

S for   STICK TO IT;

T for   THINK IT THROUGH;

R for   RISK, RESPONSIBILITY and REWARD;

A for   AWARENESS of yourself and your competitors;

T for   TALKING to each other to communicate your strategies;

E for   EVALUATION of each step as you proceed;

G for   GROWING your people through training programs and hands-on studies; and

Y for   the winning attitude of YES-I-CAN.

Taken together these ingredients will lead you to the level of strategic thinking and management that should give you the inside track for regaining and holding on to that competitive edge.

New Venture Management in an Electric Utility

Gilbert D. Harrell and George O. Murray

After describing current challenges facing mature industries, with a close look at one electric utility company in particular, this article offers a means of stimulating business growth through new ventures. It describes salient aspects of new venture management, and then provides a procedure that companies in mature industries can use to efficiently evaluate new venture proposals. Examples of how the process has worked for Detroit Edison are given as evidence of the effectiveness of the system.

Introduction

Many business executives have recently found more favorable environments after steering their companies through troubled economic water. For most who managed to survive the storm, their businesses have shown recent growth. Still, some firms are simply holding their own against the harsh realities of higher costs and uncertain consumer demand. But an alarming number of American companies have not only failed to grow with the economic upswing, they are still declining and may eventually go under, swallowed up by the trough of previous recessionary forces.

While a hostile economic environment may affect all industries to some extent, mature industries are especially vulnerable. Weakened from cash drains due to higher costs, many have tried to rely only on their traditional products or markets to sustain the needed growth. Minor course corrections are often inadequate. Instead, companies can chart new courses in their long-range planning. Some companies in mature industries are seeking ways to develop new products and services, which can boost profitability and stimulate growth. Utilities, in particular, face difficult growth environments because many have matured to a point where their success is closely tied to economic conditions in

their trading areas. In times of economic upturns some utilities are seeking new ventures to provide a more constant growth base.

A Case in Point

The Detroit Edison Company began searching for new sources of growth when its management recognized that the traditional markets for its electric power and ancillary products had reached maturity and might be expected to grow or decline according to the economy of their region. New ventures would help the company and the economy as well, perhaps, to some degree, producing a positive upward economic spiral for both.

First, in the industrial sector, electricity sales to steel producers in southeast Michigan were flat during the recession and fell dramatically in the automotive industry from their highs in 1973. Future growth in this sector is up significantly but still uncertain in light of three trends: (1) world competition with Detroit's industrial and automotive industries, (2) the introduction of more energy-efficient production processes in the U.S. and (3) population shifts to other parts of the nation. Historically, declines in the auto industry have played economic havoc every few years balanced with spurts of prosperity.

In the commercial sector, where energy use is tied to overall population growth and business activity, there has been only nominal growth over the past several years in southeast Michigan. Growth in the residential sector is also low; population has reached a plateau, resulting in slow sales of new major appliances. Responding to consumer concerns, appliance manufacturers have begun producing more energy efficient water heaters, refrigerators, dish-washers, and so on. While these models seem to please the cost-conscious consumer and are consistent with utility company desires for energy conservation, they don't generate high levels of utility growth. Furthermore, residential customers

Gilbert D. Harrell is Professor of Marketing and Transportation at the Graduate School of Business, Michigan State University, and George O. Murray is Manager of Utility Technical Services Inc.

sensitized by the previous inflationary squeeze of spending more and having less to show for it have conscientiously changed their energy use habits to conserve.

Nationally, electric industry revenues are still lagging behind rising costs. As of the late 1960s and early 1970s, new technologies and economics of scale no longer produce declines in the unit cost of electricity as they used to during the previous four decades. Since staggering amounts of capital would be required to finance new construction, many companies find it impractical to continue building new, more efficient power plants to cut their cost of producing and distributing electricity. This is particularly the case when you consider that utilities now have excess capacity and several utilities have stopped construction on plants underway. Although a strong growth market could build in the future, demand today in many areas is flat.

Like some other innovative companies in mature industries, Detroit Edison has discovered marketing opportunities through a variety of new business ventures which are strategically important in their maintenance of historical growth patterns. And like certain other companies, Edison is taking active steps to insure against plateaued growth by means of a venture management program.

Preliminary Steps in Venture Management

Venture management techniques, that are significant parts of the strategic plan, enable mature industries to discover and realize entrepreneurial opportunities that often reduce costs of their base business by spreading overhead and increasing revenues. The preliminary steps required to establish a venture management program are crucial. They involve top management , answering the fundamental strategic questions about the company: 'Who are we?' and 'What do we want to be?' In Theordore Levitt's classic *Harvard Business Review* article, 'Marketing Myopia' (September–October 1975), the importance of first defining the direction for growth is emphasized. This definition establishes limits for the types of new venture proposals which may be considered.

But before a company can chart new business growth directions, it must have a clear understanding of its present situation, including its mission and its capabilities. In many cases, the mission must evolve toward new aspects of business service. As a company broadens its mission statement by including more technological capabilities, more types of products, and alternative markets, the possibilities for business expansion multiply.

Returning to the example of an electric utility company, the importance of this preliminary self-examination can be illustrated. Traditionally, Detroit Edison, like most electric utilities, defined itself as being in the electric power production and distribution business. Its technological base included coal, petroleum and nuclear power technologies. Its markets included residential, commercial and industrial customers within the area which the state had franchised it to serve. Today Edison is in the *energy* business, and is thereby allowing for the broadening of its technology, product and market bases. For example, an apparent opportunity might be to extend capabilities to include solar power technologies. And the company can expand its market by deciding to serve certain customers outside the franchised area of southeast Michigan, for example, by marketing its expertise to other utilities.

An inventory of unique programs and skills required in a major utility provides an impressive list of resources that could be the base for expansion once these resources are viewed from the perspective of their value outside the company. For example, the utility has been a leader in applications of high technology for mapping, construction, systems design and many other areas.

Thus, by rethinking the purpose of the company, the necessity for new business growth directions is apparent. And a corporate culture that is more responsive to entrepreneurial thinking can develop. However, the management policies and procedures which take care of the current business are in some ways inappropriate to cultivate new ventures. New ventures which might be launched must be evaluated beforehand to ensure that the venture is consistent with the company's goals and will likely contribute to fulfilment of the company's mission. The following procedure was developed to be entrepreneurial and strategic in nature and yet provide the checks and balances required for responsible utility management.

A new organizational structure was chosen at Edison in order to have flexibility in developing resources to examine new types of businesses and respond speedily to directional opportunities. A strong knowledge of utility management in the group has primarily been beneficial in examining the companies resources that are grounded in a range of utility activities. At the same time, a definite strategic marketing orientation in the management group was sought and charged with a market focus as their driving force.

The New Venture Evaluation Process

When management has completed the examination of the companies focus and mission, as described above, it should seek a clear picture of the technological, financial, human and other resources at its disposal. Traditionally, these vast and sometimes diverse resources have been seen in light of their contribution to the operations of the utility, as we mentioned—an inward focus. By looking outward, these resources can provide the basis for numerous ventures aimed at new markets and businesses. But a means of evaluating the resulting new venture ideas in light of the company's strengths and weaknesses is needed. The Detroit Edison Company has successfully utilized a new venture evaluation process to take advantage of diversification opportunities, while recognizing and managing the risks involved. The evaluation process consists of the 10 steps illustrated in Figure 1. The launch of any new Detroit Edison venture depends on the successful completion of each of these stages.

The first stage, new venture product growth

directions, is obviously an outgrowth of management's desired business growth philosophy, which has already been discussed. However, the remaining nine stages merit description and examination, which follows.

Project Proposals
New venture opportunities seldom surface without extensive effort. They are the result of concerted activities on the part of management and others within the organization. While new venture ideas can originate from many areas within the company, and from outside it, an identifiable and clearly receptive company organization to generate and process ideas, and define the nature and scope of each opportunity is a critical element. Without a

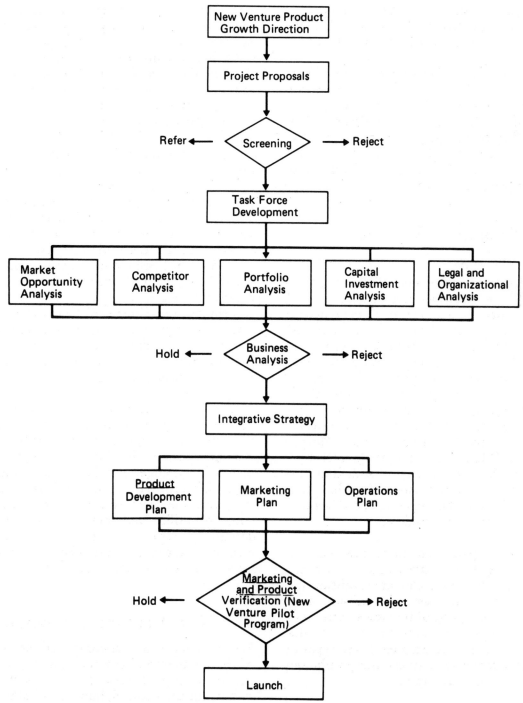

Figure 1. New venture evaluation process

formal group, good ideas bounce around from group to group until they are either championed by an aggressive executive or (more often) lost. Unfortunately many strategic plans that call for growth for new products, do not pay enough attention to provisions for a group of people who encourage exploration and collect ideas.

At the proposal stage, all new ideas that have been received from throughout the organization should be handled in a way that facilitates screening according to a predetermined set of criteria. Since individuals who generate the ideas may not have enough information to fully complete a new product proposal, the new venture team is asked to work closely with them to assist in developing the idea well enough for screening. Usually discussion with the individuals who have the idea is enough to develop the new venture proposal with information to get started.

The project proposal should include a brief description of the new venture, whether it be a product or a service. The description should consist of at least five important elements:

(1) A clear description of the product or service, including the key benefits the product will offer the eventual user.

(2) A description of potential customers and the major potential market segments, whether they already exist within the company's market base or are new segments.

(3) Likely competitors that may provide similar products or substitute products that could affect the marketing opportunity.

(4) Governmental or regulatory activities that may impinge on a particular product or service offering.

(5) Current resources the company possesses for actualizing the technical or marketing aspects of the new venture.

At Detroit Edison, a two-page proposal form includes enough information to take most ideas through the next phase, which is the screening process.

Screening

In the third stage, a screening guide is completed to determine the fit between the new venture opportunity and the company's long-range goals and resources. It is important for the screening to seek and refine ideas rather than simply provide a means of rejecting them.

This screening guide simplifies the comparison of proposed new ventures using a relatively clear, yet subjectively responsive scale. The scale carefully categorizes and quantifies a new venture on each of the relevant points. A weighting is used to deter-

mine the relative importance of, for example, competitive factors vs technological factors in arriving at a total score. Each new venture idea is given a score. Some can be eliminated on the basis of a very low score in any one of the critical areas and others can be advanced because of clear potential advantages in selected areas. After the first several new product ideas were evaluated, Detroit Edison developed an analytical base to determine the relative merits of each subsequent new venture idea. Additionally, they obtained the qualitative sensitivity to combine and refine existing ideas to generate useful new ideas. An in-depth discussion of all the screening factors is beyond the scope of the paper, however the following table provides a list that is suggestive of all the types of consideration given.

Table 1. Screening factors in the new venture process

I. Consistency with corporate mission
  A. Within philosophy of business
  B. Contributes to enhancement of mission

II. Competitive advantage and position
  A. Market niche
  B. Proprietary position
  C. Current competitors
  D. Market share position available

III. Leads to knowledge and skills desired for longer term
  A. Technical
  B. Executive
  C. R & D

IV. Cash flow and financial requirements
  A. Use of cash
  B. Generation of cash
  C. Return to shareholders

V. Enhancement of market area
  A. Contributes to growth of local business
  B. Reflects social responsibility

VI. Industry characteristics
  A. Regulation climate
  B. Probable long-term industry structure

VII. Use of current resources or additional resource requirement
  A. Management availability
  B. R & D availability
  C. Uses current channels and sales force
    1. within company
    2. to hire
    3. on contract basis

VIII. Risk management factors
  A. Entrepreneurial opportunity
  B. Clarity of future situations
  C. Risk/return range

Task Force Development

If the new venture proposal passes screening, a task force can be formed to further explore the idea. A new venture task force is generally a multi-functional group, organized for the express purpose of pursuing the commercial potential for the new product.

There are two main requirements of a task force, and the absence of either will jeopardize the new venture evaluation process. First, there should be a leader with clear responsibility for the output of the task force and the authority to assemble a functioning organization. Ideally, the task force head should have broad functional knowledge required to orchestrate the new venture analysis process. Depending on the amount of new venture activity, it may be desirable to have one individual head over all or many of the company's new venture task forces. However, for each potential venture, one leader should have ultimate responsibility for the successful application of the venture analysis procedure.

Second, the task force members are given some release time from current assignments to properly function and be recognized for their work. The time commitment makes their participation a clearly defined responsibility. In assembling a new venture task force, the following additional guidelines may be helpful.

First, in selecting the venture team, it is important to keep in mind that high risk/high payout opportunities require aggressive and creative thinking. Lower risk opportunities can generally be managed with less creativity and aggressiveness. Thus, the task force members themselves will influence the nature of many evaluations and no process will protect a company from stagnation of timid, excessively risk aversive managers.

Second, the task force should involve individuals from specific functional areas within the organization. The relevant functional areas and their responsibilities generally include:

(1) Marketing—to develop projections on market size, market growth rates, market segmentation and competitor analysis.

(2) Finance—to ensure that the proper cost and revenue projections are completed.

(3) Engineering and Production—to assess the technologies required and the proper and probable cost of producing relative capacities.

(4) Personnel—to assess the manpower requirements for each new venture.

(5) Purchasing—to ensure the supply of raw materials or component products, where needed.

(6) Legal—to identify regulatory constraints.

Third, the task force should tap those individuals who are experts in the technology, product and market being considered. If expertise is unavailable within the company, it should be acquired through consultants or other sources.

Finally, although representatives of several departments lend their expertise to the task force, the task force members should be viewed as an integrated team involved in each step of the new venture evaluation process. All of the principles of team building such as clear objectives, responsibilities, open communications and so forth apply.

Business Analysis
Business analysis involves five important activities, each of which is described. These five critical inputs are: (1) market opportunity analysis; (2) competitor analysis; (3) portfolio analysis; (4) capital investment analysis and (5) legal and organizational analysis.

Market Opportunity Analysis
The market opportunity analysis, begins with market segment definition, the relative magnitude of each, and finally evaluates existing opportunities. Market opportunity analysis is typically conducted using published data where available, to initially predict the magnitude of the overall market anticipated during the period of market entry and growth. But in this case, most of the data at this stage should be collected to provide a picture of key market *segments* the organization might be able to attract and the relative sizes and needs of buyers within those segments.

Careful attention should be paid to buyer behavior variables such as why people might buy, where, how and so forth.

Competitor Analysis
Potential competitors should be investigated in terms of their current status, as well as their potential strategic movement in markets. If there are no competitors identifiable for the new venture, usually there will be competitors in the near future. Thus, in many cases, competitive analysis must anticipate who those competitors are likely to be, and what their strength might be in the market place.

It may be useful to isolate market leaders and complete a preliminary cost analysis of their products. Published information on capital expenditures, number of employees, plant sizes, and current production can provide the task force with reasonable estimates of those competitors' per unit cost.

Analysis of industry structure can provide another basis for examining potential competitive strategies. Industry structure, i.e. whether oligopolistic or otherwise, quickly promotes insights into potential pricing, promotion and other competitive activities.

Portfolio Analysis
Portfolio analysis has become a standard part of the executive's vocabulary. It refers to a category of procedures that are useful in evaluating the relationship between the companies resources and business opportunities. Portfolio analysis is particularly robust for new venture analysis. These procedures

help investigate and visualize the relationships between a particular company's strengths and the market opportunity being evaluated. In terms of business strengths, the organization must determine for itself what constitutes a strong business. For example, a business that is likely to gain a strong market share or could produce a new product at an economical rate with available raw materials and resources might be considered a business with significant strengths.

Portfolio analysis also forces the organization to define what it considers to be a strong market opportunity, a necessity in venture analysis. Important considerations might include the size of the market, the stage in the life cycle of the market, whether the market is growing or declining, the number of competitors in the market, the type of competition and the amount of value added likely to occur from products in those markets.

Of course, a first step in this process is the classification of existing businesses in the portfolio. This allows the examination of the relative cash flow implications of new ventures within the context of existing businesses.

By using the familiar matrix shown in Figure 2 to evaluate the portfolio of strategic business units, it is possible to rate the new venture in light of other potential opportunities and current businesses within the organization. For instance, many are familiar with the categorization of businesses, strategic business units or products on such a resource/opportunity matrix. The same concept is an excellent tool in estimating the strategic potential of a new venture, as well. In the A category are ventures for which the organization has a few business strengths, but which represent a potentially great market opportunity. The B category describes ventures that are attractive to the company and for which they expect to be particularly well suited. C category ventures are generally mature businesses wherein the company has many business strengths but which suffer from low market growth and mature competition. Businesses classified in D have a few market opportunities combined with few business strengths.

Thus, portfolio analysis subjectively characterizes

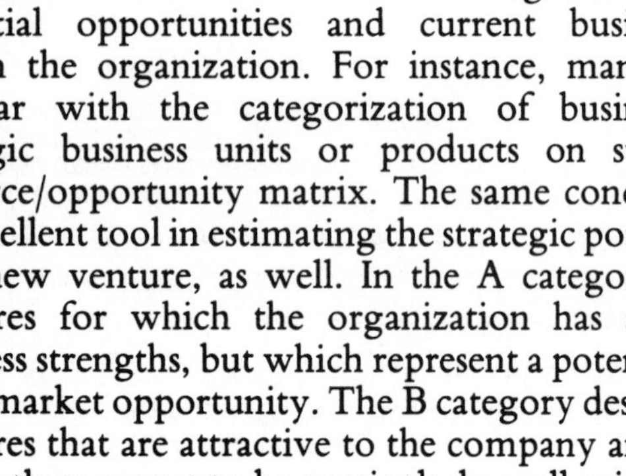

the new venture according to its place on the grid. To consider the extremes, those ventures classified as B suggest much stronger opportunities than those categorized as D which should generally be avoided. On the other hand, it is a little more difficult to judge ventures which fall into the grey areas. Careful consideration is needed to determine the practicality of launching a business in category B that could require a great deal of cash to realize the opportunity.

Capital Investment Analysis
Capital investment analysis is the fourth input required for a complete business analysis. Capital investment includes standard items such as plant equipment, working capital and personnel required to launch and maintain a new venture. Assumptions regarding levels of productivity can be used to establish levels of capital commitment for varying market shares. It is best to look at fixed costs, semi-fixed costs, and variable costs as they relate to levels of a new venture commitment.

Accurate anticipation of costs provides a major ingredient in evaluating profitability. There is a great deal of controversy over alternative funding approaches used for utilities to diversity that should be considered. Make vs buy decisions and opportunity casting need to be addressed creatively.

Legal and Organizational Analysis
Public utilities are heavily regulated. As such, they must carefully evaluate the impact of the new venture organizational possibilities to ensure that the organization forms within legal limits and in the public interest. Most new ventures are distinctly different from traditional utility businesses because unlike the electrical distribution business, for example, the customers are a smaller percentage of the total population and more competitors are generally present or on the horizon. Thus, in many cases, a subsidiary, joint venture with another company or other structure, is required.

Results of the Business Analysis
Completion of the previous five steps provides information necessary to complete a proforma financial measure of the profitability of the potential new venture. It combines the inputs from market opportunity analysis, competitor analysis, portfolio analysis, capital investment analysis and legal and organizational analysis. The business analysis should provide quantitative data for proforma income statements, cash flow projections, estimates of profit and loss and internal rates of return. Additionally, qualitative information is presented so the judgments and assumptions used for financial analysis are inclusive. In this way, the task force can estimate the impact of the new venture on total operating profit for the company.

Many assumptions must be made in order to project useful figures for a break-even analysis, cash flow

Figure 2. Portfolio analysis

analysis and profit calculations. By clearly listing assumptions (e.g. sales levels, number of customers, size of orders), all interested parties have an opportunity to judge the accuracy of the business analysis. With the help of a business analysis computer program, the task force can examine the effect on the bottom line of various changes in their assumptions, ranging from pessimistic to optimistic. These scenarios help them to anticipate trouble spots in advance.

The business analysis results in a recommendation for further action. If additional information is required, a recommendation may be made to hold the project. If the proposed venture is rejected, the analysis is kept on file and used as a benchmark study for other similar proposals. If the business analysis indicates the project might provide the kind of growth the organization wants, the task force moves into the strategy formulation phase of the new venture analysis process.

Integrative Strategy
For the purposes of the new venture analysis process, strategies are defined as qualitative statements which indicate how the new venture will compete in the market. Perhaps the most important aspect of the probability of new venture success is based on the launch and longer-term strategy. Strategies integrate the product development plan, marketing plan and operations plan to provide a unified thrust for the new venture. A few comments on these component plans follow.

Product Development Plan
Although, up to this point, the new venture analysis has investigated market wants and needs, it generally has not been specific enough for careful product development. Thus, the product development plan involves the careful design of a product or service to match the target market's needs. This process brings together technology and market analysis to create a viable market offering.

In some cases, product development is simply a matter of adjusting an existing product concept to meet specific segment needs. In other cases, it involves development of new technologies and support services to satisfy new market demands. As a general rule, however, it is a jointly held responsibility of the research, development and marketing departments.

Strategic Marketing Plan
Marketing strategy involves clear statements of marketing mix factors, such as price levels, channel of distribution, product line breadth and depth, and promotion. Equally important is a clear identification of the market segments at which marketing efforts will be directed, both in the short run and the long run. The strategy also requires concise statements of how competitive forces will be met to win market support and ensure profitability.

In order to blend marketing mix factors and achieve market entry, careful timing is necessary. Thus, timetables should be established for market entry and coordination of activities over the longer run. Commitment of resources, expected sales and market-share levels are parts of this program. At this stage, additional market research may be necessary to provide information to help with the marketing program.

Operations Plan
The operations part of the strategy involves determining the organizational form and size, as well as cost projections of operations required for market entry and growth. An important aspect is to coordinate the amount of market penetration expected with the type and level of production or service development. In other words, operations strategy coordinates the product development and manufacturing in light of expected sales levels through human resource plans and organizational structures.

New Venture Pilot Program
Once the above steps are completed, the new venture can be turned over to an existing or new business unit that will develop a pilot program and new venture launch. Whether the new venture is managed within the existing corporate structure or through a subsidiary is largely dependent on whether the articles of incorporation allow for a broadened definition of the business.

The pilot program represents the first time the new product or service is pilot-tested for market acceptance. It involves text market programs and/or follow up studies to make sure the product actually meets the needs of the market. If a problem with the new venture is identified at this point, adjustments can be made prior to full-scale launch into the marketplace.

New Venture Launch
Obviously, all new venture ideas are not going to make it through the analysis process. They shouldn't. Only those that can provide growth consistent with the organization's mission should find their way into the marketplace.

How Detroit Edison has Used The New Venture Evaluation Process

Detroit Edison has several new venture analyses going at this time, and are gaining perspective in this type of business. Two short examples help illustrate how the process has functioned to date.

An entrepreneur approached Detroit Edison with an idea to transform an Edison fuel by-product into a form of insulation. At first analysis, the opportunity looked as though it couldn't loose. The by-product was available in large quantities and on the surface it appeared that there was a need for low-cost insulation. The idea was consistent with Detroit Edison's energy related mission and was carefully documented for the proposal stage. During the screening process, the idea received high scores regarding most of the criteria. There were several potential key benefits of the product which differentiated it from traditional insulation including a higher heat flame point and lower cost possibility. The evaluation regarding potential customers involved looking at both residential and industrial users, and although market size varied considerably, clearly, it appeared that there might be a large and growing segment. The competition consisted of three strong companies but was well within the guidelines of acceptability. Government and regulatory aspects looked supportive, certainly not negative. Finally, Detroit Edison possessed the raw materials, could easily acquire the manufacturing (in the form of a joint venture partner). The screening process suggested that the only weakness was in marketing strength and channels of distribution, but those weaknesses were to be expected for many ventures and not a strong liability given possibilities of using selling agents to reach some segments. Overall the venture looked promising.

A task force of seven people were assigned to further evaluate the product. Again, at first glance, the task force felt optimistic about the product; their experience in energy had given several of the members a working knowledge of technical aspects of insulation.

The task force quickly entered into information gathering for the business analysis, this included portfolio analysis, market opportunity analysis, competitor analysis, capital investment analysis and legal and organizational analysis. Early in this process, two cautionary flags were raised. First, the market analysis indicated that the market was currently somewhat smaller than expected in the residential sector. Secondly, competition of three large firms were operating at about 60 per cent capacity with a price softening expected in the near future. The industrial market was found to be very fragmented with very specialized needs. Further analysis indicated that the product offered a significant differential advantage but in volumes too insignificant to warrant Detroit Edison's attention. At this point, the project was turned over to a small but very interested local firm. That firm now has plans to enter the business and Detroit Edison will gain because the manufacturing process for small amounts to product the specialized insulation for a few industrial applications should increase their electricity sales to the business. At the same time, it will probably provide a product of significant volume to the local manufacturer but of little interest to a large operation.

A second opportunity seemed to emerge from several areas in the firm simultaneously. A giant utility requires many computerized systems for operational efficiency. Detroit Edison had for years taken a lead in developing automated mapping systems to locate power poles, lines and customers. Many of these systems had been extended for use in architectural design and energy generation construction. Several suggestions regarding computer applications in these areas were received by the new venture group during a short-time period. An opportunity for automated mapping systems might exist.

This time, several synergistic ideas were combined and a viable new venture idea rapidly made its way through the process. The resources that would be required if successful commercialization was to take place were revealed as the process proceeded. Detroit Edison already had a reputation among potential customers for excellence in this area and all of the technological expertise. Marketing was needed. But Detroit Edison was able to join with other companies to form an important part of this high tech area. At this time, the results are not in, but it would appear that Detroit Edison has an opportunity to provide other utilities as well as non-utility industrial customers and governments with important computerized mapping systems.

Conclusion

Any new venture management process must take a long and continuous look at growth to help ensure systematic moves. The new venture management technique just described provides the needed mechanisms for efficient evaluation of a broad range of opportunities for growth outside the traditional scope of industries. No process can ensure success, but a process that efficiently addresses the critical elements in venture management can speed the amount of time required to find and launch potentially successful ventures.

In the final analysis, the New Venture Process is a people intensive business activity. The philosophies used to take ventures from idea to actualization can be important. The challenge is not to reject ventures but to find ways to make them positively contribute to the firms mission. The process should search for several viable alternatives so top management can select the best. Yes, when a good strategy can not be found the rejection should be made.

Today, old administrative approaches that stress rules and procedures which have evolved over the years as a business matures can strangle new ventures in red tape. Generally, there are no 'hot buttons' or single ideas to provide a critical success factor in new ventures. Many factors—technical, financial, production and marketing are needed. The process suggested here benefits from the integration of all of these inputs, in ways that seek opportunities.

Acknowledgments—The authors wish to thank Mary E. Gerbig and the Detroit Edison Comapny for their support in developing the material presented in this article.

How Elf Aquitaine Provides Technological Assistance to Small Businesses

Jean-Pierre Turbil

Elf Aquitaine offered its accumulated knowledge and expertise in research, development and innovation to other small and medium size businesses in the Aquitaine area. Its success led to a similar service being offered in the Rhone–Alpes region, and other large industrial groups have followed the lead in other districts. The scheme has benefits all round. Elf Aquitaine's research benefits from a widening of outlook: the area sees an increased industrial activity: and smaller businesses find technological support.

The Creation of Regional Technical Centres

Conscious of the difficulties that small and medium size businesses encounter in improving their products and creating new ones, Elf Aquitaine agreed to put its scientific and technical resources at their disposal. However dynamic it may be, a firm cannot make the indispensable technological developments needed for its growth and survival without research. Unfortunately, most of the time, this is a luxury for the small and medium size business. To maintain a research team is costly, and it is not justified unless the enterprise is capable of assimilating and developing the results which come from its laboratories. Elf Aquitaine has accumulated knowledge and capabilities many of which lay outside its field of industrial activities. The idea was born to let individual enterprises, which base their development on technological innovation and technical progress, benefit from this pool of skills and technology. This thought, coupled with the desire to develop the economy and employment in the Great South West part of France lead the Group* to create the Technical Centre in the Aquitaine region (CETRA)

The author belongs to the Research Development and Innovation Division of Elf Aquitaine.
*The term Group refers to the Elf Aquitaine Group.

constituting thus, the first experience of its type in France, Within 5 years, this centre has enjoyed an important development in collaboration with the industries of the Aquitaine area. This success induced the Elf Aquitaine Group to repeat the experiment in the Rhone–Alpes region in 1984 by creating the technical centre of Rhone–Alpes (CETRALP).

A Light Structure

Contrary to what the name suggests, CETRA and CETRALP are very light structures since they consist of four and three people, respectively. As the spearhead of the research staff, the Technical Centres are the interface with the small businesses. Their strength lies in the fact that they are able to speak the language of the enterprises as well as that of the laboratories.

They are Industrialists at the Service of Industrialists
They help the industrialist to formulate his problem and to translate it into a research project. The Technical Centres give a good deal of time to the first step because the quality of the later discussion depends on this. As they come from industry, the personnel of Technical Centres know the importance of a cost estimate or a delay, the value of an investment, the competitiveness in the market; these are qualities that the senior personnel in small businesses are very sensitive and attentive to. The Technical Centres are in continuous contact with private and public organizations that exist to help the small businesses to finance their research work.

They maintain a close relationship with other organizations in the Elf Aquitaine group, such as SOFREA (Society for the Regional Financing of Elf Aquitaine). They are in touch with the Bureau of Economic Development whose aim is to provide financial aid related to job creation for the industrial development of the south-west and south-east regions of France and INOVELF which is a venture capital company. They are also in contact with ANVAR (National Agency for Validation of Research), other associations to assist small businesses, the chambers of Commerce and Industry, etc.

Varied and Adapted Services

Once the problem submitted by the enterprise is thoroughly formulated, the Technical Centre looks for the right team in the Group which could best solve the problem, and the problem is submitted to them. A proposal is then submitted to the small business. The Technical Centre simultaneously informs the enterprise of the financial research help it could request. The Technical Centres have agreed on 'tax credits for research' and Elf Aquitaine scientists can participate in the 'technological expertise programmes' of ANVAR.

The Services Offered

These are primarily differentiated by the time taken, from a simple consultation to the complete development of a process or a product.

Short-term Studies
These imply a response to a specific question by a piece of advice, a test or a literature search.

Medium or Long-term Studies
These services are related to more complex problems, improving a manufacturing process, using alternative raw materials, developing new products. In each case the enterprise's competitiveness is at risk; so it is necessary to provide the small businesses with sound answers at the right time. Increasingly, research work is preceded by a feasibility study allowing the entrepreneur to appreciate the technical risks, the competitiveness, the marketing scope and the price levels.

Financial Aspects

The services given by the Technical Centres are costed. It is one of the conditions of the contract to establish a clear relationship with industrialists. However, as part of its policy of helping regional development, Elf Aquitaine pays for the direct expenses of each Technical Centre team, which reduces the costs to the small businesses. In addition, the Group shares the financial costs of the consultancy services.

Ownership of Results

This important point is agreed at the beginning of the assignment in the terms of a contract between the two parties. The attribution of proprietary rights may be arranged in several ways: to the small business with or without royalties to the Group, to the Group with a licensing agreement in its territory; to the two parties, with possible royalty payments for the applications that each would have.

Areas of Competence

The size and diversity or the Group's potential for research allow the Regional Technical Centres to respond to a large number of enquiries. However, among the areas in which our researchers possess a specific competence, some are specifically of interest to small businesses:

☆ *Materials:* Rubbers, plastics (thermoplastics, thermosets), filled plastics, composites

☆ *Surface treatment:* Paints, varnishes, corrosion

☆ *Glues and adhesives:* Characterization, formulation, transformation, testing

☆ *Automation:* Improving the productivity of production machinery. The Technical Centres perform the first two steps of the research; the analysis of the problem and the assessment of feasibility. The development of prototypes is generally undertaken by the specialized small businesses under the Technical Centres' direction.

☆ *Energy:* Analysis and development proposals for the utilization of energy (generation, combustion, economy thermal diagnosis); energy generation from waste.

☆ *Fine chemicals:* Formulation and compounding of products for specific uses.

☆ *Environment:* The diagnosis and production of proposals to combat nuisances and the disposal of products in their consumer usage cycles.

The CETRA and CETRALP

The Technical Centres provide assistance in terms of both know-kow and research facilities.

This is not as one-sided as it seems. The research workers who are responsible the the contracted studies, participate in the development of innovations in a complimentary environment to the one they already know. They benefit by widening their outlook and this is frequently helpful to their research work for Elf Aquitaine.

Also the knowledge of the regional industry thus acquired, helps in the creation of jobs (SOFREA) and in the promotion of innovation (INOVELF) in a better environment and with increased efficiency. Experience at CETRA shows that that cooperation between a large enterprise like Elf Aquitaine and small businesses can be helpful in the creation of industrial activity and therefore jobs. This is a fact of great economic importance, because it allows small firms to increase their competitiveness through having access to know-how they could have never acquired by themselves.

Our Group has decided to extend this work by creating the Technical Centre of the Rhone–Alpes region (CETRALP) with the same objectives as CETRA.

Other large industrial groups have followed our example: Saint Gobain/Pont-à-Mousson in Lorraine, the CEA and the SNPE in Aquitaine, Lafarge Coppee at Montélimar, PUK in the Isère and many others. The French government is actively interested in these experiments. An informal club has been formed to exchange experiences among the various projects and to make specific recommendations.

Examples of Intervention

Combustible Additives
A company in the Aquitaine region produces and markets several additives for different companies.

In the Solaize Research Centre, Elf Aquitaine conducts research work on 'liquid charcoals' and is considering the use of this type of additive for their stabilization.

CETRA and CETRALP have succeeded in developing products and have tested them by using the resources available in the various regions.

A contract has been drawn up to fix the terms and conditions for this cooperation, particularly with respect to industrial royalties and proprietary information.

Hot Metal Adhesives
CETRA has helped an industrialist in the PAU area to develop an entirely automated process for the extrusion and conditioning of small rods of hot melt adhesive to feed applicator guns.

The studies carried out so far on the formulation now enable the company to use French raw materials, which can now replace imports.

Acknowledgement—This project has been supported by a grant from ANVAR.

Additional information about the activities of the Regional Technical Centres can be obtained through the following contacts:

Dr. Elias Agouri
ELF-AQUITAINE-CETRA
BP 34
64170 Artix
France

Tel: (59) 92.22.92
Telex: 560053

M. Gilbert Ouziel
ELF-AQUITAINE-CETRALP
Chemin de la Lône-BP 32
69310-Pierre Benite
France

Tel: (7) 251 88 00
Telex: 900540 F

Can We Plan for New Technology?

Gerard Fairtlough, Chief Executive, Celltech Limited

This paper looks at the contribution of long-range planning to the emergence of the advanced biotechnology industry during the past 5 years and notes differences with planning for semiconductors 20 years ago. Two explanations for the differences are discussed: a steady progress thesis and a long wave thesis. Some conclusions are drawn about biotechnology on one hand and about the nature of planning on the other.

Introduction

Theory and practice should nourish each other, in planning as in other fields. I will try to use what has been happening in advanced biotechnology over the past 4 years to develop some insights into the nature of planning. My starting point is a paper published earlier this year by Horwitch of MIT[1] which considers the link between planning and biotechnology. He compares the rise of the semiconductor industry in the 1950s and early 1960s with the rise of the biotechnology industry in the late 1970s and early 1980s. Using this comparison he argues that corporate strategists have in the past neglected technology as a factor in long-range planning but that this neglect is now being put right. He also claims that over the past 20 years the strategic direction of innovation has become increasingly well informed and purposeful.

My paper starts by looking at three concepts presented by Horwitch and by examining, with their aid, his thesis that steady progress in planning capabilities means that the emergence of new technologies is now being directed in an explicit and well co-ordinated way. I then propose a revision of Horwitch's scheme, which in my view describes better the emergence of new technologies.

To test the extent to which explicit strategic planning has influenced the emergence of advanced biotechnology, I review the reports published by governments in various countries, and conclude that on this evidence strategic planning has been rather limited.

The next part of the paper presents an ideal-typical model of a 'long wave' cycle with new technology as the driving force. Using this model some conclusions about the future of biotechnology are drawn. The model is then used to look at two rival theses about planning: a steady progress thesis and a long wave thesis, the latter being that planning varies with the phase of the long wave cycle.

If the long wave thesis is correct it might be explained by a variation of organization perspective with long wave phases. The final sections of the paper discuss this idea.

A description of advanced biotechnology and its industrial impact is included in the Appendix.

Horwitch's View of Planning and Innovation

Horwitch's paper presents three concepts helpful in understanding technological innovation. The first concept distinguishes between three ideal *modes* of innovation:

Mode I—innovation in small high technology firms,

Mode II— innovation in large multi-product, multi-market corporations,

Mode III—innovation in multi-organization systems usually including both the private and public sector.

Next he contrasts two ideal types of strategic activity: *implicit and explicit*, depending on whether

The author was formerly Managing Director of Shell Chemicals U.K. and then a Divisional Director of the NEB, and he is now Chief Executive of Celltech Limited, 244–250 Bath Road, Slough SL1 4DY.

or not there is conscious and purposeful strategic direction in the institution concerned.

His final concept is that of *linkage*, for example linkage between units within an organization, between organizations, whether in one country or internationally, and between the private and public sectors of an economy.

The concept of linkage covers joint ventures, research contracts, minority equity holdings and licencing or marketing agreements. It also covers those government programmes in the U.S.A., Europe and Japan which have explicitly commercial objectives and which support particular Mode I and Mode II organizations.

Horwitch argues that technology is now increasingly managed from the top; it is being directed in an explicit and linked fashion that attempts to co-ordinate all forms of innovation. He supports this contention with a review of the way in which the semiconductor and biotechnology industries developed. The early semiconductor industry had all three kinds of innovative activity— Modes I, II and III. But strategic decision making remained implicit. All institutions were distinct and acted rather separately so there was an absence of linkage. In contrast, he sees in biotechnology a very different pattern with participants acting strategically across a broad front, involving long-range planning for all functions, not just R & D. He points to the strong and formal links between Modes I, II and III organizations and to statements which explicitly demonstrate strategic management.

My first criticism of Horwitch's schemes concerns his Modes I, II and III. I doubt whether this is the most revealing classification. Abernathy and Utterback[2] have studied the innovations made by industrial organizations at different stages in their development, and suggest the distinction between two ideal types: product innovation and process innovation.

Product innovation is stimulated by newly available technology rather than by the market. It depends on a group of people who together have a creative understanding of a wide field of technology. This enables the group to make connections between technical possibilities which together create something really novel. Getting groups to work together in this way and providing a receptive climate for the ideas that emerge is best done in a small, but very well informed organization.

Process innovation depends more on market-pull than on technology-push. It starts to become dominant later in the evolution of an organization as the production process becomes critically important, perhaps because of automation or the need for the lowest possible costs. Process innovation is much less a matter of creative interconnections between widely dispersed developments and much more a matter of day-by-day improvement of familiar activities and the accumulation of experience in an organization. Figure 1 shows how the two ideal types of innovation change over time.

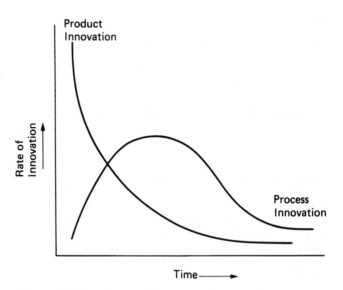

Figure 1. Product and process innovation

It is clear that Horwitch's Mode I organizations are likely to be the most adept at product innovation and in both the semiconductor and the biotechnology industries there is strong evidence that this is so. Mode II organizations have the choice of sticking to process innovation (in the case of biotechnology this could mean concentrating on say a fermentation process rather than genetic engineering) or of trying to create an enclave of product innovation in their midst.

The Abernathy and Utterback model suggests that product innovating organizations are essential in emerging, high technology industries. It does not suggest how these come into being. One necessary condition seems to be committed and energetic individuals; product champions if you like. Perhaps another condition which is necessary is a sponsoring organization of some kind, a meta-innovator. A striking feature of high technology innovation in the U.S.A. is the specialist venture capital company, knowledgeable in the industry and willing to provide help to the infant product innovating firm. During the past few years companies of this kind have also started in the U.K. and very recently Japan has announced a policy of encouraging them. I would therefore propose a model for product innovation along the lines of Figure 2.

Process innovation, since it relates to existing industrial activities, is in less need of meta-innovators.

	Venture Capital Company	Large Industrial Firm	Government
Country with Best Examples from Biotechnology	U.S.A	Japan	U.K. France
Biotechnology Examples	Genentech Hybritech	Suntory's γ-Interferon	Celltech Transgene
Other Examples		3-Ms	

Figure 2. Type of meta-innovator

The identification of meta-innovating organizations supports Horwitch's claims for an increasing degree of linkage in high technology industry since these meta-activities are undoubtedly quite recent and are growing rapidly. But is his identification of increasingly explicit strategic planning also correct? At one level it certainly is. Many people and organizations have felt it essential to do something about biotechnology. Conferences, studies, reports, newsletters and databases seem at times to occupy more people than the actual practice of advanced biotechnology. This has lead to an unusual awareness of the field spreading into the popular press and to TV which has resulted in unrealistic expectations in some places. But strategic awareness is not the same as strategic planning and the evidence of such planning is not so strong. A good test, because the data are publicly available, is to look at the reports commissioned by governments in various countries.

Government Sponsored Reports

Reports commissioned by government and published between March 1980, and mid 1981 include those from the U.K., the U.S.A., France, Canada and the Netherlands.[3] The U.S. report is from the Office of Technology Assessment, which serves the legislature rather than the executive arm of government and this consists of an agenda for discussion rather than proposals for action. The rest were executive commissions. All the executive reports recommend changes in education and training and in development of specialist researchers often by international exchanges. They also emphasize the need for better links between universities and industry, for better methods of technology transfer and for government funded research to become more industrially orientated.

They usually contain recommendations aimed at improving co-ordination between different departments and at keeping up to date the regulations governing genetic manipulation and the licencing of new drugs. Overall measures affecting industry particularly tax write-offs for R & D are also advocated.

However, an explicit industrial strategy is lacking in most reports. The French report identifies gaps in the country's biotechnology (e.g. enzyme production) and recommends concentration on specific areas (e.g. the agriculture/food area) but without revealing how these areas were chosen or what should be done in them.

The Canadian report is entitled *Biotechnology: A Development Plan for Canada* and therefore claims to be a planning document. The analysis is simple but perhaps sufficient for a country which the report admits had virtually no industrial biotechnology at the time of writing. The Dutch report also identifies some half dozen industrial areas on which to concentrate (e.g. veterinary vaccines, process control equipment) and is backed by a brief examination of the strengths and weaknesses of the Netherlands in biotechnology.

The overall impression from these published reports is that governments are not engaging in strategic planning for industry. There could be a number of explanations for this.

(i) Governments do not consider industrial planning to be their job. If so the claims of Horwitch about the planned emergence of the biotechnology industry would not be supported, at least as far as governments are concerned.

(ii) There is a plan, but it has not been published. This may well be the case in France and also in Japan, where in spite of the lack of a published report, there is plenty of evidence of government support for biotechnology.

(iii) The writers of the report were not skilled in long-range planning, in which case the reports again fail to support the Horwitch thesis.

(iv) The reports are, at least in part, designed to impress the public that something is being done to encourage innovation without actually doing anything much. This could be called pseudo meta-innovation.

For obvious reasons I had to survey government

reports. No doubt among the many private sector ones there are some excellent examples of first class professional planning, but I suspect that the overall picture may not be too different. And the private sector is not without its pseudo meta-innovation either, in this case intended to impress gullible investors.

A Long Wave Model

Kondratiev, Schumpeter and others have produced a variety of *long wave* theories[4] in which phases of economic prosperity are followed by phases of depression. The cycle time is around 50 years. Long waves might be generated by a variety of factors including wars, revolutions and international economic rivalries, and long waves must also be influenced by the 'short waves' of the traditional business cycle. But the factor most frequently postulated as the generator of long waves is technological change and I will concentrate on this. This simplification allows me to perform another simplification: that of dividing the long wave cycle into four ideal-typical phases.

In the *growth* phase the economic motor of the industrialized world is envisaged as the rapid development of a limited number of key industries all exploiting fairly recent technical advances. Although based on recent technology, these key industries already have well identified products, and business opinion agrees that demand for these products will grow massively. Sustained investment in those industries takes place everywhere where the technological skill and the financial resources are available. Although the product innovation has taken place much potential for process innovation remains and this continues throughout the growth phase (product and process innovation are used in Abernathy's and Utterback's sense of these terms). Process innovation plus the economies of scale following from continuously growing markets leads to lower and lower costs, which in turn feeds market growth. Those firms which were in at the beginning of the key industries make large profits during the growth phase.

The phase of *limits to growth* then takes over. High profits attract newcomers into the key industries and over capacity results. Raw material shortages, pollution and other environmental problems emerge. Trades Unions gain greater bargaining power and governments intervene with higher taxes and more stringent regulations. Profitability declines, demand falters and various crises shake the world economy.

The *retrenchment* phase follows. Disastrous profits force firms and also governments into closing capacity. Unemployment rises, raw materials go into surplus and the bargaining power of workers and raw material suppliers weakens. But some of the costs of retrenchment are once-off, and this, plus the lower input costs due to firms' better bargaining power, leads to a recovery of profits.

This brings in the fourth and final phase: *new industries*. In this phase the emphasis is on product innovation. The increase in profitability and in business confidence towards the end of the retrenchment phase means that investors are looking for industries into which to put their money. The key industries of the previous growth phase are mature and do not need much investment beyond that generated by retained profits. So any new industry with reasonable prospects seems attractive, and a good many try to come up with enough product innovation to rate as a key industry of the future. By the end of the new industries phase several key industries emerge as having excellent prospects for steadily increasing market demand. Thus the growth phase starts again.

This model is certainly over-simplified and differs in a number of ways from those put forward by others. Freeman,[4] drawing on the work of Perez, suggests that the growth phase of a long wave depends on the right match between key technologies and the institutional framework of society. If what he means by this is that innovation needs meta-innovation, I would agree. I would be less ready to accept the notion that new technologies somehow lie around until society becomes ready to use them. Certainly the way advanced biotechnology has emerged is not like that. In fact, I believe that, to a large extent, the development of technologies and of institutions is a mutually interactive process.

But how does the model match with recent history? The immediate post-World War II period, the late 1940s and early 1950s, can be seen as a new industries phase. Pre-war technologies (automotive, energy) were revived and civilian uses were sought for wartime developments (atomic power, valve-based electronics). In the late 1950s and the 1960s a few key industries emerged, particularly obviously in the world's leading economy, the U.S.A. They were automobiles and consumer durables, metals and plastics to make them and oil and electric power on which they all depended. What was good for General Motors was thought to be good for America and, for example, synthetic fibres were hugely profitable to ICI and DuPont. The years from 1958 when the Suez crisis was over, to the raw materials crisis at the end of the 1960s may be seen as the growth phase of the cycle. The phase of limits to growth took up most of the 1970s with the OPEC shock of 1973–1974 as its most critical point. We are now in the retrenchment phase.

Long Waves and Biotechnology

I intend to use the model as the basis for an alternative explanation for the differences noted by

Horwitch between the emergence of the semiconductor and of the biotechnology industries. The *long wave* explanation of these differences is that while semiconductors came in during a growth phase, biotechnology emerged during a retrenchment phase. The reason for the apparently unplanned and disjointed emergence of semiconductors is that they were not the key industries of that growth phase. Compared to cars and dishwashers the application of semiconductors looked difficult and the resulting markets uncertain, so the focus of attention by decision makers in government, financial institutions and industrial firms remained elsewhere. When advanced biotechnology emerged at the end of the 1970s the context for these decision makers was different. Retrenchment was starting and to locate possible new industries for the future was a general ambition. Hence the abundance of official studies and the media attention, sometimes superficial and based on wishful thinking rather than careful analysis.

I admitted earlier that my model of the long wave was a highly simplified one. Although growth is generated by the key industries, they need not be the only ones to grow and this growth need not be only during the growth phase. Obviously semiconductors grew rapidly in the 1960s and 1970s and biotechnology is growing strongly in the 1980s in a particular sector: health care.

It does not need the long wave model to forecast a strong future for biotechnology in the health care field, since the advantages which its products have in diagnosis and therapy are already apparent and are already creating a growing market. However, in fields outside health care, including agriculture, overall economic factors need to be taken into account. Here it is that biotechnology needs product innovation during the new industries phase, which we might expect during the late 1980s and early 1990s. It would be reasonable to conclude that:

(i) Advanced biotechnology is a strong candidate for a key industry in the next growth phase, but this may not start until after the year 2000. Then indeed the prediction of the Spinks Committee may prove correct. 'We envisage biotechnology—the application of biological organisms, systems or processes to manufacturing and service industries—as creating wholly novel industries, with low fossil energy demands, which will be of key importance to the world economy in the next century.'

(ii) Biotechnology will be important before the growth phase (automobiles and oil were important in the 1930s). Biotechnological processes will be introduced into the chemical industry by gradual absorption.

(iii) Even in the retrenchment phase advanced biotechnology is developing strongly in health care. The skills and techniques being built for this application will contribute to product innovation in other fields.

(iv) On the evidence of government sponsored reports at any rate, planning may not have played a very large part in the emergence of advanced biotechnology. Meta-innovation has been essential at this stage. Planning may be needed later.

Long Waves and Planning

Switching now from analysis of biotechnology to analysis of planning I return to Horwitch's paper. His thesis has an underlying assumption that the practice of planning has over time become more valuable and more generally accepted. I will call this the *steady progress* thesis. The *long wave* thesis, on the other hand, might suggest that attitudes to planning and the activities of planners vary with the phase of the long wave cycle. Which thesis is correct?

In support of the steady progress thesis it can certainly be said that planners have a growing battery of tools and an increasingly solid experience in using them. Ansoff[5] has traced the evolution of long-range planning in a series of papers, several of which have introduced new planning concepts explicitly building on older ones. In a paper published in 1978 entitled 'The Planned Management of Turbulent Change' he first describes a sociopolitical environment of increasing turbulence and uncertainty. He suggests that management systems (especially planning systems) have evolved partly in response to this environmental change. His evolutionary scheme can be summarized as follows:

1900	Procedures manuals
1920	Short-term budgeting
1940	Capital budgeting
1950	Management by objectives
1955	Long-range planning
1960	Periodic strategic planning
1970	Issue analysis
1975	Periodic strategic management
1980?	Real-time strategic management
1990?	Surprise management

Beck[6] sees planning during the 1960s as dominated by the computer and by the erroneous belief that processing more and more data would give a better result. But the crises of the 1970s made it starkly clear the forecasts and plans made in this way could be dangerously wrong and he describes a reaction to this: the development of scenario planning. These examples support the steady progress thesis, but if the evolution of management systems is partly in response to environmental change and if this change is cyclical, then the dominant style in management systems is likely to be cyclical as well.

Burrell[7] argues that the social sciences have been subject to long term cycles in which 'positivism' and 'subjectivism' have alternated as the dominant approaches. Towards the end of the 19th century the prevailing tradition of positivism gave way to a subjectivist approach which lasted until the 1920s. Then positivism of the Talcott Parsons variety took the lead until the late 1960s when a new wave of subjectivism emerged. Burrell's cycles do not seem to correlate very closely with economic long waves, but it might be reasonable to expect a closer coupling between economic cycles and management thinking.

Perspectives on Organization

To investigate this requires a typology of management systems and a good one is provided in a recent paper by Astley and Van de Ven[8] entitled 'Central Perspectives and Debates in Organization Theory'. Their use of the term 'Organization' is a wide one and certainly includes long range planning of the kind discussed in this paper.

Their analytical scheme uses two axes: (i) microlevel vs macrolevel for organizational analysis and (ii) deterministic vs voluntaristic assumptions about human nature, to yield four basic perspectives on organizations and their management. This is shown in Figure 3.

The *system–structural* perspective includes that adopted by F. W. Taylor, Weber, Lawrence and Lorsch, Parsons and Luhmann and therefore approaches such as bureaucracy theory, contingency theory, structural-functionalism and the more cybernetic parts of systems theory. It assumes that much of what happens in organizations is as a result of impersonal force within them and that Management is therefore a *reactive* process.

From this perspective planning should be along the lines of extended budgeting with management by exception or management by objectives as the means of ensuring that forecasts are met. Ansoff's evolutionary scheme summarized above suggests that this approach was typical of the 1950s.

The *strategic choice* perspective has it that an organization's structure and strategy, and even its environment, are shaped by the intentions and actions of individuals within it, expecially those in power. Management is seen as *proactive*. Action theory and decision theory follow this perspective and writers like March and Simon are influential within it. Planning is therefore concerned with things like portfolio management and diversification. The early work of Ansoff and the approach of Henderson and the Boston Consulting Group, Shell, GE and DuPont are examples of these perspectives. Ansoff sees this approach as a feature of the 1960s.

The *Natural Selection* perspective is that of industrial economics and population ecology. The focus is on total populations of organization or industries and on concepts such as niches and barriers to entry. Those organizations which happen to fit the niches available to them will thrive, those that do not will go under. Writers such as Chandler and Williamson adopt this approach.

Management is *inactive* and planning mainly a matter of predicting the inevitable rather than influencing the future, although portfolio choice of the kind made by stock market investors would fit this perspective.

Lastly the *Collective Action* perspective is that adopted by social ecologists and social planning theorists such as Emery, Trist, Vickers and Michael. A key concept is interorganizational networks. The 'soft systems' approach of Checkland and the political analysis of J. K. Galbraith also tend to follow this perspective. Planners using the scenario approach and other 'societal' aspects of planning likewise draw on the Collective Action view of the world. Management is *interactive*.

Figure 4 suggests how the organizational perspectives as described by Astley and Van de Ven might match the phases of the long wave model described above. Why should there by any such match? As well as a *Zeitgeist* explanation, in which planning along with many other human activities is influenced by the mood of the time, there could be a functional explanation. The time horizon of planning is usually no more than 5–10 years, which

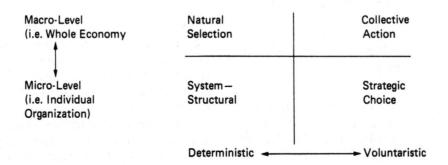

Figure 3

Long Wave Phase	Growth	Limits to Growth	Retrenchment	New Industries
Organizational Perspective	Strategic Choice	Collective Action	Natural Selection	System— Structural

Figure 4

is an order of magnitude less than the long wave cycle. It would therefore be quite rational to adopt a different style of planning for each phase of the long wave cycle. This implies a readiness on the part of the planner to change the planning perspectives and this seems to me to be some evidence that this happens. For instance Taylor wrote in 1975

'... after a decade of experience with formal planning systems it should be possible for planners to abandon the rather limited systems analysis or management scientists' view of Corporate Planning as a formal exercise in resource allocation. It is clear from numerous research studies that comprehensive formal planning systems are of limited use. The management of a highly volatile activity may be better advised to develop broad strategy and contingency plans.'

A few months later Taylor was writing that corporate planning would have to be adapted 'to give more emphasis to non-economic values, the quality of life inside the organization and in the communities outside ...'. Here is an influential academic advocating a change in planning style.[9] I believe that papers like these had a powerful effect at the time. Today others are stressing the need to give more emphasis to *economic* values; no doubt they too are having a powerful effect.

Organizational Perspective and the Two Theses

I will conclude this comparison of the 'steady progress' and 'long wave' theses by looking at them from each of Astley's and Van de Ven's perspectives.

From the system-structural perspective the long wave thesis might be favoured since it has a deterministic bias and provides a functionalist explanation for observed changes in planning practice. The steady progress thesis would get support from this perspective if it could be shown that the discipline of planning with its practitioners, researchers and teachers, constitutes an autonomous system capable of generating steady progress. In either case planners are seen as reactive.

On the other hand from the perspective of strategic choice the steady progress thesis looks the more attractive. The thesis fits with the picture of planners building up by experience a set of planning techniques and then choosing the one they prefer for a particular job. They are seen as proactive.

Supporters of the natural section perspective might see nothing to choose between the two theses since from their viewpoint planning makes little difference to the fate of an organization. They would agree with Ackoff's remark: 'Most corporate planning is like a ritual rain dance: it has no effect on the weather that follows but it makes those who engage in it feel they are in control'. They will ignore Ackoff's further remark that planning need not be like this if planners overcome self-imposed constraints.

It is worth noting that long wave theories themselves may be a product of the natural selection perspective. The fact that they are popular during the present retrenchment phase would fit in with the long wave thesis.

From the collective action perspective both theses might be supported, as contributors to an interactive management style.

Clegg[10] sees management techniques primarily as an instrument for control, ensuring the loyalty or obedience of employees at all levels. Planning might be aimed at persuading middle managers to follow the top management line. He argues that management techniques do become more effective over time but also that they are modified through each long wave cycle.

Michael in his book *On Learning to Plan and Planning to Learn*[11] argues that long-range social planning should be accepted as a learning process rather than as social engineering technology. He also emphasizes the need for all concerned with planning to be open to change. They should question their commitments and objectives. This questioning should be informed by and should in its turn inform their evaluation of what is happening at the present and what might happen in the future.

In the conclusion to the paper from which I have drawn so extensively Astley and Van de Ven say: 'Because contradictions are pervasive in organizations, the theories that capture and reflect discrete segments of organizational life must also inevitably be contradictory and can be reconciled only dialectically'. I think this conclusion applies to the rival theses I have been considering. Both approaches should be useful to planners who seek to understand the nature of their work. Both, at least in the form I have presented them, are capable of much improvement. But I hope that to have stated the two theses, and to have compared them in some depth may have thrown some light on the nature of planning and of innovation. I hope too that using the specific context of biotechnology may have contributed to the nourishment of theory by practice and practice by theory.

As I did earlier for biotechnology, I will try to draw some conclusions for planning and for innovation:

For planning these are:

(i) It is worthwhile debating the nature of planning as this should make planning more relevant and more likely to succeed.

(ii) As a contribution to such a debate two theses can be compared: the steady progress thesis and the long wave thesis.

(iii) Using the example of biotechnology both theses receive some support.

(iv) Taking each of the four perspectives of Astley and Van de Ven leads to a similar conclusion—both theses are supported.

(v) A dialectical approach, aimed at a higher level synthesis of the two theses, could be followed.

For innovation these are:

(i) Debate about the nature of innovation is also of great importance.

(ii) The distinction between product innovation and process innovation is valuable.

(iii) So too is the concept of meta-innovation.

(iv) We should, however, watch out for pseudo-meta-innovation.

Freeman in speaking about economic change resulting from technological innovation says:

> However, it is essential not to under-estimate the vast scope of institutional change which is needed. It will involve enormous changes in the pattern of skills of the work-force and therefore in the education and training systems; in management and labour attitudes; the pattern of industrial relations and worker participation; in working arrangements; in the pattern of consumer demand; in the conceptual framework of economists, accountants and governments, and in social, political and legislative priorities.

My paper may make a modest contribution towards changing the conceptual framework of planners and managers. I hope I have offered meta-innovation and not pseudo meta-innovation.

Acknowledgements—This paper is based on a talk to the Scottish Regional Group of the Society for Strategic and Long Range Planning. I am grateful for their invitation. I would also like to thank Celltech's Library and Information Service for their valuable support and Beverley Marlow for secretarial help.

References

(1) Mel Horwitch, Changing Patterns for Corporate Strategy and Technology Management: The Rise of the Semiconductor and Biotechnology Industries. Paper presented at the Mitsubishi Bank Foundation Conference on Business Strategy and Technical Innovation, 26–29 March, Ito City, Japan (1983).

(2) William J. Abernathy and James M. Utterback, Patterns of industrial innovation, *Innovation/Technology Review,* **80** (7), 59–64 (1978).

(3) References to these reports and an extensive bibliography on biotechnology can be found in *Information Sources in Biotechnology* by Anita Crafts-Lighty, Macmillan (1983).

(4) Professor C. Freeman, *Keynes or Kondratiev—How can we get back to full employment?* Presidential address for Section X of the British Association for the Advancement of Science, August, University of Sussex (1983).

(5) H. Igor Ansoff, *Planned Management of Turbulent Change,* European Institute for Advanced Studies in Management. January (1978).

(6) P. W. Beck, Corporate planning for an uncertain future, *Long Range Planning,* **15** (4), 12–21 (1982).

(7) Gibson Burrell, Systems thinking, systems practice: a review, *Journal of Applied Systems Analysis,* **10** (1983).

(8) W. Graham Astley and Andrew H. Van de Ven, Central perspectives and debates in organisation theory, *Administrative Science Quarterly,* **28**, 245–273 (1983).

(9) Bernard Taylor, Strategies for planning, *Long Range Planning,* pp. 27–40 August 1975; Bernard Taylor, Conflict of values—the central strategy problems, *Long Range Planning,* pp. 20–24, December (1975).

(10) Stuart Clegg, Organization and control, *Administrative Science Quarterly,* **26**, 545–562 (1981).

(11) Donald M. Michael, *On Learning to Plan—and Planning to Learn,* Jossey-Bass Publishers, San Francisco (1973).

Appendix

Biotechnology may be one of the corner stones of the next industrial revolution. The impact of biotechnology will certainly be profound and promises to provide new food, new sources of energy, medicines and methods of pollution control.

But, what is biotechnology? The Spinks Report[3] defined it as 'the application of biological organisms, systems of processes to manufacturing and service industries', a definition which has met with general agreement. He suggested there are three generations of biotechnology:

(1) the first generation stretching back to Roman times with processes such as baking bread, brewing beer, making wine, cheese and yoghurt which, by this definition, are all biotechnological;

(2) the second generation starting in the 1940s with the production of antibiotics, and highly dependent on the sciences of microbiology, biochemistry and microbial genetics;

(3) the third generation beginning in 1975 when recombinant DNA techniques had avanced sufficiently for practical applications to become clear.

Classical genetics, improving organisms by selection, has been important in the first and second generations of biotechnology, but the third generation depends on molecular genetics, the directed manipulation of genetic material and the transfer of genetic information between species which cannot interbreed. The two main techniques of molecular genetics are recombinant DNA and cell hybridization. It is the use of these techniques together with a few others such as enzyme immobilization which can be called advanced biotechnology.

Recombinant DNA allows pieces of DNA from plants, animals or other micro-organisms to be transferred into a host micro-organism or other cell which thereby acquires new abilities for synthesis and other biochemical transformations.

An early and striking example of recombinant DNA techniques was production in 1979 of human insulin by the bacterium E. coli. By transferring a strand of DNA which is an exact copy of that in human beings into an E. coli cell and then allowing that cell to reproduce itself many-fold in a suitable environment, an insulin-producing strain is obtained. This strain can be used to make a rec-DNA fermentation product, in this case the exactly correct molecule of human insulin. Production of the desired fermentation product follows the pattern of fermentation processes making naturally occurring products, for example, the process for making an antibiotic like Penicillin. But although the process is a bacterial fermentation, the information is from a human cell, so what is produced is a human protein. The human genome is the architect; the bacterial cells are the building workers.

Recombinant DNA is a way of transferring a relatively small amount of genetic information from one type of cell to another, but it is also possible to fuse two cells of different types so that substantial parts of the genetic material from each of the two cells is retained and reproduced in the resulting fused strain. This technique has an important application in the production of monoclonal antibodies.

Antibodies are proteins which are made by animals as a defence mechanism against foreign substances entering their bodies. Resistance to infectious diseases which people have either as a result of one attack of the disease, or because of an inoculation, is provided by antibodies. In nature a mixture of antibodies is produced which differs from animal to animal, but by fusing, for example, lymphocytes (white blood cells) with malignant myeloma cells, the resulting hybrid cell or hybridoma has the capacity to reproduce itself faithfully.

Since each clone of cells produces only one antibody, that antibody has a clearly definable specificity, in contrast to the conventional polyclonal mixtures produced by the immune response in animals or man. The way in which antibodies function as a defence mechanism is by combining with the particular invading susbstance (or with part of it) and with virtually nothing else. This selective combining power is why antibodies can be so useful, especially the pure strains of monoclonal antibodies. For example, diagnostic tests for a variety of medical conditions have now been devised using monoclonal antibodies which allow a much faster and more reliable diagnosis because of the highly specific combining power of the antibody.

The most immediate area of commercial impact for advanced biotechnology is human health care.

Genetic engineering allows a vast number of peptides and proteins to be made on a scale and at a cost not previously possible. Human hormones such as insulin or calcitonin, other therapeutically valuable human proteins such as interferon or plasminogen activator are now being produced and several have passed through the stage of clinical trials into commercial sale.

Production of vaccines will be possible by rec-DNA techniques in the near future. Vaccination introduces substantially harmless substances into the body which provoke an antibody response which is similar to that provoked by a dangerous infection. Thus immunity is established in advance. If chosen well, just a part of the protein of the infective agent will give rise to such an immune response. These proteins can be made in bacteria and are incapable of causing an infection. Infections like hepatitis, herpes, typhoid, cholera, malaria and schistosomiasis will soon be fought with vaccines of this kind.

Monoclonal antibodies produced by cell fusion are now becoming very important in diagnostic tests and are already being used in special areas for therapeutic use, since their specific combining power may enable them to deliver drugs to a specific target area in the human body.

Recombinant DNA techniques will also be of importance in some diagnostic tests and ultimately in the treatment of genetic diseases where the sufferer is missing an important gene.

It is safe to assume that by 1990 a major part of the health care industry will have been affected by genetic engineering. Perhaps a third of the present activity of pharmaceuticals and diagnostics sectors will have been replaced or greatly expanded by that year, as a result of advanced biotechnology.

Turning now to agriculture in which the long term opportunities are no less dramatic than human health care.

Agriculture must have been based on rule-of-thumb genetics since its early beginnings, and in this century classical genetics has had an enormous influence on yields, on quality of product and on the scope for raising plants or animals in new climatic conditions. So the application of genetic engineering will continue a well established tradition with the added dimension of transfer of genetic material between species, especially with micro-organisms. It is a good deal more difficult to transfer genetic information into a plant cell, since the cells not only have to replicate but also to differentiate into the various types of cell needed for a whole plant. But this is now possible.

Advanced biotechnology should enable plant breeders to produce a wider range of varieties from which genetic selection of yields and quality can take place. Characteristics such as disease resistance, tolerance of particular soils or climate, or ability to fix atmospheric nitrogen are targets for improvement in agricultural plants. For veterinary use, vaccines, hormones and fertility control agents are important targets and success in human health care is now being followed by animal application.

Non-health care, non-agricultural industries are a very large market, but margins are usually low and costs have to be kept to a minimum. This makes it difficult to do R & D work with anything other than short term objectives.

Larger volume, capital intensive industries such as chemicals, energy and minerals are at present suffering from stagnating markets and low profits.

They also have mature technologies where costs have been brought down by many years of process improvement. To make an impact in such industries will require a lot of R & D work which it is presently difficult for these industries to fund. Over-ambitious promises for biotechnology made a few years ago have also made these industries suspicious.

The way forward is to find targets which have both a shorter term commercial pay off (they will mainly be in smaller volume areas) and potential as models for larger scale applications.

An example of second generation biotechnology comes from the food and drink industry. This is the use of industrial enzymes to manufacture high fructose corn syrups used as sweeteners in soft drinks and various foods. Genetic engineering did not play a part in making these enzymes but it is clear that new industrial enzymes will become available from genetic engineering in the future and these will lead to similar changes. Sweeteners, viscosity and texture modifiers, and preservatives may well be affected during the next 10 years, with indirect influences on the world markets for agricultural products, such as sugar and maize.

Micro-organisms have been used in the chemicals, minerals, energy and allied industries for a very long time. Perhaps the best example is making industrial alcohol by the same sort of fermentation process as is used to make alcoholic beverages. Although petrochemical routes are now an important source for ethanol, fermentation production has continued throughout the period of cheap oil and gas and is now becoming the preferred route in many parts of the world. Other chemicals, such as butanol or acetone, used to be made by fermentation but are now very largely produced petrochemically. Here there is a clear potential for reversion to fermentation.

In the developed capitalist countries the firms involved in genetic engineering can be divided with some approximation into specialist firms, major groups and auxilliary suppliers. A fair number of specialist firms, usually with close connections to one or more university departments strong in the science, have been found recently, the majority of them in the U.S.A. The longest established started in genetic engineering around 1976 and some now have a total staff of over 200, most of them qualified scientists. Firms specializing in rec-DNA are the oldest, while those in cell fusion are more recent. Many firms specialized in either rec-DNA or cell fusion. Some like Celltech Ltd in the U.K. have strength in both fields. The specialist firms provide contract research services and consultancy, develop and patent processes for making proteins in bacteria or modification to existing fermentation processes, and are starting to make products of their own where this can be done on a fairly small scale, e.g. diagnostic products based on monoclonal antibodies.

These specialist firms have received a lot of publicity and great expectations about their commercial success have been raised. Some will undoubtedly be very successful and will expand into medium scale production or into large scale contracting for other enterprises. Some will no doubt be less successful and may fold up or be taken over by other firms. The basis for success will be industrially orientated scientific excellence, plus the ability to choose financially rewarding projects and to commercialize discoveries effectively.

Existing groups, often very large multi-national enterprises, for example in oil, chemicals, minerals, food and pharmaceuticals, have become involved in genetic engineering, either with in-house research and development units (occasionally on the same scale as those of the specialized firms, but sometimes more modestly so as to have a window on the new technology) or by taking a minority stake in one or more of the specialized firms. The large pharmaceutical companies are at present most advanced in this process and mostly have followed the in-house R & D route. The giants of oils and chemicals have the financial and commercial resources to play a big role in the new genetics but, if microelectronics is any guide, it may be that the most radical innovation will come from specialist firms rather than the giants.

Suppliers of auxillary materials to the emerging genetic engineering industry include suppliers of laboratory instrumentation, equipment and consumable materials; suppliers of tissue culture and fermentation equipment, including process control and data-logging instrumentation; and also data processing hardware and software. An example is suppliers of what has become known as the gene machine. This is an instrument for the synthesis of strands of DNA which are built up chemically by adding base after base to the growing strand. These machines are fully automated and computer controlled, and some are being built by the research groups of genetic engineering companies as well as by instrument supply firms.

Postcript

This paper was written without the benefit of having read Perez' paper on 'Structural Change and Assimilation of New Technologies in the Economic and Social Systems' (*Futures*, p. 357, October 1983). Perez' model of long wave cycles is more sophisticated than mine, which leaves out her emphasis on the interaction between technical and social systems. In her model a 'key factor' gives rise to a 'technological style' which drives the upswing of the long wave and she claims that the technical inputs needed for the key factor are probably available long before it emerges. I would argue that this has not always been the case. For example, the discoveries of nylon, polyethylene and other synthetic polymeric materials made in the late 1930s and the 1940s were fundamental advances taken up rapidly, often by the firms in whose R & D laboratories the discoveries were made, and were significant contributors to the key industries of the 1950s and 1960s (or to the technological style of those years, to use Perez' term).

But this does not detract from Perez' model as a whole. In it the upswing of a long wave begins when technology and the socio-institutional climate complement each other. This insight could be very fruitful. The cyclical changes in organization perspective which I postulate in my paper might help to create the socio-institutional climate required for the subsequent long wave phase. If so, I was right to emphasize the importance of understanding the nature of planning, including the influence of perspective on the practice of planning.